FATHER/LAND

ALSO BY FREDERICK KEMPE

Siberian Odyssey: A Voyage into the Russian Soul

Divorcing the Dictator: America's Bungled Affair
with Noriega

FATHER/LAND

A Personal Search for the New Germany

FREDERICK KEMPE

G. P. PUTNAM'S SONS

NEW YORK

G. P. Putnam's Sons
Publishers Since 1838
a member of
Penguin Putnam Inc.
375 Hudson Street
New York, NY 10014

Library of Congress Cataloging-in-Publication Data

Kempe, Frederick.
Father/land : a personal search for the new Germany /
by Frederick Kempe.
p.   cm.
ISBN 0-399-14497-8 (alk. paper)
1. Germany—Historiography.   2. Political culture—Germany.
3. National characteristics, German.   4. National socialism—Moral
and ethical aspects.   5. Germany—Politics and government—20th
century.   6. Nazis—Psychology.
7. German Americans—Biography.
I. Title.
DD290.24.K46   1999   98-51837 CIP
943.087'01'9—dc21

Printed in the United States of America

1   2   3   4   5   6   7   8   9   10

This book is printed on acid-free paper. ♾

BOOK DESIGN BY JENNIFER ANN DADDIO

ACKNOWLEDGMENTS

This book had various purposes, but one was particularly important to me: that non-German readers gain a more nuanced and personal understanding of a country that is back on history's hot seat after a half century on ice. I also hope German readers find something beyond self-recognition: a better understanding of the content of their current success and of the dangers and opportunities that lie ahead.

In my efforts to achieve those purposes, I owe a particular debt to all those Germans who have befriended me and helped educate me over the years, many of whom are sources in this book. To list them all here would require its own chapter. So I'll instead limit these acknowledgments to those who helped specifically with this manuscript.

I will never be able to repay Peter and Maria Bagley for their friendship and safe harbor. More to the point, Peter's editing and suggestions helped produce much of what is good about this book. I am responsible for whatever is not. I still haven't found a more skilled and thoughtful editor—or a more loyal friend—than Kyle Gibson (unless, of course, it is Peter Chase).

The German Marshall Fund, the Bosch Foundation, and the Körber Foundation provided assistance without which this book wouldn't have been completed. I am specifically grateful to Ulrich Bopp and Frank Theiner at Bosch, and Ulrich Voswinkel and Wolf Schmidt at Körber. Thanks also to Jack Janes, who has done so much to increase American understanding of Germany, and to his American Institute for Contemporary Studies, where I was proud to have been a fellow. Hats off to Craig Kennedy of the German Marshall Fund, whose support and camaraderie was only exceeded by his profound understanding and appreciation for things German.

Almut Schoenfeld, Kathleen Brown, and Sandra Shapshay provided valuable assistance at various stages of the project. Dieter Wolf, a talented German reporter, took time from his own writing to provide some remarkable sleuthing. Claudia Kleinert generously shared her time and vast knowledge about Germany's Turkish population.

I couldn't believe my luck at having Neil Nyren once again as my editor at Putnam, a man of unique wit, grace, and editing prowess. He long encouraged me to do "my German book," and gave generously of his time in saving me from less ready projects. And any writer is fortunate to be represented by Esther Newberg.

My greatest debt is to Dow Jones and the *Wall Street Journal Europe*, a unique setting of the highest possible journalistic standards. Thanks are not enough for Karen House, my long-time boss and friend. As Dow Jones international champion, she has consistently directed me and many others to produce journalistic excellence "über alles." Thanks also to Peter Kann, an inspiration and leader for so many reporters over the years, and to Phil Revzin, who tolerated my leave of absence in the middle of his successful efforts to remake the *Wall Street Journal Europe* into the excellent paper it has become. A personal thanks to Jeff Burke and Craig Copetas for the time they took to coach me on an earlier manuscript of a different sort.

A good reporter never underestimates the importance of his sources, but in this case I will only specifically name two: my cousins Manfred and "Franz." They have shown me more clearly than anyone else how much good can grow from such sorry seed. I am proud to call them family.

For the comforting memory of my parents,
Fritz Gustav and Johanna Schumann Kempe

For my sisters, Jeanie, Patty and Teresa

What sets this Germany apart from those of the past is that we are the chil-dren of the Nazis. It has an impact on almost everything we do. That his-tory will stay with us a long time. When you look at these twelve years with some distance, they are decisive years in German history, years in which Hitler exploited the grandest feelings of the German people for the most ter-rible crime of modern history. But we are also America's children. What my generation has in the way of democratic experience, what we have learned about democratic culture, we have to thank America and no one else. And that is a heritage we can build upon.

—JOSCHKA FISCHER, FOREIGN MINISTER

CONTENTS

*nellay of horse and hoofe and
ware, and mangles, and scatters to
seen beneath and the blue above,
lack and danger, and life, and
Racca, — Racca used to ride
mouse-gray mustang close to my
blue eesape and bright-belled lep
ghed with joy as I looked at*

PROLOGUE

FATHER'S LAND

My father, as I told my childhood friends in Utah, was an American war hero. Though he was born in Germany, he fought for Uncle Sam at the Battle of the Bulge, where he was injured and decorated for his bravery. His exploits there were so bloody that he didn't like to talk about them much.

But I had his photo proudly hanging on my wall, in his American army uni-form with the sergeant's stripes. That was evidence enough that my father, despite his thick German accent and birthplace in Dresden, had fought against the German pest.

There was only one problem: the story was a lie.

My father never fought in Germany with the Americans. The closest he ever

Father

came to the rumble of cannon fire was as a cook at the U.S. army base in Richmond, Virginia. He only saw the whites of the enemies' eyes in Laramie, Wyoming, where he was posted as a guard at a POW camp in the final weeks of the war.

So why didn't I tell my childhood friends the truth? Because the truth wasn't large enough or powerful enough to neutralize my father's accent, a thick one from his home region of Saxony that most Americans associated with the Nazi villains of *Stalag 17* and *A Bridge Too Far.* The truth wasn't dramatic enough to separate me sufficiently from my German roots. My father hadn't been heroic enough to protect me from bullies who labeled me an alien child.

Even as a young boy, I knew that Germanness was something to conceal. In rewriting my father's history, I fought my own war against Germany; I blew up the bridges between our family and the country that had caused the world so much heartache and bloodshed.

Years later, when I became a foreign correspondent, first for *Newsweek,* and then for the *Wall Street Journal,* I still was uneasy with my German heritage. I preferred reporting in Poland, Israel, Russia, and Latin America. I felt more warmth toward these people than toward the cooler, grayer Germans.

Even after I learned German in college, even after I lived in the country as a reporter, I couldn't embrace the place of my family origins. My first two books were about Panama and Siberia—their issues intrigued me more.

Germany was never my land.

It was my Father's Land.

It was "the old country," a musty and outdated place. My parents' families had abandoned Germany for a better life in America, their land of opportunity, so I could only reason that the country was an undesirable place to live. It was the home of unknown relatives who sent indecipherable letters in thin blue envelopes bearing exotic stamps. It was the past. Not the future.

My Ukrainian-American friend Alexander Motyl grew up speaking two languages and fiercely wanting freedom for his parents' homeland. My Greek-American friend Michael Chaus lived a childhood of Greek family parties, Greek Orthodox church socials, and Greek holiday celebrations. But I never considered myself German-American. My immigrant parents rarely spoke their native tongue to each other, and almost never spoke it to me—a conscious effort to render me as American as possible.

I owe this mostly to my mother, who began the work of Americanizing me from the start by blocking my father's effort to name me after himself: *Fritz Gustav.* "Can you imagine naming an American child *Fritz?*" my mother said to me later in life. "And so soon after the war! I wouldn't allow it."

My mother had been a second-grade school teacher, and she understood how cruel children could be about anyone who didn't fit. By the time I was born, she had already stopped teaching German at home to my three older sisters; they had been harassed and bullied as "little Hitlers" in school. Taught by experience, she was determined to make me as red-white-and-blue-blooded as possible.

My mother preferred the ethnically neutral name of Paul, after a beloved uncle of hers who had fallen in world War I. My father backed off his insistence that I be named Fritz, but he wanted a name that more closely approximated his own. So they landed upon Frederick, or Fred for short. My mother later told me that, in her own mind, she was naming me as well for the great Prussian monarch, Frederick the Great. He had been a relatively enlightened ruler by German standards and for that reason was her favorite.

My mother successfully imposed her will on my middle name— Schumann, which was also her maiden name. Her side of the family is related to the composer Robert Schumann, a matter of family pride for generations, and all three of my elder sisters carry Schumann as their middle names as well. By my mother's reckoning, Fritz was a German branding that would have exposed me to ridicule. Americans only named their dachshunds Fritz, after all. But who could quibble with Robert Schumann? My mother preferred her Germanness à la carte.

And that is how I became Frederick Schumann Kempe. Even my name was something of a New World compromise that had its origins in German history.

Yet I only learned all this after I had grown older. The derivation of my name wasn't an important issue in a childhood full of Little League baseball games, summer vacations at Disneyland, and high-school proms.

I couldn't have been more different culturally from my father. While he used his free time to work through trunks and boxes full of family records, I memorized the batting averages of every player in the National League. My father collected stamps and coins from Germany—I had the best baseball-card collection in my entire school. My father's study was decorated with old drawings of Dresden and daguerreotypes of nineteenth-century family ancestors in black suits. I had hung a poster of San Francisco centerfielder Willie Mays on my wall beside a large photograph of President John F. Kennedy.

As I grew older, my father frequently tried to interest me in his genealogical research, which traced back our family three centuries. But I never saw what good these roots could do me. As a teenager, I found his fascination with all these dead Germans to be a little creepy. When he died, in 1988, I knew he was still upset that I had never properly learned to value his life's work. He willed his records to me, for he was a traditional man and I was his only son. But he had no reason to think I would value this treasure.

Eventually, during my college years, I grew more interested in history and in Germany. I began to ask my father more questions about his Fatherland and his role in the war against it. I knew my invented version of his heroics needed correction. It mystified me that my father wouldn't talk about the war years, and I began to wonder if he had something to hide. When I pressed him, he sidestepped my questions. When I asked him what had made his Germany go wrong, he said the Versailles Treaty's punishments after World War I had turned his countrymen desperate, ripe for a *Führer* who would create jobs and tell them they were special—that they were *Übermenschen.*

"The West created Hitler," he once said to me.

"And what about the Germans?" I had replied, with a teenager's sarcastic sneer. "You think maybe they played some small role, too, *Dad?*"

"Think what you like," he huffed.

And that was the end of it for many years.

I grew closer to my father in his last years, as is often the case between father and son. It was appropriate that it was Germany and my study of his mother tongue that allowed us to grow closer. In 1985, we traveled together to his home state of Saxony, which fate had placed in the Soviet bloc's East Germany. We strolled the trails of the Ore Mountains where he had whiled away what he called the happiest days of his childhood. We visited the bakery in which he had been born in a small village called Leubsdorf. We walked through his old school yard in the town where he had been raised, Kleinzschachwitz near Dresden.

The trip put him in a reflective mood—and me in a receptive one.

He spoke of his prewar childhood, in the 1920s, in a Germany suffering hyperinflation and postwar depression. He told me how his mother pushed wheelbarrows full of marks to the market to buy goods quickly before the money lost its value. He spoke of how Mormon missionaries—local Germans and not the American boys in their white shirts—walked into their hopeless world and offered a way out. He talked of how his father dispatched him, as the first member of his family, to the New World in America when he was just seventeen. He was to establish the beachhead for his family immigration that would then follow.

During a break at a roadside café during our time in Saxony, I asked him again about the war. His voice bore a curious sadness as he finally told the story. The American military intelligence unit at his Virginia camp was trying to recruit him and other native Germans. It wanted them, among other things, to debrief POWs, decipher intercepted communications and, if he were chosen as one of the more capable candidates, to operate behind enemy lines. The Americans, my father said, wanted these German immigrants "to serve in some secret war against our Fatherland."

I am sure that is the way he said it because I jotted down what I could remember of the conversation that evening in my journal. My father said that the Americans didn't understand the difficulty their German recruits might have in betraying the country of their birth. "Hitler had given simple Germans so much hope."

My father was to deploy his Saxon dialect, his charm, and whatever else popped into his mind to break down the enemy. "The Americans were not so civilized, either," he told me. "They told us we could ignore the Geneva Convention if we had to use other means."

"So you became a spy?" I asked excitedly, hoping my father's true story might be even better than the fib I had deployed against my childhood enemies.

"No, Fred," he said. "I didn't."

I remember even now how he sighed and then paused before continuing.

"I failed the tests they gave me, on purpose. I didn't want to carry out dirty tricks against the Germans."

To sell him and the others on the necessity to work against the land of their birth, the recruiter did everything possible to convince them of how evil the Third Reich had become. My father recalled one session during which the lecturer showed the men photographs of railway lines that he said were leading to a concentration camp. He said many prisoners were dying in the camps, some from overwork and malnutrition. And the Germans were systematically killing many, he said, particularly the Jews.

"We knew the Jews had it bad, but there was nothing about this in the newspapers," said my father. "This was a sensation."

"How did you respond?"

My father looked away. I repeated my question.

"I didn't believe it."

"You didn't *believe* it?"

"How *could* I believe it? My father, your grandfather, had told me about the French propaganda during the First World War." The French, wanting to demonstrate that the Germans were barbarians, had invented stories about how the Germans cut off the heads of French soldiers they killed or captured, even showing photographs as proof—though the heads weren't real; plaster of Paris, his father supposed. "The Germans never would have cut off anyone's head," said my father, "and I was sure they wouldn't murder Jews, either. I was certain this was American propaganda, just like the French."

"You told the officer this?"

"I did." He said that most of the other Germans in the room agreed with him. After that, he figured, the American officers decided he was unreliable, even if he hadn't done so badly on his test. He never joined their secret society. They never asked him to sign up.

So it was that he never came face-to-face with German soldiers, except in Wyoming, guarding German POWs toward the end of the war. He had kept a cigarette lighter that one of the POWs had given him there. It was smooth and heavy, of simple but sturdy construction. My father had carried it on our trip to Germany for some sentimental reason he never told me—and he gave it to me that day.

"He made it from spent bullet casings that he'd melted down," said my father. "Few American soldiers could ever produce something this perfect with nothing but a few crude tools. The POWs there were mainly from the Afrika Korps. Rommel's group. They were healthy and of the highest morals. Better than the Americans."

Father at the POW camp in Wyoming (far right)

"Better?"

"Better as men."

I was troubled by the comment, but I let it pass.

We talked about many other matters as we continued our drive through East Germany. My father was disappointed at how quickly we motored from Dresden to his mother's village of Krummenhennersdorf on the plush banks of a small stream. It had taken us less than an hour to reach there by car, but when he was a child the trip had been a day's adventure that included a ride on a narrow-gauge train.

Back in Dresden, he was saddened at how little of his "Florence on the Elbe" had survived the Allied fire bombing and soulless East German reconstruction. When we reached the river itself, he recalled the spot in it where he had been baptized a Mormon.

At one of the bridges, he recounted for me how each time the family came to Dresden they would put on their shoes before crossing the span and then walk into town. "Shoes were expensive, especially to replace the soles, so we'd walk barefoot until here. Then we'd put on the shoes, so that the 'city slickers' wouldn't make fun of us." The recollections fell one over the other, the mosaic of memory that makes up one's life.

What remains most in my mind, however, was an elementary-school class reunion staged for his visit, attended by the remnants—almost exclusively female—of his lost generation of Germans. Most of the men had already died, either during the war or in Soviet prison camps thereafter. Those few who survived World War II rarely had the energy or health to live into their seventies, as my father had done.

The only other male at the reunion sat angrily in his wheelchair, snarling at the world. I reckoned he was too mean to have died earlier. He had been a ranking Communist official, and he lectured us on the benefits of life in East Germany: good education, no poverty, little crime. He was sure East Germany was superior to the American hell of violence and ghettoes. His lines seemed memorized from some party manifesto—none was based on experience, because of the restrictions on Western travel.

The old women ignored him and flirted with my father, who was full of mirth and life, having aged far more gracefully. They also spoke adoringly about the school's other surviving male, acknowledged as the richest school alumnus, a man who had fled to Peru after the war.

No one had to ask why. They winked when I tried.

My father left the class reunion confused that afternoon. By leaving Germany early he had escaped the hardships that had been his classmates' lives. He had opened a world of opportunity to me and my three elder sisters. He had spared us the burden of lugging around the weight of German history all our lives.

Yet my father was oddly melancholy as we drove from the reunion to yet another stop in Saxony. Even in drab East Germany, my father said he felt more at home than he had done for years. "There is something about *Heimat*," my father said, using the German word that best captures the deeper meaning of home.

It was on this trip that my father finally decided to reconvert to Lutheranism after years of grumbling about Mormonism. He'd been studying the two religions for some time and had often agonized with me about the choice. He made his move in a typically exacting German manner, demanding that the Mormons excommunicate him. The responsible church authorities in Utah didn't see any cause to do so—my father hadn't committed any sin that would require such a measure. He didn't drink or smoke, and hadn't committed adultery. In the end, however, my father got his way. This religious "coming home" brought him enormous peace, much as his trip to Saxony had done before it.

As we began to drive away from Dresden at the end of our trip, my father said to me, "Do you remember the needlework on your grandmother's wall?"

I did. She was a woman who spoke no English, so the English words she had stitched into this decoration had been particularly memorable to us: *East or West, Home Is Best.*

"Well, this is the closest thing there is to home for me," he said. "I understand the people here. I think they understand me. Did you see how much we laughed together? Didn't you feel their basic goodness?"

I did. There was something so decent about them. That, I told my father, was the mystery. How could such an apparently good people with such a rich cultural history have done such evil things?

My father couldn't explain it any better than the army of historians before him. It was a part of German history he hadn't directly shared in. At the end of that trip, he told me he wished I would someday write a book that would help him grasp modern Germany. I wrote about so many things, he said. Why didn't I write more about Germany? He had so many documents he could share with me.

I promised him that I would, though it has taken me a long time to do so. Three years after that trip to Saxony, my father dropped dead of a heart attack at age seventy-nine. It hadn't been four months since we'd buried my mother. Yet another nine years would pass before I felt ready to face whatever family secrets, whatever family identity my father's trunks and boxes contained.

By then the Berlin Wall had fallen and the unification of Germany had made it, once again, Europe's determining force. My father had missed all that. The end of the Cold War had placed his reconstituted country at the center of a reconnected continent, geographically and politically. Europe's two primary tasks—integrating itself more closely and spreading its stability eastward—demanded German leadership. After years on ice, Germany was on history's hot seat again: the subject instead of the object of European decision-making.

But was Germany ready? That it remained haunted was not open to debate. The ghosts of the past defined the German political conscience; they hovered over every debate about Germany's role in the twenty-first century. The central question was whether the famously tortured and talented Germans were likely to find some sort of redemption now that merciful fate had provided them a new chance, perhaps the best chance in their history to do well and to do good.

Surrounded by friendly neighbors, anchored in Western institutions, made rich by the postwar economic miracle, they were a rock of stability at the middle of the European map. Their wartime horrors had made them eager to cede sovereignty and power—even their beloved currency—to European institutions. Their postwar successes had made them loyal Western allies and friends of the same countries that had in the end defeated their continental ambitions.

Germans' readiness to lead was and is a critical question, and not only for Germans, for Germany's destiny is Europe's destiny. Twice in the last century, a Germany gone wrong has been at the core of world wars. How would it turn out this time?

And this leads to other, more philosophical questions. What causes evil, and what breeds good? And can so much evil become so good in such a short span of time? I wondered about the nature of change, of self-improvement and national improvement. After only half a century of reeducation and reconstruction, could the strength of German democracy and liberalism be as great as it seemed?

The possibility of a redeemed Germany—a new Germany that neither hid from its ghosts nor succumbed to its past—emboldened me. So it was that I decided to entwine a personal odyssey about the significance of my German heritage—what it meant to me to be linked to this tragic and extraordinary country—with a search into the future: a search for the New Germany.

I had so many questions, so much to explore.

Demographic change had brought the country its largest ethnic minority ever, the Turks, and they were so much more foreign than the Jews had ever been. Whether they and the Germans could happily coexist was a core question for the future. That was all the more the case because one of the country's chief foreign policy challenges would be how to keep Turkey from turning anti-Western, which in turn could unsettle Germany domestically.

At the same time, thousands of new Jewish émigrés had arrived from Russia. Would they be embraced and made to feel at home? It seemed as though some dramatist, by sending a new Jewish population to Germany, was inventing a plot whose drama and importance only few Germans comprehended.

And Germany's military was dispatching its troops abroad on a combat mission for the first time since World War II—to former Yugoslavia, a place of heart-stopping German atrocities. It was a mission whose symbolism spoke both of the country's growing influence and of its shrinking self-constraints.

Germany's youth seemed to be lurching toward the modern world and lurching to the right at the same time. East Germany was testing the country's ability to integrate itself before it integrated the rest of Eastern Europe into the European Union. And each and every one of my German friends was acting out some private drama. They called themselves "normal" Germans, but could Germans ever be "normal" again?

America's missionary-like remaking of Germany after the war dramatically altered the country: perhaps no land in Europe or the world has been Americanized so deeply and in as many different ways. But had Germany truly grafted on the open, democratic national traits of the World War II victors? Or was it all a façade, one that a new national crisis could wash away?

And there were all the old questions of German history and what sort of role such an ever-present past plays in shaping the future of a newly intact Germany.

I was determined to avoid making my search a weighty academic treatment. Leave it for others to write ponderous chapters about Germany's economic modernization, its growing investments in Eastern Europe, its central role in a more integrated European Union. Certainly, one needed to study such affairs. But what intrigued me were the people and the issues that would shape the future, the Germans who were the texture of the fabric of this newly unified country.

And I knew any book I'd write about Germans was also an act of self-exploration: did my German blood place any special responsibility on me? Was there anything particularly German about me? I had long since stopped bragging about my father as a war hero, but I had no idea when I began this book that I would soon be grappling with a family war criminal. After years of denying my own Germanness, I would have to confront it.

I sensed my father's presence as I began to sift through his things in search of the New Germany. Little did I know how much, at the same time, I would learn about myself.

ullay of horse and hoofe and
ware, and mangles, and scatters ...
...en beneath and the blue above,
...ach and danger, and life, and
...acca, — Lacca used to ride
...mouse-gray mustang close to my
...blue serape and bright-belled ...
...shed with joy as I looked at ...

ONE

HITLER'S OFFSPRING

Two souls, alas, are lodged within my breast,
Which struggle there for undivided reign.
  —JOHANN VON GOETHE, *FAUST*

There are not two Germanys, a good one and a bad one,
but only one, whose best turned into evil through devilish cunning.
Wicked Germany is merely good Germany led astray . . .
It is all within me. I have been through it all.
  —THOMAS MANN, BEFORE THE
    LIBRARY OF CONGRESS, 1945

My first shock lies at the bottom of my father's old army footlocker, among the yellowed sheets of a dog-eared scrapbook.

Pasted to the front page is a reproduction of a painting labeled "The Naked Truth" by Fougeron. An unclad figure holds a burning torch toward a crowd, the crowd turns its head from the glare. The caption reads: *A Curious Fact Has Been Established by Scientific Investigation That Many People Really Do Not Want to Know the Truth . . . When the Truth is Presented, They Turn Their Backs on It.*

So this was to be my father's collection of unrecognized verities.

While my father lived, the heavy, olive green trunk sat untouched at the back of a deep closet underneath the stairs beside his study. It was as if he considered it to be safer there in the dark, away from prying eyes. When he died in 1988, I inherited it with a number of other small and large boxes, steel containers, and bulging envelopes stuffed with family history. I'd carted the locker from our family home in Utah to my apartment in Washington to the next one in Berlin and to the next one in Brussels, never opening it for a decade.

My father had been a private man, secretive. He never talked much about personal affairs. His life's regrets—his meager formal education, his humble job as a baker in a supermarket, his strained relationship with my mother—the effect of all this on his psyche was something an Old World Father didn't discuss with a New World son. So for most of his life I knew only the broad outlines of his life history: The facts were clear enough: it had been my father's duty to prepare the ground for his family's immigration when he arrived in New York in 1927, at the age of eighteen. He worked first in a Chinese laundry before finding an all-night job as a baker, the profession for which he had apprenticed in Dresden.

The Mormons promised prosperity in Utah and, over time, most of my father's newly converted family would relocate there. But my father would never know such bounty. Until his last days, he worked as a baker in a supermarket. His younger brother would be the one to experience the American dream—he went to college and became a well-paid engineer for a diamond-products company. It had been my father's task to make that sort of life possible for his brother and ultimately for me and my sisters. My father often spoke of how he, as a child, yearned to join one of the ships passing by on the Elbe, as a carpenter. But his father refused him the permission or the money for the tools. His life was to be sacrificed to fish all of them out of the dreary dead-end of post–World War I Germany. And as a baker, his father had said, his family would at least always have enough to eat.

During the trip I took with my father to his homeland in 1985, three years before his death, I unearthed evidence that this overly responsible father of his had gambled away the family bakery in Leubsdorf in a game of cards. Alcohol had played a role. This had apparently been the reason they moved to Dresden and why my grandmother had been attracted by the cleansing influences of Mormonism. My grandfather was running and hoping for a new start.

For all my father's genealogical research, he wasn't eager to learn more from locals in Leubsdorf about this aspect of his father's history.

"I could tell you many stories about my father," he told me at the time. "He could be a weak man. Very weak."

"In what way was he weak?" I had asked.

My father's eyes darkened. A long pause, a pained sigh. "Some matters are best left buried," he said. "What good would it do anyone if I told you now?"

With the memory of that conversation in mind, I rummage through his footlocker, a musty realm of old photos, postcards, black binders full of records, shoeboxes containing old letters, and scrapbooks pasted to bursting with newspaper clippings.

My father always had been a collector. There were the stamps, *National Geographics*, scrapbooks filled with his favorite political cartoons, and booklets justifying his belief that the world was under the control of a global cabal of elites unified by such organizations as the Trilateral Commission, the Council on Foreign Relations, and the Freemasons.

After his death, I had discovered a large suitcase containing a copy of every article I had ever written, from sports columns in my high-school newspaper to war reporting for the *Wall Street Journal.* It had been his unspoken way of expressing pride in my work—a pride I rarely heard from him.

More curiously, my three sisters and I happened upon a number of coffee cans, filled to the brim with coins, hidden in the rafters of the garage. I recognized them immediately as my father's shield against the ravages of a new monetary crisis, which he had always been certain would come. He often had told me about his Germany of 1923, when his mother rushed to the market with wheelbarrows of his father's hard-earned marks, hoping to translate them into goods before inflation could devour their remaining worth.

So it doesn't surprise me that one of his scrapbooks, stuffed with German and English clippings from newspapers in New York, reflects this apocalyptic thinking. The articles mostly reported natural and man-made disasters: a deadly tornado in the Midwest, the worst floods ever to hit China, earthquakes in Japan, France, Nicaragua, and the Transcaucasus, almost everywhere. And assorted reports of ship disasters and revolutionary violence, evidence of a world gone mad. I imagine a headline over it all: *"The End of the World Is Near."*

I vaguely remember my father quietly uttering the odd apocalyptic thought or another throughout his life.

We live in a decadent world headed for the rocks, Fred.

Rome collapsed when its politicians grew as corrupt as ours, Fred.

I don't envy what you'll have to live through . . .

That sort of thing.

Yet nothing in those pages, three years before Hitler came to power and less than three years after my father had immigrated to America, predicts that the twentieth century's worst disaster was brewing back home in Germany. There is nothing about the Reichstag elections in 1930, when Hitler's party scored its first big success—18 percent of the vote. There is nothing about the German jobless rate rising toward a high of some 30 percent of the working population by 1932, setting the stage for the ugly history that was to follow. At eleven in the morning on January 30, 1933, Hindenburg appointed Hitler Reichskanzler. My father's scrapbook doesn't include that event, either. But it is about then that it adopts a more nationalistic tone.

A large clip catalogues the contributions of German immigrants to America, ranging from scientific breakthroughs to great literature. Other articles follow the young and dynamic Hitler: a fully illustrated announcement of the new Third Reich flags with their swastikas; reports of growing employment throughout the land; Josef Goebbels opening a new bridge that was said to be a testament to German engineering.

My father also appeared to share in Germans' chafing against post–World War I punishments. He had collected accounts of Russians and French arming themselves to the teeth while the Germans remained "defenseless" because of the Versailles Treaty's restrictions. Hitler's propaganda seemed to be infecting my father in Manhattan, four thousand and eighty miles away from his birthplace, with both German pride and resentment, the ingredients of a war to come.

With each page, the evidence grows more compelling, until I reach a collection of dog-eared pulp pamphlets bunched together at the back of the scrapbook. The tracts denounce the West for the Versailles Treaty's injustices, condemn French and Jewish propaganda against Germans, and deny all German guilt for the "Great War."

A particularly strident pamphlet bears a heroic front-page drawing of a vibrant, handsome Hitler sporting a swastika armband. The Führer himself had written the article under the headline: "Hitler's Appeal Against the Madness of Versailles."

I was born more than two decades after my father had collected these papers. I try to imagine his thoughts back then, when as a young man he first would have read these German diatribes against an unjust world. Nothing he had said to me while he was alive suggested he had been a Hitler fan, but he also had never spoken out against him, as had my mother. Now I fear I know why.

I can only imagine him nodding his agreement as he had underlined sections of the pamphlets, such as the one quoting Viscount Rothermere from London's *Daily Mail* of July 10, 1933: "Something more significant than a new Government has arisen among the Germans," he wrote of the then forty-three-year-old Hitler. "There has been a sudden expansion of their national spirit like that which took place in England under Queen Elizabeth. Youth has taken command. . . . It would be both futile and unfair to resent this revival of German spirit. Each nation has the right to make the most of its own resources. It is Germany's good fortune to have found a leader who can combine for the public good all the most vigorous elements in the country."

I look at the return address at the bottom of the last page of each of these tracts. They were mailed to my father monthly from Hamburg by an organization called the "Fichte-Bund," whose name betrays its views. After the Prussians' humiliating defeat by Napoleon at Jena, the German philosopher Johann Gottlieb Fichte's "Addresses to the German Nation" preached regeneration. Fichte exalted the German spirit which, unlike the decadent Jews and French, would create a new era under the leadership of a small elite untroubled by conventional morals. The Bund was apparently trying to rally German emigrants to their country's new cause. My father was a paying subscriber.

I imagine my father sorting through his mail upon returning home to his one-room Brooklyn apartment. I recall his stories of the exploited German bakers, who were well trained, hard working, and prepared to labor viciously long hours. He had sacrificed much for his family, for his parents, his children. For me. Like many postwar offspring of German fathers, I wonder if I really wanted to know what my father's innermost thoughts had been during the Hitler era.

My father had come to America as the child of a beaten and internationally despised country. He carried an inferiority complex his entire life. I had always thought it had mostly to do with his working-class roots. He was self-taught and well read, but my mother was the family intellectual, the teacher and college graduate. He had always been defensive about that.

But perhaps, I think, as I leaf through the pamphlets, it was his Germanness that had bred the inferiority complex. The scrapbook is a collation of reasons to believe in himself and in Germany. He was more a product of his times than I had ever imagined. I wonder what he might have become if not for the luck of immigration. I ponder about how different my life might have been.

The scrapbook takes another turn in 1934. My father's obsession shifts from natural disasters to Jews. He records Hitler's decrees forcing the firing of all Jews as civil servants. By 1935, new laws dictate that Jews can't visit public swimming pools, cinemas, or theaters. The Nuremberg laws, "to protect German blood and German honor," provide official sanction to generalized discrimination and the humiliation of Jews.

Foreplay to the Holocaust.

My father has collected clippings on good Jews building Palestine, bad Jews endangering Germany, fearful Jews under growing attacks in Romania.

I cannot read my father's emotions in these pages. His only personal notes are coolly transcribed from some unnamed "yearbook," a bloodless listing of increasing anti-Semitic incidents for each of the years from 1935 to 1939 in Austria, Romania, Poland and, of course, Germany.

The clips my father has included from the New York German-language paper, the *New Yorker Staats-Zeitung und Herold*, are particularly poisonous. I read them slowly and with some difficulty in the ornate German script then still used in printing. One outlines how Jews are conspiring to seize political power in Moscow. The language is clear. "The Communist enemy is a Jewish enemy." Another explains how Jews control New York's organized crime. It includes photos and names of the leading Jewish mafiosi and claims that eight out of ten such crimes are Jewish-inspired. "That is the contribution of Judaism to the building up of America!" it sneers in bold print.

Mother and father, newlyweds

Another article compares the German-Jewish problem to the American black problem—races that will never quite fit in.

Sprinkled throughout are accounts from various papers of growing violence against Jews. A large photo in 1939 shows Orthodox Jews building the last barricades against Nazi invaders in Poland. Another portrays the scene at Havana Harbor, where some 907 Jewish refugees aboard the German liner *St. Louis* are being turned back out to sea. A small 1939 article quotes Goebbels saying, "The fate of Jewry indeed is hard but no more than deserved."

All appear without comment from my father.

I recall only one confrontation ever with my father over race. I had returned from a high-school scholarship competition in Washington, D.C., with a photograph of a dazzling black woman I had met. I was smitten. My father discovered the photo, and told me I should stay clear of "Negro" girlfriends because their brains were smaller, inadequate for breeding. The statement seemed so out of character for my father—I responded with stunned rage.

"You bigoted bastard!" I fumed.

I remember the words well, for I never had had reason to say them before or afterward. He struck me across the cheek. Not hard, but the shock was all the greater since he had never hit me before, aside from the occasional, well-earned childhood spanking. I left home for a week until my mother begged me to return.

On issues of minorities and race, my mother had always been our role model. She spoke tirelessly of our obligation toward the world's less fortunate. She had been a second-grade teacher who had favored the underdog student: the child with a learning disability, an immigrant child struggling with English, the fearful victims of broken families or parental abuse.

As I sort through the clippings, it occurs to me that our family's experience after the war was a metaphor of sorts for what had occurred in postwar Germany: the worst of its character had been altered or at least censored, and its better sides won time and opportunity to flourish. The war's outcome had censored my father's probable racism; the allied victory created more space for my mother's liberal spirit. Yet until this moment I never thought of my father as representing the "bad" German and my mother the "good."

More memories from my childhood rush back: my mother had been a Roosevelt Democrat, who valued what Franklin Delano Roosevelt did for America's unfortunates. My father hated him for selling out eastern Germany in his negotiations with Stalin. I recall angry dinner table fights over such subjects. Mother adored Kennedy. Father, Nixon. Mother instilled an optimism in us about the future. Father wanted us to be braced for the worst. Following my mother's death, nothing I found in my mother's affairs surprised me. Her humanity, her emotional traumas, her loneliness, her fears—she was an open book. But my father's life had always been more of an encrypted code. I was beginning to break it.

Had he been anti-Semitic? A racist? If so, how did his views change with time and experience?

I grasp for memories that contradict the image of my father suggested by the scrapbook. I had never thought of my father as anything other than a deeply good man.

I recall my father's support for Jesse Jackson as a candidate for President. I argued that Jackson was too radical for America, but my father said the country needed someone who would look after the elderly and disadvantaged. I find myself to be relieved by this recollection. And now I consider closing the trunk and setting it back in the attic, into oblivion. How much do I really want to know?

And how much am I willing to share in a book? Will my friends and acquaintances treat me the same way afterward? Or will they instead begin to view me—horror of horrors—as a *German.*

That is, of course, the last thing I want.

And it goes right to the heart of the problem of twenty-first-century Germany. Even if Germans have become a better and reformed people, the Holocaust isn't an event one forgives and forgets.

How many mitzvahs must one perform to undo a Shoah?

Not an eternity of good deeds.

One long-term side effect of the Third Reich is that none of my German friends has a natural relationship with a Jew; the link between victim and perpetrator is by definition unnatural. Even a generation or two on, they can't sit easily at a common table without ghosts taking up the free chairs.

Yet my own relationship with Jews has never carried German baggage. When I have disliked a Jew, or one has disliked me, the relationship has never borne the mark of history. I never went out of my way to seek Jewish companionship, as do many of my German friends, nor have I ever focused much on the Jewishness of my Jewish friends.

By contrast, my German friends either love Jews too much, subconsciously compensating for past crimes with an obsession for Yiddish plays and Klezmer music, or their resentment festers in a hidden pool, to seep out in the occasional stench of an offhand remark. ("Don't you think there must be something about them if people have persecuted them for so long," a youngish German company board member once said to me.)

By chance, a Jewish friend of mine, Ed Serotta, visits my Berlin apartment on the day that I am scouring my father's scrapbook. Ed and I have known each other for years. He sees I am shaken.

"You look like you've seen a ghost," he says.

"Something like that," I say. I pick out pages of the scrapbook for him to read—choosing the most damning possible excerpts. I want him to hate me for what I have found.

Ed's own family had emigrated to America at the turn of the century from Czarist Russia. He is a photographer and author, and he'd recently published a book on Germans and Jews. The book is a moving documentation of what has become one of the world's most neurotic relationships.

"So what's the big deal?" he says as he reads.

"Ed, don't you see what this means? All these years, I thought I was clean. I knew I had German blood, but this stuff"—I point to the scrapbook as to an object of disgust—"had nothing to do with me. I never even thought of myself as a German-American when I was growing up. Now I've got to deal with this *shit*. And you see what it's done to *them*."

Them.

Them. That's how Ed and I—how all we of the adjudicating American press—had always regarded the Germans. I had to find my way back to that. I was not one of *them*.

Ed tilts his head. "Don't you think you might be overreacting just a tad?"

"No, I don't," I say. "Read more."

So he does. And I wait for his response.

Many American journalists cover Germany with a cloak of superiority they dare not wear in other countries: we generally agree that "these people" are humorless, inflexible, unhappy, and to be studied in their natural habitat as a phenomenon. I often detect a form of racism among American reporters. In other countries and cultures they would never generalize from small incidents the way that they do about Germans.

Journalists live in Paris and London because they like it there. Reporters live in Germany, by and large, because it is a better, more important story. I know many reporters who have become Francophiles, Anglophiles, and even Russophiles. The Germanophile is a rarer breed.

American reporters learn early on that the easiest way to get copy into the paper from Germany is to find some peg that recalls the past: a torched asylum home here, neo-Nazis in the military there. The result has been that, for years, each new reporter has reinforced stereotypes because it is a cheap ticket to publication. One of the most important signs of changing international attitudes toward Germany is that this practice has begun to lose some currency.

My own newspaper, the *Wall Street Journal*, covers Germany closely because it is the world's third-mightiest economy and has some of the globe's most important companies. But even we don't mind a historical peg—the rebuilding of Hitler's Olympic stadium for modern times, Deutsche Bank and Volkswagen coming to terms with their Nazi past, the in-depth portrait of an eastern German skinhead . . .

Yet Ed and I are different from many in the American press: we hold German culture and the state's support of the arts in high regard. We respect Germans for the new society they've built on such foul ashes. We share a distaste for the cheap short cuts our colleagues often take to sell a story. Yet we also know that in reporting Germany we are often watching the walking wounded.

And now, I tell Ed, I feel I've been hit by the same late-falling shrapnel.

Ed shakes his head in disbelief at my reaction to the scrapbook. He has always watched modern Germans with bewilderment as they agonize as perfectly over the Holocaust as their fathers and grandfathers had once organized it. At times, Ed had praised Germans for dealing with their past more completely and commendably perhaps than any other people in the world. On other occasions, Ed had sneered at them for so eagerly bathing in their own guilt, hardly able to contain their relief at finding another Jew before whom to supplicate.

Ed hasn't any patience for anyone's tendency—whether, Jewish, German, or German-American—to lose perspective. Even if my father had shared the views of the articles he pasted into his scrapbook, says Ed, such opinions in those days had been no more unusual or socially unacceptable than a taste for two lumps of sugar in a cup of coffee.

"Fred, don't fall into the trap," he says. "This is nothing." He flips through some more pages. "Nothing conclusive here at all. And what has any of this got to do with you or your life now?"

"History . . . is a nightmare from which I am trying to awake," says the protagonist in James Joyce's *Portrait of the Artist as a Young Man*.

A historian would be hard-pressed to find a country where a mere dozen years of history, between 1933 and 1945, has cast such a long shadow. History plays a more critical role in the conscious present in Germany than perhaps any other Western country. As Germany expands its influence in the twenty-first century, it will be constantly balancing its potential power against its history-taught self-constraint.

When Germany sent combat troops to join NATO allies in Bosnia in early 1997, it was the overcoming of history that gave the story its importance: the *Bundeswehr* for the first time was treading on territory where the *Wehrmacht* had goose-stepped before.

When Germans balked at accepting a single currency, Helmut Kohl told them it was a matter of war and peace. A unified Germany could not stand alone as the mightiest country at the middle of the continent—history had taught that. And it was a German who was saying this most loudly.

The French desire for a single European currency was also born of history—they would be neutering a larger, unified Germany's two primary instruments of sovereign power in Europe: the Bundesbank and the Deutsche Mark. Even as the Germans won the agreement to put the bank in Frankfurt, at the same time they accepted that its head would perhaps never be German.

So even Europe's single currency, in a way, is Hitler's Offspring.

And for the Germans, the expansion of the European Union and the North Atlantic Treaty Organization to the east is part of paying an historical debt. Then-Defense Minister Volker Rühe more than once defended the widening of these Western institutions on moral grounds—Germans owed East Europeans, to whom they had done so much harm, the same embrace the West had offered to Germans after the war.

German fascination with history is, quite literally, as old as the modern study of history. The historian Fritz Stern, who influenced much of my early thinking on Germany through his books, notes that it was the German Leopold von Ranke who in the first half of the nineteenth century established history as a central and autonomous discipline that would depend on the cold facts of primary sources.

"The Germans have taught us history as they have lived it: sublimely and cruelly," Stern writes in his book of essays, *Dreams and Delusions.* He says the "German Question" in all of its guises "has had a decisive bearing on the history of the world" for well more than a century. "There is no denying the centrality of German history, and fascination with it requires no apology."

Yet history for the German is more of a nightmare than a foundation. As continental leadership is thrust upon it, history suggests that Germans shouldn't embrace the opportunity. History is a wagging index finger. And that sets the Germans apart from their neighbors and allies.

Contrast that to the French, who celebrate "La Grande Nation" despite Napoleon's excesses and Vichy's collaboration. Britain's fallen empire and tarnished royals don't alter patriotic instinct. America's misadventures in Latin America and Vietnam don't dull a flag-waving pride that has been reinforced by a wealth of heroic moments when Americans marched forward as the globe's White Knights.

Not so with Germany. One could cheer a tennis champion like Boris Becker or Steffi Graf, one could celebrate a World Cup soccer champion, but to scream "Go Deutschland" remained somehow unseemly. When German thugs beat a French policeman into a coma during the 1998 World Cup, it was a history-laden, national event. The country's top tabloid, *Bild,* gave the policeman's family 50,000 DM and ran a fund-raising campaign that produced tens of thousands more. Germans, in short, wanted to show they weren't *that sort* of German again.

History has made Germanness as much a personal drama as a nationality.

Happily for me, my own wounds—and those of my family—weren't so deep when compared to most of my German friends.

Or so I thought as I dug more deeply into my father's footlocker . . .

My eyes stop short on a gray envelope, upon which my father had written: Arthur Schumann, 1932—*private.*

The brittle seal of the old envelope breaks easily, and several yellow clippings from newspapers fall into my hands. I pick up the largest, from the New York *Daily News* of April 1932. The photograph shows my Grandpa Schumann—a far younger version than I had ever known but unmistakably handsome. He stands in the dock of a New York city court. Beside his own photograph is a second frame showing my aunt, his young daughter Ingeborg, whom the newspaper properly called "a strikingly attractive blonde."

The headline reads, in screaming letters: "Preacher Jailed for Beating Daughter, 15."

"Enraged because his pretty 15-year-old daughter had stayed out all night," wrote the reporter, "an elder of the Mormon Church in Brooklyn last night beat the girl into insensibility with a broom handle. The elder, the Rev. Arthur T. Schumann, 37, of 292 Kosciusko St., one of the leaders of the Church of Jesus Christ of Latter Day Saints, at Gates and Franklin Aves., Brooklyn, was dragged from his battered victim by two policemen and jailed on charges of felonious assault."

Arthur Paul Thomas Schumann had been my grandfather, on my mother's side. He was my childhood hero, the man who took me on long boat rides in the park, the man who showered love upon me unconditionally, the man for whom I could do no wrong, or who for me could do no wrong. He called me his Pathfinder. There was no safer place in the world than on his lap.

I learned later from my mother that my father sometimes resented my closeness to my grandfather. I also knew that the two men were cool toward each other. My instinct had always been to side with my grandfather. He played the violin, wrote poetry, and was so filled with love that one could easily consider him the proper blood descendant of the great composer Robert Schumann. If ever there was a "good German," in my eyes it was Grandpa Schumann.

The envelope in my father's footlocker shakes me. I wonder why my father had saved it. The year 1932 was a dozen years before my father would marry Arthur Schumann's daughter, my mother.

The clippings provide more troubling facts. One says Ingeborg was rushed to St. John's Hospital, where physicians said they feared a spine injury. "Examination of her body revealed more than thirty welts, police reported," says the article. And according to another article, my grandmother told police that her husband had "frequently practiced brutalities upon a younger daughter, Johanna."

My mother.

A clipping from a later edition of the same day's New York *Daily News* carries a photo of her sad and frightened teenager Ingeborg's face beside that of my grandmother, who looks stern and angry. The tabloid had somehow got them to pose with the broom handle that had been used on Ingeborg.

My grandmother vowed to police that she would never return to live with her husband again, and that she intended to institute separation proceedings. (They would, in fact, spend the rest of their days together.) At the Gates Avenue police station, my Grandpa Schumann—who had come to America just a year and a half earlier—defended his right to beat his children on the grounds that it was the German way.

"Ingeborg is a good girl," he told Lieutenant Joseph Scheidler and Sergeant Albert Farrington. "But she is so pretty I was afraid she might get into trouble with boys. So I beat her to make her good. My father beat me and that is why I am a good man."

Berlin 1927. Grandfather Arthur Schumann and his wife. Ingeborg is on the left. My mother, Johanna, is on the right.

Another article identifies my grand-father as "a roofer by trade and a musi-cian by avocation who came to this country 18 months ago." The paper quotes him: "I have not much education myself. I gave my stepson, who is now 22, a good education. I only beat him once. He has told me many times since then that he thanked me for the beating. It made a better man of him."

At a court hearing, my mother was a witness. It turned out that her sis-ter had been sitting over her lessons one morning after she had come in so late. My grandfather struck her then without warning, by way of punishment. When Ingeborg protested that her father didn't have the right to beat her in America, a place where children had more rights, he grew even more angry and reached for the broomstick.

Further articles, in the *Daily News* and a local German-language paper, de-veloped this German theme of proper upbringing. Judge Dodd at the Supreme Court lectured my grandfather that Americans no longer raised their children with the rod, according to the *New Yorker Staats-Zeitung und Herold,* a one-cent German-language newspaper. The paper reports that Grandpa "weeped like a child" as he was led to the courtroom in handcuffs, not understanding why he would be incarcerated for trying to make his daughter a good girl.

The German paper is on his side. In a commentary alongside the article, it notes that Americans were hardly the people to tell Germans how to raise their children. "Every right-thinking family father must clench his fists when he reads this report. Nowhere is there as much corruption and crime as in free America, crimes that are primarily committed by the young. Judge Dodd says that parents here don't have a right to use the rod on their children. Yes, Judge Dodd, you can experience the fruits of this American upbringing daily. It is hair-raising that Schumann should be treated like a dangerous criminal by the court, when he only wanted the best for his child . . . Who is responsible for his children, you, Judge Dodd, or this family father?"

The article sarcastically poses the question to Judge Dodd of how he would have reacted to his teenage daughter staying out all night. Would he simply have asked her in the morning if she had had a good time? "Every child needs a firm hand now and again," it concludes. "It doesn't matter how well you raise a child, the daily contact with other (American) children teaches them other things. I have deep sympathy for Schumann . . . He has the right to bring home the bacon, and otherwise he must shut his mouth and dance to his children's music. A fine state of things."

For context, I search the New York *Daily News* on the day of my grandfather's crime for reports on Germany. An inside headline reads: *"Hitler's Storm Troops Raided."* The text: April 14 (1932): Police raided 150 gathering places of the fascist storm troops, carrying out President von Hindenburg's order for the dissolution of the organization. Adolf Hitler told the Associated Press, "We'll be back six hundred thousand strong. Our storm troops were suppressed once before when we had only twenty thousand. When the ban was lifted, we had sixty thousand." He added, prophetically, "We'll take over the power and the ban on the troopers will be lifted."

My grandfather's crime is trivial compared to the transgressions that would come.

When I began to explore my German roots during college, I wrote an essay for a German literature class that argued that my Kempe and Schumann sides represented the two sides of the German soul that had wrestled with one another throughout history. The Schumann in me, I wrote, represented liberal, free-thinking democrats. The Kempes were the solid, obedient foot soldiers for whatever movement led the country.

Schumann was the dreamy Utopian and Kempe was the cold realist, Schumann the poet and Kempe the peasant; the writer and the worker, the musician and the soldier, each playing their accompaniment to German history. Hitler had demonically soldered together these otherwise positive attributes. He abused the romantic notions of Germans to seduce them into seeing themselves as a master race. (What could be more romantic than to think you are of that race?) Then he tapped the efficiency of the Kempe to create factories to rub out those who threatened this genetic Utopia.

I argued in my essay, not very originally, that the Holocaust captured the world imagination because an advanced industrial country with a rich culture had committed the crimes. It was because of Goethe that we were horrified by Goebbels. It was Brahms that made it so hard to understand Buchenwald. Genocide, one would think, should have been the monopoly of illiterate barbarians. Stalin's Russia hadn't reached Germany's level of development when it built the gulags, and Pol Pot's Cambodia never produced Beethoven. Yet only Germany achieved the brutal efficiency of Auschwitz.

On the few occasions when I thought about it, I considered myself the happy outcome of a better mix of the two sides of the German character. Without the Kempe genes, I was certain I would be a crazy Schumann (my father often reminded me of the madness that consumed the composer at the end of his life—and how it infected my mother's line). But lacking the Schumann side, I wouldn't have been able to tolerate my own colorless company. Being a Kempe always seemed a matter of duty to me, but being a Schumann was a pleasure. Kempe was a military march; Schumann a joyful dance.

This view was reinforced by family parties. The Schumann family Christmas, presided over by my boisterously loving Grandpa Arthur, was always vibrantly alive. Children laughed and frolicked beside parents locked in spirited conversation. Each year's high point was American football in the snow, a gloriously sloppy and chaotic affair.

I recall the Kempe gatherings as more scripted. The homes were tidier, the children more obedient, and the matron Grandma Kempe was distant and un-approachable. My mother always felt uneasy with the Kempes, who had difficulty fathoming her emotional highs and lows.

It struck me later in life that these two families never would have known each other in Germany—their worlds and natures were too distant. It was only the upside-down world of immigration and their common conversion to the Mormon religion that brought them together in Brooklyn in the early 1930s. My father met my mother when she was just a young teen, for his younger sister had married her older brother.

My mother's clan had their roots in Leipzig, Berlin, and Breslau—city folk who were cigar merchants, business people, photographers, poets, playwrights, composers, and musicians. They were of the German intellectual and educated class. My great-grandfather had been a prominent Social Democrat in Breslau, which became Poland's Wroclaw after the war. He mixed with the city's finest, who bought the hand-rolled cigars he supplied to the best hotels.

Most Schumanns were proud of a heritage that connected them to the composer Robert Schumann, a bloodline that reached us through the composer's uncle. My father's tribe were the more predictable Kempes and Bartschs, country folk who originally hailed from the Ore Mountains in what is now Germany's federal state of Saxony. They had been farmers, coal miners, and, when the industrial revolution gave them the chance, workers. The closest they had come to white-collar work before immigration to America was when my grandfather opened a bakery—a profession he then handed down to my own father. They were simple people with humble lives, the polar opposite of the Schumanns.

Grandpa Schumann had been a professional photographer in Berlin before he'd emigrated. He had been a handsome and charming man, something of a ladies' man. He took whatever jobs he could get in Depression-struck America, though he was most proud of being a draftsman for Franklin Roosevelt's WPA—among other projects, laboring on the Guggenheim Museum in New York.

My inheritance from him was a trunkload of poetry, dripping with emotion. He poured out epic poems about the church to which he had converted in Germany—the American Mormons. If God didn't love my grandfather, it wasn't for lack of expressed adoration from his side—volumes of it. His other passion was the violin, and he could play for hours without end, Schumann of course. His favorite piece was, perhaps predictably, "Traümerei"—"Dreaming." He paid one of my cousins fifty cents an hour for the right to give her violin lessons.

In my college thesis, I argued that the success for the future of Germany was to find a combination of Schumann and Kempe that tapped the best of both sides' qualities.

I talk over this Schumann-Kempe theory of German history with a friend who toils at Bonn's Defense ministry, Vice Admiral Ulrich Weisser. In a French fish restaurant in Bonn, we gab for hours about the divided German soul.

I note that Robert Schumann's writings describe his own split personality in the two imaginary characters Floristan and Eusebius, one the external and impetuous performer and the other an internal and brooding thinker. I say that what the Chinese call Yin and Yang has been tearing Germans apart, and not unifying them, for ages.

My friend the admiral calls upon Goethe's Faust, the most *ur-Deutsch* of all characters. He recites a few of Faust's most famous lines, spoken in the play to the student Wagner, who can't share Faust's deep, exalted urges.

> *Thy heart by one sole impulse is possessed;*
> *Unconscious of the other still remain!*
> *Two souls, alas, are lodged within my breast,*
> *Which struggle there for undivided reign.*

The waitress, tossing us a curious nod, delivers two flutes of champagne as Weisser completes the excerpt:

> *One to the world with obstinate desire,*
> *And closely cleaving organs, still adheres;*

Above the mist, the other doth aspire,
With sacred vehemence, to purer spheres.

It is typical to me of Germany that Admiral Weisser, then the chief of the military planning staff, is as well versed at analyzing the two sides of his German soul as he is at determining the pace and structure of NATO expansion.

On the day after our dinner, Admiral Weisser mails me a copy of a speech that a seventy-year-old Thomas Mann delivered at the Library of Congress in Washington. *"A little more insight into our divided German nature,"* he has scrawled upon it.

Thomas Mann, a refugee from the Third Reich, had been an American citizen for several months when he delivered the speech just after the war had ended in 1945. Germany's recent history weighed on his every word.

Mann speaks of the tugs tearing at the German soul as being cosmopolitanism and provincialism, worldliness and world-wariness.

He visits Faust as well—it is a German national sport to agonize over one's Faustian character—with his "two souls, alas, lodged in one breast." (In the original German, "alas" is actually "ach," which generations of actors have interpreted in a manner ranging from a groan of pain to a primal scream.) Mann focuses on Goethe's devil, who toys with the German soul. For him, it is this devil who is the villain of the Third Reich.

"Wherever the arrogance of the intellect mates with the spiritually obsolete, there is the devil's domain. The Devil, Luther's Devil, Faust's Devil, strikes me as a very German figure, and the pact with him, the Satanic covenant, to win all treasures and power on earth for a time at the cost of the soul's salvation, strikes me as something exceedingly typical of German nature. A lonely thinker and searcher, a theologian and philosopher in his cell who, in his desire for world enjoyment and world domination, barters his soul to the Devil. Isn't this the right moment to see Germany in this picture, the moment in which Germany is literally being carried off by the Devil?"

Yet Mann in this vein also attacks the musicality of the German, the Schumann in me. I had always viewed a love of music as the ultimate German redeeming value. One could offset at least some of Hitler's heritage with

Bach. What differentiated my family most from that of our Utah neighbors was the way music dominated our Sundays—my mother's classical records spun all day on the hi-fi. She played Schumann most often, of course, but the record cabinet was filled with so many others: Beethoven, Mendelssohn, Schubert. She particularly loved the Schumann and Schubert "Lieder," that most poetically beautiful of German musical inventions.

Mann argues in his text that music is "the most unrealistic and yet the most impassioned of arts, mystical and abstract." He says Faust had to be musical, "for the relation of the German to the world is abstract and mystical, that is musical—the relation of a professor with a touch of demonism, awkward and at the same time filled with arrogant knowledge that he surpasses the world in 'depth.' "

Germans, he says, gave the Western world "its most beautiful and socially binding, but also deepest and most significant, music, and for that they haven't been denied gratitude and fame. At the same time it felt, and today feels stronger than ever, that such musicality of the soul is paid for dearly in other spheres—in the spheres of politics and human relations."

Mann then delineates the two strains of the German psyche: his version of "Kempe versus Schumann" is "Martin Luther versus the wood-carver Tilman Riemenschneider."

Mann calls Luther the "pure incarnation of German nature," and he doesn't mean it positively. Luther was "Germanness in its purest form," says Mann, ". . . anti-Roman, anti-European . . . in the guise of evangelical freedom and spiritual emancipation. And the specifically Lutheran, the choleric coarseness, the invective, the fuming and raging, the awful crudity coupled with tender depth of feeling and with the grossest superstitious belief in demons and changelings, arouses my instinctive antipathy. I should not have liked to have been Luther's dinner guest."

But Mann, knowing German history, recognizes Luther's greatness. Luther's translation of the Bible into German created the language that writers from Goethe to Mann himself built upon. Luther also broke loose from scholarly chains and did much to introduce philosophical speculation, criticism, and freedom of research into all sorts of questions. Germans have much to do with the way the Western mind analyzes and thinks, and Luther had much to do with this German influence.

Many critics of Germany say it faces danger now because democracy has such shallow historical roots—forced upon the Germans, as it was, as part of their penance after World War II. But even Mann recognizes that Luther in his teachings was one of the earliest democratic thinkers.

"Every man his own priest," says Mann. "That is democracy. [Luther] was a liberating hero—but in the German style, for he knew nothing of liberty, of political liberty, that is, the liberty of the citizen—this kind of liberty not only left him cold, but its impulses and demands were deeply repugnant to him."

Mann condemns Luther for a historical betrayal for which he felt Germans were still paying a price.

"Thus Luther hated the peasant revolt which, evangelically inspired as it was, would, if successful, have given a happier turn to German history, a turn towards liberty. But Luther saw in it nothing but a distortion of his work . . . The peasants, he said, should be killed like mad dogs, and he told the princes that they could gain the kingdom of heaven by slaughtering the peasant beasts. Luther, the German man of the people, bears a good share of the responsibility for the sad ending of this first attempt at a German revolution . . . and for all its consequences."

Luther, this "conservative revolutionary," was in favor of freeing the religious soul, but he favored keeping the political beast in chains. This bad start at popular uprisings continued, says Mann, with failures again in 1813 and in 1848.

So often when I have complained to a German friend about some surly service or nasty experience I had experienced during the day, the friend will blame this on the fact that Germany never had a revolution.

Many historians and lay observers continue to trace Germany's often sour national mood to Luther. For whenever Germany has tried popular revolt, it has failed. An arguable exception is East Germany's final months, when mass protests led to the fall of the Berlin Wall and unification, but few Germans celebrate that "revolution" and unification as a national triumph of some positive popular spirit. They are more likely to grumble about the higher taxes, the political strains, and the clashing cultures that have come with unification. The rise to power of National Socialism, at first through elections, was as close as Germans have come to a successful grassroots uprising, and that ended in the worst sort of populist dictatorship.

The hero of Mann's speech is Tilman Riemenschneider, ultimately a loser. He was a pious artist and a Luther contemporary. I, like so many American tourists, had visited his finely cut altars, sculptures and reliefs along the Romantic Road in southern Germany. He never strived to be political—naturally modest as he was. Yet his heart went out to the poor and the oppressed—like my mother with her troubled students.

Seeing the plight of the peasants, Riemenschneider left his coddled life to fight alongside them against the bishops and the royals, whom Luther was defending. "Riemenschneider paid dearly for it," writes Mann. "For after the crushing of the peasant revolt, the victorious powers whom he had opposed took cruel revenge upon him; they subjected him to prison and torture, and he emerged from the ordeal a broken man, no longer capable of awakening the beauties in wood and stone."

Mann notes that this person, this Riemenschneider, has always existed in Germany. And he has most often failed.

As I dig deeper in my father's footlocker, I grow uneasy about the idea of this neatly divided Germany.

I have no doubt that my mother, my nearest Schumann, represented something good: I think of her, sitting late at night at her work table, agonizing over how she would help a new immigrant child learn English, how she could rescue a little boy who had lost the desire to learn because of a broken family. My mother fought the demons of melancholy that drove the composer Schumann mad and then rose above them to initiate creative writing programs for a new generation of Americans. Her tearful students read poems at her funeral. Some of hers. Some of their own.

But as I search further through my father's things, it grows clear that my father couldn't be considered dark to my mother's light. I found IOUs from siblings and parents, whose first stop when they arrived in America was my father's wallet. Though far from well-off himself, he bankrolled the purchase of his sister's first house, the wedding of a good friend, and the first days in the country for many others.

I also find a telling exchange of letters between my father and his own father. In one, my grandfather, who by that time was living in New York, announced to his son in early 1940 that he was returning to Germany because he expected America to join the war against the Reich. He wanted to be with his homeland, where he noted there was more work anyway. And he feared how Germans in America might be treated once war broke out—he didn't want to be caught on the wrong side of the fighting. He said he would leave alone, so it would continue to be his son's job to support his mother and siblings.

My father had kept copies of his own return correspondence. He ignored the politics of the time and focused only on his father's familial obligations. My father said that he had supported the family alone for long enough: it was time for his father to get to work. I don't know what impact that specific letter had, but I do know my grandfather never left America. However, I recall family tales about how Grandpa Kempe would linger at the docks wistfully looking at ships heading for Europe.

Among my father's letters I found love notes from a struggling poet named Hildegard, who seemed swept away by poems my father had written to her. And I unearthed the first shy jottings of my own teenage mother to my father, who was ten years her elder. They were teasing, flirtatious, sent from a summer camp in Milford, Connecticut, where she was a cleaning girl.

Dividing the world into good and bad Germans wouldn't work for me any more than it did in the end for Thomas Mann.

Says Mann, "There are not two Germanys, a good one and a bad one, but only one, whose best turned into evil through devilish cunning. Wicked Germany is merely good Germany gone astray, good Germany in misfortune, in guilt, and in ruin." For that reason, Mann doesn't put himself in the white robe and leave it to someone else to exterminate the wicked. "It is all within me, I have been through it all," he says.

A good lesson for the new Germany—it is all within it. It has been through it all.

Mann is merely baffled how a people so predisposed by self-analysis "could ever conceive the idea of world domination."

I didn't get it either, though I understood why Mann seconded Goethe's almost prophetic wish of so many years earlier that perhaps there should be a German Diaspora. "Like the Jews," he said, "the Germans must be transplanted and scattered over the world . . . in order to develop the good that lies in them fully and to the benefit of nations."

I talk to my German friends about the secrets I had found in my father's footlocker, hoping they will share with me the results of similar searches through their own family histories. Most had more reason to question their parents' pasts than I, but none had spent much time investigating. Why look for trouble?

It is easier for most Germans to accept vague collective responsibility rather than to look too close to home. German friends regard my search for individual responsibility, for family stories, as something curiously American.

Yet I was coming to have a great deal in common with this people I had always considered so foreign. The natural pride that most offspring feel for earlier generations was rendered impossible by the Third Reich. My father's footlocker casts new shadows over him and my beloved grandfather, though they hadn't been involved in the Third Reich at all. Back in those bad old days, even glancing association with matters German had a tendency to stain.

Then I remember the words of my friend Ed Serotta.

Perhaps I am making too much of all this.

I was born in America, after all. I listen to country music. I eat Mexican food. I had played Little League baseball. Nothing I found in my father's trunk was all that terrible, considering the times. I had a father who might have had some prejudices, but he had led a good life. I had a grandpa who had been arrested in Manhattan as a child-beater, yet I had known nothing but a lifetime of love from him.

When I tell my eldest sister Jeanie about what I had found, I expressed some relief to her that at least I hadn't unearthed any evidence of family complicity in the Holocaust. She then tells me a story that I hadn't heard—of my mother's return trip to Germany in 1936 to see the Olympics, when the Third Reich was just beginning to roll.

My mother had told my sister of an awful relative whom she had met during that time. My sister thought he had been an uncle of some sort, whom my mother had portrayed as a quite terrible Nazi—and quite a senior one. I'd never heard the story before. I make a note to check it out, but I had enough of history for the moment.

I return my father's heavy trunk, with some difficulty, up a wobbly ladder to the attic of my apartment. Goethe's Faust, Thomas Mann's Martin Luther, some phantom uncle in the Third Reich, even my father's footlocker—what did all of this have to do with twenty-first-century Germany? One German friend argues that I must draw a *Schlussstrich*—a dividing line delineating the bad German past from the better German future. He says I should write about "normal Germans."

Yet even as I launch my search for present-tense Germany, I know the past will return again and again as an irresistible magnet, as it has been for Germany for so long.

TWO

NORMAL GERMANS

In every German there is a touch of the wild-haired Beethoven striding through forests and weeping over a mountain sunset, grappling against impossible odds to express the inexpressible.
—STEPHAN EHEBALD, PSYCHIATRIST, READING FROM
THE XENOPHOBE'S GUIDE TO THE GERMANS

The German cannot afford to live from his gut. Within the German resides an unbearable pride. What's positive is that time has weakened this flaw. At the moment, our democracy is stable because of this. Germans have become less German.
—NORBERT HELDERMANN,
MATHEMATICS PROFESSOR

When I first fly back to Germany after four years absence, I am rushing through the Frankfurt airport when the sight of new rubbish bins stops me cold.

They are sleek and shiny, attractively curved on their long, low sides, so aerodynamic that they seem to have been styled by the designer of those jets out there on the tarmac. One yearns to have trash in hand, just for the joy of putting it into one of those four, equally-sized compartments for glass, cans, paper and *Restmüll*—other refuse. Atop them is a circular launching platform awaiting the fuel of stray ashes. I imagine the thought that went into this refuse complex: the airport authority drawing up specifications, the architect finalizing his blueprints, and the rubbish-bin maker deploying space-age metals to produce the highest-end garbage cans I'd seen anywhere in the world.

As I study them, I weigh two contradictory conclusions about Germany:

1) The bins demonstrate the environmental consciousness of Germany's advanced civilization. Germans have seen to it that thirty percent of their land is covered with protected woods. Each tree is safeguarded like an albino whale; each public place is littered with recycling points of one sort or another. No other country's Green party is such a potent national force.

2) Or less generously: the receptacles say more about the German obsession with order than about any love for the environment. The national ritual of recycling is so all-pervasive and far-reaching that one fears that form conquers substance; for no one has the capacity to properly process the mountains of neatly sorted refuse.

Germans busy themselves to an extraordinary extent sifting trash: green bottles from white, plastic from paper, cans from cartons. When I arrive later that day at my new Berlin residence, I see a half-dozen different garbage cans labeled for separate purposes in the apartment house's common courtyard. I marvel at the societal discipline this presupposes.

The one for colored bottles bears an announcement informing residents that nothing may be deposited there before seven in the morning—a protection against noise pollution. My neighbors apparently share such passion for waste disposal that one has to restrict the hours they may indulge in it. Within days, I determine by the clinking of bottles at just past seven that some of my cohabitants had been waiting all night to join in this recycling mania.

Germans' lust for sorting their waste is so great that no recycling company can keep up with it. I've read that there is so much excess segregated garbage that it is often recombined and cast away in a common dump.

Germans want recycled paper so badly that mills had been known to pulp perfectly new paper in order to serve market demand.

Yet Germans are untroubled by such stories: it isn't the system's imperfections but rather its principle that counts. *Prinzip über alles.* Recycling is a beautiful and noble concept. It brings order to the natural chaos of garbage.

Yet perhaps one can make too much of the airport receptacles, I think to myself. The foreign reporter often errs in trying to turn everything he sees into some epiphany about the nature of the Germans. Germans, I tell myself, have no special gene that caused the Holocaust, designed the Mercedes Benz, composed Beethoven's *Ninth,* or developed Frankfurt Airport's trash cans, any more than Americans are genetically predisposed toward gum-chewing, fast food, or technological genius.

Sometimes garbage is just garbage.

My basketball club—*Deutscher Basketball Verein Charlottenburg*—is so pleased by my return to Berlin after four years away that two of its members, the surgeon Herbert Kindermann and the schoolteacher Gerhard Stockheim, volunteer to help me move in. The flat itself belongs to another club member, Frank Schuldt, who had been posted by his company to Slovenia. When urged by other *Verein* members, he made his apartment available to me. After all, the *Verein* could always use a big man inside. Though age had slowed me, my six feet three and two hundred twenty pounds still took up valuable territory.

The *Verein* for years has been one of the most important levels of German social organization. Literally translated as "association," a *Verein* is actually much more than that. It seems that virtually every German belongs to at least one, and he often takes his obligations to its members as seriously as he does those to his family.

One German friend is a member of a *Verein* for garden cottage owners, another belongs to a darts-playing *Verein*, a third has joined a nudist vacationers' *Verein* (for which she receives all manner of travel discounts), and yet another dances in a tango *Verein.* Though these clubs revolve around some specific activity, the friendships formed there often follow members through a lifetime. They vacation together, raise children together, and generally settle life's problems together.

If all my club did was play basketball, we would merely have been a team. But most had already known each other for years, having started playing basketball together as teenagers. It wasn't the sport but the camaraderie that held them together. After I first joined this *Verein* in 1990, I quickly learned that to tell a secret to one member of the *Verein* was to tell them all. A particularly critical point in my private life coincided with a tournament in Innsbruck. After the first day's play, a handful of fellow members gathered late at night at a sausage stand to sort out my problem over vast quantities of beer. One could trace our humiliating loss the following day to the after-effects, but no one blamed me—it had been the *Verein*'s duty to attend to my affairs. The advice proved fruitless, but friendships were solidified and the *Verein* had done its duty.

And that was the point.

Germans take their friendships more seriously than any nationality I have known. I have never been trusted entirely by *Verein* members due to my peripatetic lifestyle, which requires that my friendships receive irregular attention, certainly not the *Verein* norm. As I am American, the *Verein* has forgiven this shortcoming. I am expected to be superficial, and my conformity in this respect is at some level welcomed. The *Verein* keeps me on its roster and I play when I can.

Following the weekly Monday practice during my first month back in Berlin, I satisfy the team's unwritten requirement that I attend the *Stammtisch*— a regular but informal gathering lubricated by tall, cold glasses of beer. I update *Verein* members on my life and book plans. They also challenge me to write about "normal Germans," not Helmut Kohl, not Boris Becker, and certainly not the neo-Nazis or the Scientology-bashers then in American headlines.

It often seems the fondest ambition of the modern German is to be "normal." Or, in German, nor*Mal*, with the accent on the last syllable like an exclamation mark. When the Germans were unified in 1990, they celebrated becoming nor*Mal* again, no longer abnormally divided. When their troops joined allies in Bosnia, it was a sign of normalization—the first such combat troop mission abroad since the war. Above all, many of the elites wanted to be normal Europeans, allowing their singularly tragic nation-state to disappear in a borderless Europe. Yet it was also growing nor*Mal* to demand that

Europe increasingly satisfy German interests and that Germans pay a more "normal" (smaller) share of the budget.

One can only fully understand this desire to be like everyone else when one observes Germans' discomfort at their own singularity. Some crazy Americans blow up a building in Oklahoma. An American sect poisons itself en masse to join a quickly passing comet. The whole country grows obsessed by O. J. Simpson's trial or President Bill Clinton's sexual misadventures. We Americans might be troubled by these stories or eat them up, but rarely would one think they define our Americanness.

However, when a rogue German burns down a synagogue, when a right-wing party wins a surprisingly large share of a local vote, when recently drafted GI's raise a Hitler salute, the world often calls a whole society in question.

The conclusion is often that *they* are at it again.

They. Those Germans.

Those *Ab*-normal Germans.

Accent on the first syllable. For emphasis.

And that is what my German friends resent. What do they—a stockbroker, a doctor, a computer software specialist, a psychiatrist, a mathematician, a chemistry teacher—have to do with contemporary neo-Nazi ugliness?

In truth, my *Verein* doesn't represent "average" Germans. By the nature of the game of basketball, they are taller, more worldly and more educated (basketball for their generation was played most enthusiastically at universities). They are also a little cocky, many of them having played on the team I joined that won the German National Championship in 1993 (for players age thirty-five and over). But these men of my *Verein*—height, education, cockiness notwithstanding—considered themselves nor*Mal*.

So I spend a few weeks combing the group for specimens to study; ultimately, I pick a representative from these self-proclaimed "normal" men to begin my research.

The team's resident psychiatrist is Stephan Ehebald, who, though forty-five years of age, can slice through far younger defenders on the basketball court with a young man's speed.

Fellow players note that he is more selfish than some on the team, as testified by the rarity of his passes and his singular focus on the basket. His life partner, a South African of French and Indian descent named Rokaya, tells me before dinner at their apartment that to understand Germans I should look at Stephan's most troublesome characteristic: obsessive orderliness.

"Sometimes it is just awful how anal he is."

Stephan smiles. "Anal is normal in Germany."

It is asparagus season, and Stephan promises us the freshest, fattest, tenderest white spears in the land. He and Rokaya differ on whether they are better boiled or steamed. But Stephan, citing the Germans' genetic superiority in deciding matters of asparagus, boils them, not without a remark about Rokaya's inadequate peeling of the outer skin, which he judges as being far short of perfection.

The *Verein*, which participates without hesitancy or apology in members' personal affairs, has some doubts about whether Stephan can make this relationship work, or any relationship, for that matter. We all agree that Rokaya handles him better than the many who have come before her—she stands up to him. The *Verein* generally agrees that Rokaya has lasted because she doesn't allow Stephan to feel the boredom or the superiority that have always prompted him to move on in the past.

While Stephan pours champagne to prepare our palettes for the asparagus, I apologize that I will be drinking water. I am driving that night. German law is sufficiently strict and broadly enough enforced with random police checks to cast a sober pall over many parties.

Yet before I decide to teetotal entirely, Stephan wants to provide me some statistics to better inform my decision. Stephan reckons that I weigh roughly a hundred kilos, which I nod is correct. He will base his calculations on only eighty of my kilos because "alcohol won't dilute in bone matter," he explains, "and bones make up about twenty percent of your body mass."

He holds up the bottle of champagne, which he says holds ninety cubic centimeters of alcohol. (He reaches this figure by using a formula based on the bottle's 750 grams of content, or three-quarters of a liter, of which twelve percent is alcohol.)

If I drink the whole bottle, he figures, "you will not only be quite jolly but also at a 0.11 percent alcohol to blood level," considerably over the allowed percentage at the time of 0.08 percent. He performs a little more math to land upon the portion of the bottle that I may safely drink and still drive.

I tell him to shut up and pour. By this time, I have a ferocious thirst. But he will not be dissuaded from further calculations.

"Ah, but perhaps you can drink more than my calculations allow," he says. "A fit liver is capable of processing ten to twenty grams of alcohol per hour." He takes the lower end of this scale "to be on the safe side." Though I can't recall all the details of his reckoning, I do remember the result: I would be allowed an entire bottle of champagne if I would stay for three hours. Stephan recalls that the length of my usual stay is about that, so he concludes the bottle is mine for the drinking.

By now I've lost my appetite for the wine. I tell him he's become "tiresome."

Ah, but to be "exhausting" is part of German normality as well, he smiles, replacing my word with his own.

And Rokaya agrees. The German, she insists, feels a need to impart whatever wisdom he holds on whomever will listen.

The operative word, agrees Stephan, is *Lehrmeister*—master teacher. Yet history has put the Germans, as a nation, in a bind: though they are well able to tell the world how to run itself, they have disqualified themselves. They feel great pain at how little the world wishes to listen to them as a nation.

As individuals, however, they don't feel the same limitations.

Rokaya's twelve-year-old daughter Roxanne, who has joined us for dinner, complains that Stephan just can't stop trying to teach her. He counters that she is lucky in that he is willing to share his experience and wisdom with her at such an impressionable age.

Stephan informs us all that he hasn't yet finished his lecture on alcohol, and he wonders if Roxanne would mind if he continued.

"You won't stop no matter what I say, so why do you ask?" she says.

"Clever girl," he says. "Naturally, you are right . . . Now, alcoholics who consume two and one half bottles of spirits a day, or six hundred grams per day—not unusual for them—often have an exceptional liver capability that can keep them alive for some time."

"Boring," sighs Roxanne.

"Eat your asparagus," says Stephan, unfazed. "Alcoholics have the ability to burn up to twenty-five grams or more of alcohol per hour. The liver exerts itself heroically, but over months, years, and decades it wears out. Then comes cirrhosis. The alcohol won't be metabolized properly then. The liver has nine hundred and seven jobs, and it can't do any of them, so self-poisoning occurs as toxic waste can't be eliminated any more."

"Nine hundred and seven?" Roxanne asks skeptically.

"I made that up." He smiles. "Maybe it is only one hundred."

Stephan is serious about his math, but he's poking fun at his pedantic self at the same time. In the New Germany, tongue in cheek describes more than anatomical placement. One notices the emergence of a hipper, subtler humor, I tell the table.

The country is becoming lighter with every year. Home-grown comedies have become big hits, and some of them are even funny. Stand-up comedy—quick lines and sharp humor of the New York variety—has found its place beside the more set-piece cabaret acts. A friend of mine who designs foreign policy for the Christian Democrats is a German blonde who peppers me by e-mail with dumb-blonde jokes.

"One of the welcome changes among Germans these days," I say, "is that they take life less seriously—they are readier to laugh."

"As long as it is not at themselves," says Stephan's partner Rokaya.

To help me understand, she retreats to the bedroom and retrieves a thin book she picked up at London's Heathrow Airport: a sixty-four-page pamphlet called *The Xenophobe's Guide to the Germans* (its cover is decorated with a beer stein, an Iron Cross, and a bulging sausage).

It's clear the book has been passed back and forth between them. It is dog-eared and heavily marked with underlines and exclamation points.

"For a small and insignificant pamphlet," says Stephan, holding up the book before me, "it delivers a profound knowledge of the German condition."

Germans are often surprised when wisdom can be delivered in but a few words.

Rokaya reads: "Germans are square-jawed robots whose language sounds like something awful in the drains, whose cars out-perform all others and whose football team seldom loses . . . But behind the facade lies a nation distinctly uncertain about where it is, where it is going, even how it got there. Seeking refuge from the world's uncertainties, on the one hand, they rely on order and system, the State and the Bundesbank; on the other they retreat into the Angst of the soul, psychoanalysis, and high culture."

Rokaya stops and exclaims, "Don't you see! This is Stephan. They are writing about Stephan!"

Stephan nods in agreement. Germans have been an easy target for so many years partly because they have become so willing to absorb the indignities of foreigners.

Rokaya reads on: "None of this anxiety should be mocked; humor is a quite separate category to be viewed in a serious light . . . The German's sense of humor is no laughing matter."

Stephan interrupts. He turns to a page that he prefers: "Generally speaking, the Germans regard themselves as a modest, rather ordinary sort of people. Give them a beer, a wurst, a bit of *Gemütlichkeit* (coziness), and another German with whom to argue politics or bemoan the stress of life, and they will be content."

He flips to an excerpt he likes even more, his self-description: "In every German there is a touch of the wild-haired Beethoven striding through forests and weeping over a mountain sunset, grappling against impossible odds to express the inexpressible. This is the Great German soul, prominent display of which is essential whenever Art, Feeling and Truth are under discussion."

In Stephan, I had always seen a bit of this wild-haired Beethoven—or, in his case, Freud—weeping over the sunset. His house is filled with photographs brought home from his many tours throughout the world—always of children. African children laughing, Latin American children playing, Indonesian children sadly studying the lens.

Stephan figures Germans' problems begin with their anal nature, which commences early in life. "Parents, as an expression of the perfect order that Germans seek, force toilet training on their children at too early an age," he says. "That is what happened to me."

"I wondered what it was," says Rokaya playfully.

Stephan smiles at his beloved and continues. "My father tried to stop it—this early toilet training. He was a more flexible man. He knew the world. But my mother imposed this training on me anyway. You have to understand child development to understand the Germans. It is only in the third year of life that you learn the difference between wrong and right. An infant of one or two years old is totally immoral, without conscience. That's why he can rip the wings off insects or the legs off grasshoppers. If there is no structure, small children can be tyrants. They don't fully foresee the consequences of their actions until ages ten or twelve."

"What's the point?" I wonder.

"Sorry, I digress. There is something anal in the German character and personality. There is a desire to control and that results in a search for power. We put the emphasis on being clean far too early. It is this anal fixation. It is in the third year that a child should learn most about controlling bowel movement. If you train him in the first or second year, it can harm the personality for later life."

Whenever I rail against the world for being prejudiced against the Germans, I recall that often Germans are prejudiced against themselves. It is difficult for me to imagine a discussion with intellectuals of any other nationality—or race, which the Germans are clearly not—that would speak in such negative generalizations about itself.

Stephan opines that this anal characteristic has receded a great deal in the West but less so in eastern Germany where, shortly after unification, Stephan visited nursery schools where a long row of potties was lined up for mass training. "And you know what kind of society that can create, preparing the newborn as early as possible for the 'benefits' of socialism. The worst insult your mother can give your apartment is—this place looks dirty. She can say it's uncomfortable, even *ungemütlich*, but it is when she says it is dirty that you are really hurt."

Rokaya remembers the horror of her first stay with Stephan in Berlin, during which he lectured her on how to handle the contents of his home. He told her she'd have to learn quickly how to treat his many kitchen gadgets properly "or I would be declared 'un-gadget minded' and be asked to leave."

I chuckle at a threat that I assume was in jest.

"He wasn't kidding," Rokaya says.

"No, I wasn't," agrees Stephan. "Like many Germans, I was prematurely nappy-trained."

By the end of my night with Stephan, I fear that I am reinforcing old stereotypes rather than unveiling the "new Germans." Stephan must have felt it, too, for within days he invited me to accompany him on one of his "emergency doctor" outings, not so much to observe him as to glimpse the varied profiles of those who beckoned him for help.

In a country that has been reported to have more sick days per capita than in any developed country in the world, the state has provided the all-purpose doctor. He is only a distant cousin to the American emergency paramedic who rushes from drug overdose to violent car crash. Though Germany has such emergency teams as well, Stephan is of a separate breed. He and dozens of others acting as general practitioners drive about Berlin streets day and night in wait for calls that range from the critical to the (far more frequently) trivial.

Anyone may dial the designated number. Got a cough? Leg acting up? Something wrong with your circulation (the most frequent of all German complaints)? Just call. In response, Stephan, with a driver in a yellow car marked *Notarzt*—emergency doctor—turns up.

Our first stop is at the home of ninety-three-year-old Gertrud Schneider, who is hyperventilating when we arrive. She tells Dr. Ehebald of her swollen legs, her leaking bladder, her five stomach operations. Despite her age and Stephan's youth, she bows before his medical credentials as before an altar, beginning virtually every sentence with a reverent "Herr Doktor."

Stephan's abilities stretch far beyond psychiatry, as they must for any emergency doctor, but here he is sure that he is treating an ailment of the spirit. Frau Schneider is afraid of death, he confides to me in an English she can't understand while she ticks off names of friends who have recently died. He also ascertains that the call to the emergency service was a means of gaining some attention from a kindly neighbor who wasn't visiting as often as Frau Schneider thought she should.

"It is a weekend, a particularly bad time to be alone, isn't it?" Stephan says sweetly to the old woman, placing a stethoscope on her chest.

She nods.

The heartbeat is too fast, but close to regular. Stephan provides her a pill—which he describes as a *Scheiss-egal* tablet—roughly translated as a "doesn't-make-a-shit's-bit-of-difference" pill. It is a small dose of Valium, to calm her and let her sleep. He takes the neighbor to the side and tells her to keep the old woman out of the hospital as long as possible. "It is always in the hospital where they give up," he says.

The old woman is calm until we begin to leave, and then she panics and screams from pain.

But Stephan has a dozen other patients already sitting in his virtual waiting room—the list provided him by the dispatcher. He must move on.

The next stop is the home of Lothar, a male nurse, who when we arrive is in the midst of an anxiety attack. He has worked in a psychiatric hospital for twenty-five years but is now unemployed. He has called because of back pains.

Stephan provides his diagnosis while his patient is briefly out of the room. "You can see by the way he acts that he isn't sick physically but spiritually. Psychological stress can lead to long-lasting backaches. Ninety percent of back pain is from that."

Ninety percent? I ask.

Give or take, Stephan smiles.

Lothar has been through this routine before. It turns out that he's a regular caller. He recognizes the *Scheiss-egal* tablet Stephan offers him and eagerly swallows it.

And so it continues.

We make one stop after another through anxiety-ridden Deutschland. There is the sixteen-year-old teenager who has moved away from home to live with a boyfriend who seems to be mistreating her. There is the waitress in her mid-twenties whose stomach difficulties Stephan quickly traces to her relationship with a married man. There is another old woman whose leg pain seems related to her move from her life-long home in eastern Germany to the apartment of a daughter who had moved west to marry a West Berliner. There is the twenty-seven-year-old advanced biology student who has smoked too much hash and is shaking with fear when we arrive.

And there is the unemployed bricklayer who has been an asthmatic ever since his marriage broke up three years earlier following a move from the

North Sea coast to Berlin. Sitting on an uncertain stool in his one-room apartment at a local flophouse, he shows us his two oxygen bottles and nine sorts of medicine. He lived for his wife, he says. And for his job: "We know how to build homes to last an eternity in northern Germany. Stone houses to stand the salt air." He inflates his lungs and coughs. He finds the women and the buildings in Berlin to be far less reliable.

As we walk away, I turn to Stephan and ask doubtfully, "These are the normal Germans I should write about?"

Stephan apologizes. "It seems the whole city today is in the midst of a nervous breakdown. It's unusual, but not infrequent. We have some full-moon nights where we simply go from one lunatic to another."

But are Germans more angst-ridden than other nationalities? I ask.

On matters of anxiety, he reckons, they have plenty of competition for world-leader status. Everyone who breathes is angst-ridden, he says. It is what motivates most of us. "Anxiety can be a source of energy driving you from one goal to the next," he says. No German specialty here, Stephan is sure.

I feel a sense of relief as we make our last stop of the day to a truly injured person: a young woman, lying on her bed wincing with pain from a fall off a horse.

Stephan probes and decides: she hasn't any breaks but does have a severe bruise to the hip. He provides her a pain reliever to get her through the weekend and suggests she visit a doctor on Monday for further treatment if the pain doesn't diminish.

We walk down our final set of stairs for the day.

I turn to Stephan. "Thank God for that."

"For what?" he asks.

"Finally, a patient whose injuries aren't psychologically induced. My faith in Germany is restored."

"Ah," says Stephan, "but we don't know what she was thinking that made her fall from that horse."

His diagnosis: probably a pondering of the wrong kind.

The members of *Deutscher Basketball Verein Charlottenburg* are horrified that Stephan has guided my search for the normal German. They recite his various imperfections, condemn his skewed, quasi-Freudian outlook on life, and declare him unfit for the task.

The team intellectual, Norbert Heldermann, appoints himself Stephan's successor. He is a mathematics professor at a technical university in Lemgo and publishes mathematics books, but he is willing to volunteer expertise on most matters.

For me, Norbert embodies two frequent German conditions.

First, he has a passion for *Bildung,* that particularly German concept that suggests a life-long pursuit of higher education and culture. He is a resourceful enough guard on the basketball court, but his favorite sport is verbal jousting. He deploys his vocabulary, ideas, and intellect like rapiers—or, his detractors argue, more like blunt clubs.

Second, he is a dreamer. There is a mismatch between his estimable intellect and its distance from reality. In late-night banter, he often rambles on about Utopian worlds and constructs that have no practical purpose beyond the sheer joy of working his gray matter.

Norbert's ways make me think of Heine's famous poem describing Germans:

> *The Russians possess the land,*
> *The British possess the sea.*
> *But we have over the airy realm of dreams*
> *Command indisputably.*

Norbert also embodies another trait that his team members describe as uniquely German: *Besserwisserei.*

He is so certain of his opinions that he quickly dismisses those who don't share them. When accused of this trait by one club member, Norbert argued revealingly that he isn't a *Besserwisser,* because in German one regards such a person as one who believes he knows better but who doesn't actually do so. He, on the other hand, isn't a *Besserwisser* because he truly *does* know better.

Verein members loathe or love Norbert. There is no in between. Stephan remains his close friend, despite the fact that Norbert spent some considerable effort to woo Rokaya away from him, including an outing to Frederick the Great's Sanssouci castle in Potsdam—where he endeavored to convince her of his own greater suitability.

Although Rokaya was shocked by Norbert's ultimately failed seductions, Stephan was merely amused. He, like Norbert, considered the flirtation to be more intellectual jousting than true betrayal.

To introduce me to his Germany, Norbert invites me to Lemgo, a medium-sized northern German city that has a well-preserved old town, but which is otherwise dull enough to serve the purpose of a search for "normal" Germans.

On the Sunday I arrive, Norbert is engaged in the final throes of a neighborhood fight over the fate of a narrow patch of grass and dirt in front of six identical townhouses, of which his own is one, running up a narrow slope from a small suburban road. The homes had been British officers' quarters before the troop withdrawal that followed the Cold War's close and German unification.

Norbert and one of his neighbors, a schoolteacher named Claudia, prefer that the area remain "wild," or be seeded with grass to make a play area for children. Three of the other neighbors, and potentially a decisive fourth, want to convert the space into a gravel or cement parking lot. The showdown, I decide, is between two German clichés: the primordial German love of green areas and the German passion for cars.

"There are plenty of parking spaces on the road," Norbert sneers, "but that isn't enough for the true German. He wants to be able to see his beloved machine each time he looks out of his bedroom window."

The coalition against Norbert, however, is formidable.

Its leaders are a young couple in the first of the townhouses running up the hill, the only one directly on the road. They are a handsome and fit couple, whom Norbert calls Hartmut and Gertrude, and are members of the local soccer *Verein*. Hartmut is an auto dealer. They had already indented a gravel parking space into their backyard as a safe retreat for their new 500-series BMW. But they sought another slot for whatever other new car Hartmut might bring home.

The couple had allies that included the construction worker, of Russian origin, who lived in the next house up the hill, an unemployed house painter who lived beside him and, newly, yet another Russian who worked in a metal factory and lived at the top of the hill. They outnumbered Norbert and his schoolteacher-ally Claudia who lived in homes number four and five running up the hill, poised between the painter and the metal worker.

I sit with Norbert and Claudia over Sunday morning coffee to plot strategy for a neighborhood meeting that evening which might be critical to Norbert's last-ditch efforts to block construction of the parking lot. He assesses the enemy.

He won't be able to win over Viktor, the Russian-born construction worker. But how could one take such a man seriously? Viktor had applied for disability pay only a short time after arriving in Germany from Russia in 1991, as part of the large post-Soviet emigration of ethnic Germans. Ever since, says Norbert, he has been living off state aid. It was complaints of a bad back that stopped him from working, but Norbert points out that this hasn't stopped him from constantly adding improvements to his own home. Norbert's view is obvious: this is not the kind of émigré the country needs and certainly not a man fit to decide important neighborhood matters.

Norbert recounts how Viktor responded to his first appeals to join the stop-the-parking-lot movement. He drew Norbert's attention to a city blueprint that accompanied the sale of the houses, on which the existing green space was marked *Stellplätze*—literally, "standing spaces" for cars. "The higher-ups have told us what they want," Viktor told Norbert at the time, "and we must obey."

Claudia recalls that Norbert made it worse by pointing out to Viktor that perhaps his German wasn't of sufficient sophistication to understand that the word *Stellplätze* didn't necessarily refer to cars. It could as well mean "places for cows to stand," Norbert had said at the time, straight-faced.

Viktor hadn't been amused. Given a monkey wrench, he might have rearranged Norbert's intellect a bit. He groused that Norbert was talking down to him.

"You think Viktor dumb," Norbert mimics his broken German. "You are professor. You are intelligent. But Viktor sees what you do. You play with our heads. This is game for you. But not game for Viktor." Upon which Norbert angrily walked out of the meeting, bristling that he couldn't discuss such a critical issue on such a personalized level. It was the principle he cared about, he argued, not the man Viktor. *Prinzip über alles.*

As the odds turned heavily against Norbert, he began to be more tactical, Claudia says. He argues now, quite rightly, that Claudia can't afford her contribution to construct a proper parking area, so he is seeking a delay of the decision until her finances improve, which Norbert figures might be never. (The neighbors don't only want a level parking area, they want it professionally prepared and expertly surfaced with the best concrete available, all at significant cost.)

Yet Claudia, though she agrees on the ends with Norbert, is tiring of his proclivity to enrage those neighbors he should be winning over. She had been forced too often to mediate among the parties. Most were refusing to talk directly to Norbert, so Claudia carried messages between them.

Norbert and Claudia sip the strong coffee and recount the dramatic showdowns that had set the scene for the evening event. One night, the car faction had put up stakes where they imagined their parking places would be, and positioned their vehicles in these designated slots. When Norbert arrived home late at night from one of his mathematics lectures, he ripped the stakes down.

Norbert drew upon a statute of law in his arguments: the *Bürgerliches Gesetzbuch*, the door-stopper-thick bible of civil rights law in Germany. It regulates life among German neighbors down to the finest details.

Norbert found, to his delight, a regulation that prohibited a *wesentliche Veränderung*—a considerable alteration—of common property without the agreement of all parties. "I regarded the introduction of the posts as a *wesentliche Veränderung*," he says.

On another evening, Norbert came home at eleven in the evening from a basketball game to find his neighbors had put all of their cars back in their designated places, even though the posts were gone. He pulled his car into a position that blocked the exit, and then he went inside.

Norbert insists, as Claudia listens doubtfully, that he was merely picking up mail that he had forgotten to post—some of the textbooks he publishes. He thus parked as close to his apartment as possible to reduce the distance he'd need to carry the books from door to car.

But tempers were running so high that Hartmut, the auto salesman, knocked on his door within ten minutes and threatened to call in the police if he didn't move his car. At that point, Norbert saw it as a point of principle—*Prinzip*—to keep the vehicle in place. "I wanted to move the car—I wanted to post my mail—but you can understand that I couldn't satisfy him at that point," he says.

The auto salesman, however, had his own *Prinzip:* "I'll expect you to move your car immediately," he said. He said Norbert was endangering the lives of all the children by blocking the only exit by which they could rush their children to the hospital in case of an emergency.

"My car stays as long as I want," Norbert replied.

"I am officially informing you that I am calling the police," Norbert recalls the salesman saying, apparently figuring that informing "unofficially" wouldn't be quite forceful or legal enough. He marched off down the incline to his home in order to do so.

Norbert emerged from his door several minutes later. Hartmut acted as if he was calling the police on the mobile phone as Norbert walked by.

"So are you moving your car?" he asked, so that Norbert and, apparently, the policeman on the end of the line could hear.

"I won't comment on that," said Norbert, and then he drove off, ostensibly to mail his post.

Claudia shakes her head: "It became a power struggle. Men."

Norbert regards his actions more as the expression of that old-fashioned German trait: the defense of *Prinzip.* He couldn't accept the principle of the parking places without having reached a neighborhood consensus. And without Norbert, there could be no consensus. As a matter of principle, he would do everything in his power to stop the project until they could convince him to go along. "Democracy," he says, "is just a word in the *Grundgesetz* as long as we don't live it in the seemingly unimportant matters of every day."

In all my world travels, I have rarely met a people who talk more about *Prinzip* or who will more blindly sacrifice pragmatic considerations in their pursuit of the perceived *Prinzip,* something that dates back at least to Kant's "categorical imperative."

"Norbert's real problem," says Claudia, "is that he always talks over their heads." She turns to him. "You should speak their language."

"That I won't do," says Norbert. "As a matter of *Prinzip*."

Claudia sighs.

What the neighbors had put on the agenda for the evening discussion was a provisional, lower-cost alternative that would get around the schoolteacher's funding problem: they'd dump gravel atop the grass until they could finance a more permanent fix. Norbert had an answer for this as well: "I am arguing that one should either do this properly or not do it at all."

An appeal to German perfectionism was hence Norbert's last, weak straw. He knew the building could only take place if there was a consensus of all neighbors.

Yet if blocked again by Norbert, the neighbors threatened to take the issue to a local court. Norbert knew that was a risk. "The judge's response will depend on whether he has just built a parking place for himself or whether he is a Green." Given the nature of Lemgo, Norbert feared the court case could only turn against him.

Yet how to back off from war after such heady escalation? His approach had assured that his neighbors would resent him for the rest of time whether he won or lost.

The evening's meeting would be difficult. Claudia says the neighbors don't like the idea of the American reporter attending. They figure I'm part of Norbert's trickery.

"Why should I care?" says Norbert.

"Sometimes the German is so arrogant I can hardly stand it," says Claudia. "Now, *that's* typically German."

At that point, Norbert declares it is time for a Sunday excursion "in search of Germany." We thank Claudia for the coffee and tell her we'll be back for the fireworks that evening.

As we drive off, I notice that Norbert seems stung by Claudia's condemnation of his arrogance as typically German. "A better word, he says, "would be *überheblichkeit*"—more presumptuousness than arrogance.

So what's the difference? I ask.

"When a Frenchman is proud of his Vaterland, *ma patrie*, he thinks about the beauty of his mountains, about his own ways. When a German is proud of his mountains, it is because they are higher than those of his neighbors. This explains the German inclination toward the degrading or humiliating of others. It has always been at the cost of neighbors that Germans have made themselves feel great. Look at the wars. We can't just say we were good soldiers, we had to show that we could crush the British. We can't just build good cars, we had to build better cars than the Americans. That is what makes us proud."

He traces this characteristic to geography and late nationhood. Germans only became a nation in the late nineteenth century, and they have either regretted this fact or have felt too strongly about asserting it ever since. At the same time, says Norbert, Germany's central geographic position in Europe left its borders constantly open to crossing peoples and cultures.

"The German," says Norbert, "was always forced to stand up for himself. You have two possibilities when you are in such a position. You either shut yourself off, lock yourself in and build walls around yourself, or you cooperate with all the others. The politics of the past Germany was always to define one's self against others. The reason that Helmut Kohl was a great leader was because he promoted a policy of cooperating with others. That is what is special about this country now."

Helmut Kohl was a great leader? I ask.

That certainly never had been the tone of our *Verein Stammtisch,* where I was frequently the single voice singing the praises of a man I argued had been Germany's greatest postwar leader. Kohl kept the Western alliance intact in the face of Soviet threats by stationing medium-range nuclear missiles on German territory, in defiance of massive German protests. He unified Germany peacefully while remaining solidly within the North Atlantic Treaty Organization and the European Union. He stubbornly fought to create the single European currency, again ignoring public opposition. Historians will write his name large.

But not German intellectuals. On some level, he embarrassed them. He wasn't sophisticated or worldly, they maintained. He couldn't speak English at all and didn't even employ German properly. Perhaps his very size and immobility reminded Germans too much of themselves. The previous chancellor, Helmut Schmidt, was more the German they would like to be—urbane, intellectual—sticking the glob of snuff in his nose and inhaling before uttering the next profound thought. Kohl was the German they had become: consistent, steady, stubborn, and unexciting.

Hannah Arendt wrote about Eichmann as the "banality of evil." Kohl had been more the "banality of good," like the country he had represented, in that he was slightly boring, yet stable and civilized.

Before his election defeat in 1998, Germans had voted for him over and over again, but they'd never particularly enjoyed it. The man who would defeat him in a landslide, riding a Social Democratic-Green coalition, was a provincial governor from Lower Saxony who, at age fifty-four, had been but an infant when the war ended.

Any responsibility Gerhard Schröder might feel for German war crimes would be diluted through inheritance. His war scar was the fact that the fighting had cost him a father whom he would never know. That left him with a hardscrabble postwar childhood as the son of a mother who struggled as a cleaning woman to keep her family afloat. Yet by the late 1990s, Schröder's politics were so modern that they fit nicely into an American-style campaign that focused on his relative youth and personality and glossed over the vague outlines of his policies.

If Kohl was the Germany the people had become, Schröder, whom they embraced at the ballot box as their Clinton/Blair New Age leader, was the Germany they wanted to become. In the election, Norbert wouldn't vote for him, but he also didn't mind him: Schröder had stature, presence, and wouldn't embarrass Germany on the international stage. The fact that Schröder was onto his fourth wife, Norbert would say, could either be understood as a sign of his instability or proof that he could adjust easily to new situations and demands, like the country he represented.

Norbert pulls up the car to a park where he promises me a German role model even larger than Helmut Kohl. We walk a few hundred yards into the well-groomed woods until we reach the *Hermann's Denkmal,* a fifty-four-meter-high statue memorializing an early German who turned back the Romans in the first century after Christ.

It is one of the few historical pilgrimage points left in Germany that have more to do with breast-beating than hand-wringing, more to do with national celebration than remorse. As that, it isn't a monument Germans talk much about.

"Though I've lived here for nearly three years, I've never come to visit Hermann," Norbert says. "It is safer emotionally to visit such a place with a foreigner. I couldn't go on my own because such places make me too emotional—bring tears to my eyes."

Norbert informs me that he is being sarcastic. I tell him the explanation isn't necessary.

"In Germany, you sometimes have to give advance notice if you are to engage in any form of irony," he says.

Norbert explains that he has often thought of moving abroad because his form of humor is lost on the Germans. He tells a story of how he told a colleague of a joint venture he hoped to begin with an Icelandic friend to turn glaciers into a new brand of ice cream.

"He thought about it a long time as a concept instead of laughing spontaneously at the absurdity of it. That destroys every joke. The German ponders too much. He isn't quick in his thinking."

I don't have the heart to tell Norbert that, both spontaneously and after some pondering, I don't consider his concept particularly funny. I mull the difficulty of telling bad jokes to people of insufficient humor.

One thing is clear: there isn't much irony to the imposing statue in front of us, completed in 1875, just four years after Germany defeated France and while it was still feeling the full patriotic rush of its first unification. Its construction had begun fifty years earlier, Norbert explains to me, but it was only after the victory over France that the national feelings were strong enough for the conceptualizers to raise the funds to complete the edifice.

The pamphlet Norbert bought us says Hermann, known to the Romans as Arminius, was a twenty-year-old youth of noble rank, the son of the Germanic prince Sigimer, "whose radiant face and sparkling eyes revealed his extraordinary valor, quick comprehension, and power of decision." We learn of how he fought against the decadent Romans and for the purer German way of life, which at that time included "outstanding virtues" such as "boldness and bravery, chivalry and faithfulness, love of freedom, and a sense of the heroic."

His victory, the pamphlet tells us, "not only saved Germany and the

British Isles from being romanized like Gaul and Spain, but kept the way open for Germanic mind and manners in Europe."

Norbert raises an eyebrow at this: "I find it catastrophic to think that the Romans lost. They had so much more to offer us." After all, he says, it was the Romans to whom the Germans owed their first steps toward civilization, including fruit growing and viticulture, road building and architecture, coinage, and systems of measurement.

"Germans at that point of history were unable to heat a single room," he says.

I ask Norbert why he is so hard on his country. We all know about the country's crimes, I say, but aren't there German figures for whom he feels pride? Beethoven, Goethe, Schiller, all those Nobel Prize winners with their breakthroughs in medicine and science. And look what the country has made of itself since World War II.

"I am a German intellectual," he explains, "and as such I have to stand at a distance to my country. As a child, I wasn't allowed to love my Fatherland. My generation was not educated to embrace certain ideals but rather to avoid certain evils that had seduced our parents' generation. One wants to love what one esteems, one wants to love one's country, but we weren't allowed."

What one can't love naturally as a child, one can't love easily as an adult. It becomes a habit of thinking, he says.

Norbert was born in the year the Federal Republic of Germany was created. "The parents who hugged me were insecure, and that has an impact on you. Then you are insecure as well. Their ideals were shaken up. They didn't have any ideals left after the war, only needs. So they took care of these needs. And we had the *Wirtschaftswunder*. But something was missing. A normal child loves his parents, loves his Fatherland. When he hears his national anthem, he wants to put his hand on his heart. The French have a very natural relationship in this way with *la patrie*. But we weren't allowed to love Germany. You could live here, you could work here, but you weren't allowed to love Germany."

Norbert then talks about the importance of our *Verein*, and why these clubs played such an important role after the war. "Every human being needs to be imbedded in a larger unit of organization. We must identify with something. Our *Verein* provides many of us with some of this identification, but it isn't enough. I love this country—I identify with this country. I love the language. I love the fact that it is small enough to be manageable. I couldn't love America in this way. And everywhere you look there are intelligent people. Most things in Germany function. Trains leave on time and arrive on time."

He says this without a trace of irony.

"I've been running my publishing house for twenty years, and not one letter has been lost in that time."

Norbert frowns as he looks up at Hermann hovering over us. It reminds him of the German proclivity to overdo. "No one can have a simple relationship with Germany," he says.

He recalls a six-month trip he took around the world that started in Cairo and took him through Africa and then to India, where he came down with a bad case of dysentery. He finally gave up trying to get well in India. With relief, he boarded a sparkling Lufthansa plane to fly home. He was happy, at first, to be among the German flight crew and passengers.

"You look ill," said his seatmate, a German engineer.

Norbert told the man the story of his long trip and sudden illness, expecting sympathy.

Yet before the plane could take off, the passenger had complained to the flight attendants that he was seated next to someone who was ill. He wanted the man removed. The flight attendant relocated Norbert to a vacant row in the back of the economy section, where he could infect no one.

The next image of Germany came upon his arrival home. He drove away from Frankfurt airport with his father and noticed that every turn was well-marked, every road properly lined and lighted.

"Not a square centimeter of German territory goes unplanned," says Norbert. If anything is wild, it is because it has been planned to be so. "Planning is an addiction of the German. It is a horror, but it can also be beautiful and reassuring."

Norbert himself has a large patch of earth in the center of his backyard that he allows to grow wild, just to see what sorts of weeds and growth will occur in the natural Lemgo biosphere. It drives his neighbors to distraction. "They just can't bear it that parts of my property are unplanned."

Yet even the chaos of Norbert's backyard is planned—by him.

We look up at the inscriptions that surround the statue. Those who had conceived the monstrosity had decided to put this ancient hero into context for the contemporary German of 1875, four years after the German victory in the Franco-Prussian war. "Only because the German people were frenchified and rendered powerless by disunity was Napoleon Bonaparte, emperor of the French, able to subjugate Germany with the help of Germans. Finally in 1813, all the German tribes rallied behind the sword raised by Prussia and won freedom from shame." The text went on to tell how the Germans finally taught the French a lesson in 1871 for their "arrogance."

Norbert shakes his head. "That language! It's written in *Blut und Boden* German. Do you see my point? We can't just be proud of being German, we have to be proud at the expense of others."

Norbert and I agree that the national tone following post–Cold War unification was the opposite of the hubristic fever that came after the Franco-Prussian conflict. The Germans had embraced the 1990 unification with humility, almost reluctance.

On the drive back home, Norbert and I stop to reflect on Hermann at a Chinese restaurant, oddly installed in an eighteenth-century German manor. Folk wisdom is etched into the half-timbered facade and, inside, elk horns hang beside Chinese lanterns. The half-timbered walls are adorned with Chinese lacquered paintings. It seems a fitting place to talk about how new foreign influences are diluting Germany's Germanness.

We agree that the statue of Hermann has little to do with today's Germany. If anything, the statue stands as a symbol for contrast between Germans pre-Hitler and those post-Hitler. "The pathos of the past is impossible to bear for the modern German," says Norbert. "I am constantly shocked at how important it was to feel superior toward others. This romantic fight for unification. This same soul that produced that statue composed the music of Wagner. Awful!"

The new German soul, if such a thing exists, puts Chinese kitsch in Wagnerian settings. It complains about the costs of unification instead of building some huge Helmut statue to celebrate it. It eats Turkish kabobs on street corners instead of bratwurst, and it vacations as far away from Germany as possible.

Norbert himself married an Argentine woman, and his children are more proud of their Latin than their Germanic heritage. To be Latin American is "cool," they tell their father. Being German is boring. Even Helmut Kohl fought to surrender national sovereignty through a single currency, hardly a modern Hermann except perhaps in his physical dimensions. I wonder what is left of the *überheblich* Germans who built the statue.

Norbert picks at his egg rolls with a chopstick. "After World War II, there was a societal confusion. Two generations have followed. To a certain degree, the human race is capable of learning. When you have experienced great pain, you learn how to avoid pain in the future. When something makes you happy, you repeat it. But you can only learn within limits. That goes for people and countries. The German needs to control his feelings, his gut, with his intellect."

"So," I ask, "your view is that the German gut is still suspect and must be held in check."

Norbert nods as if to say I am a good student and have learned the day's lesson well.

"The German cannot afford to live from his gut. Within the German resides a pride that is unbearable. This feeling has been weakened, mollified. At the moment, our democracy is stable because of this. Germans have become less German."

He rattles off evidence:

Germans travel so much that "they have discovered that they are foreigners everywhere but in their own country. That makes them more tolerant. They now recognize better the discomfort their own inflexible and often humorless society can cause others."

The German role as either the first- or second-leading export country has made Germans more worldly. "Germans hardly speak German anymore. They '*updaten*' their files, they '*saven*' their work in their '*outbaskets*.' And when we go to the basketball game, we cheer for '*ein tolles Dunking*.'"

The Germans know they have to be on best behavior because everyone watches them so closely. "We often criticize ourselves before the rest of the world can get around to it. We are a people who live in fear of saying the wrong thing, of doing the wrong thing. It is the way we've all been conditioned."

He speaks of a student in one of his math classes who talked recently about solving a given problem in steps until he reaches "the Final Solution"—*die Endlösung.* The class is young enough that it doesn't recognize the faux pas. So Norbert teaches them why they must discard this term forever because of the Holocaust—it was Eichmann's term for the extermination of Jews, he tells them. "No one protested. They all understood the problem."

Part of German education is learning what one, as a German, isn't allowed to say or do.

When we return to Lemgo in the early evening, Claudia tells us the neighborhood council is off. The distrusting neighbors have apparently decided that attending would be playing into Norbert's hands. However Norbert may have planned to deploy me, they wanted no part.

I was disappointed to miss the showdown for which I had timed my trip to Lemgo. I couldn't imagine it unfolding in any other country in quite this way: the unshakable posturing on both sides, the strict adherence to the town's blueprint on the part of the pro-parking spaces faction, the passion for principle on Norbert's part, and the inflexibility of all the parties involved.

Of course there was also another possibility: sometimes a neighborhood spat is just a neighborhood spat.

It's telling that our *Verein's Stammtisch,* where we collect to drink beer after Monday practice, is at an Italian restaurant rather than the expected German pub. Berlin has little "typically German" left about it. The population is almost a quarter "foreign," and the restaurants are even more heavily so.

Verein members chuckle at the notion of Norbert teaching me about normal Germans. He's just as ill-suited as Stephan, they insist. They point me instead toward Gerhard Stockheim, a high-school chemistry teacher who all agree is not only "normal" but at the same time the model of the "good German" for the next century.

Gerhard is the soul of our *Verein;* he volunteers more of his time to it than any of us, participates in board meetings, acts as score keeper, keeps the finances, and participates in youth programs. He knows his *Verein* is part of the texture of the society he wishes to nurture.

The German term for such an individual is *Vereinsmeier*, but that word is too suggestive of a simple-minded sort with nothing better to do than club life, a description that fails to capture Gerhard.

He peppers each of our meetings with questions about life and politics that demonstrate deep curiosity and knowledge about the world. As a teacher, he volunteers time to take his students to the sort of experimental theater that teaches them about their past. Yet he also invites them sailing, each year, to better bond with them.

He approaches all his life's various obligations with seriousness and commitment: long vacations abroad, often to the United States or Latin America, are planned two years or more in advance. The team schedule and school outings are organized to the final detail.

As our shooting guard, he fires the bottom out of the net. But as age slows him down and expands his waistline, he's happiest of all swilling beer at the *Stammtisch* and sitting with his pals in the stands of the local professional team, Alba Berlin.

He and his wife, Christina, a teacher of similar values and spirit, adopted a mixed-race child in Peru, where Gerhard had been the German equivalent of a Peace Corps worker. He traces his left-wing politics, his determination to do good in the world, partly to the special obligation he feels as a German.

Even with all these demands, Gerhard volunteers time to his "guild" of chemistry workers and teachers, where he participates in the training programs of the dual system for which his country is famous. The dual system is an elaborate apprenticeship program combining practical experience and state-funded training schemes that many other countries have emulated.

When he invites me to attend one of the Berlin Chamber of Commerce's graduation tests for one of this system's programs, I balk. What could be so interesting about a chemistry examination?

When he explains that instead he is offering a seat at an examination for restaurant professions that would include a free five-course meal, I readily accept. Among those being tested will be his baby-sitter, who has been training to become a hotel chef. She has become another one of the Stockheims' "projects," a sweet girl with an alcoholic father and a broken family, whom they've embraced as a daughter.

As recently as the 1980s, Germans said the guilds were part of the reason they survived economic crises better than most—they simply had the most skilled people to provide them the greatest productivity. But the guilds had struggled to keep pace with the technological revolution and companies' demands for greater cost efficiencies. German firms, who shared the financing of such programs with the state (including the tab for our meal), were cutting back their contributions.

A buzz is already in the air when we arrive at the testing location, a socialist-era dining hall in one of the farthest reaches of eastern Berlin. The students, in their chefs' smocks and waitresses' black skirts and frilly aprons, are gathering backstage for their grand performance. The judges and we, the guinea pigs, are whetting our palates with cocktails.

Gerhard introduces me to Dieter Riechl, the chairman of the Examination Commission. More and more restaurants, Riechl says, frowning, don't feel their chefs and service staff need the level of expertise the guilds provide. They lean toward cheaper staff and American-style "on-the-job training." He relies on larger hotels and restaurants to take the program's students, but even those employers rarely tap the student's full capabilities.

Though students learn how to make sauces from scratch, most restaurants need them only to open packages and add the right dose of water. They learn to carve roast beef, chicken, and duck expertly by the side of the table—known as "English service." Or they can offer "French service"—which entails showing off the various elements that would be served later on a great platter—before retreating to beautifully arrange plates they bring back out to place before their guests.

What employers instead called for was "American service": slapping the food on the plate in the kitchen, then placing it under a warmer until an untrained waiter could rush it to a customer.

"Just-on-time delivery," says Riechl. "We face the Americanization of everything here. Everything has to be better organized, rationalized. Productivity is guiding us, the need to reduce personnel costs."

He tells me to enjoy my meal, for he doesn't believe this training program will exist for that many more years. "The position of the waiter will die as a profession. As a guild. It will merely be a job."

"So I am experiencing something of a 'last supper,' " I say.

"I believe this may die out," Riechl nods.

And a little of what has made Germany unique, in a positive sense, will die along with it. But Riechl knows that losing some Germanness isn't all bad. He is hardly the image of the up-tight examiner, in his dark blue work shirt, a yellow tie, and a week-old *Miami Vice* growth of beard. He travels a great deal abroad and understands Germans' failings.

It was because of this that he has added "friendliness training" to his course of instruction. "This was a clear oversight in previous years," he says. "I am making the effort to teach them to be friendly."

It wasn't the first time that I had been confronted with one institution or another that was busy instructing Germans on how to smile and be more helpful and kind to customers. Could one really teach this skill like mathematics?

"Making the effort?" I ask.

"Part of the problem is what lurks inside Germans," he says. "There is a reserve in many that can't be solved by instruction alone."

That said, economic uncertainty makes Mr. Riechl's job easier. Waiters, he says, are learning friendliness out of necessity. In a tight job market, employers can more easily hire someone with a ready smile and leave the frowners on the reject pile.

"Before the German will lose the job, he will be friendly," Riechl says. "And this trend is reinforced by customers who expect more friendliness." In short: world-traveling Germans are growing less willing to accept surliness at home.

Riechl speaks in wonder of Bloomingdale's in New York, where he was served happily even after he tried on a dozen pair of shoes without buying a thing. "I know this American friendliness is superficial," he says, but he still prefers it to the Germans' superficial instinct to be unfriendly. "The American understands the market. You are more in tune with the customer. We have a civil-servant mentality. People always had assured work places— they couldn't lose their jobs if they were unfriendly to you."

The examination for the students is a banquet for us. The chefs under scrutiny toil in the kitchen over the five courses whose makeup they have drawn from a hat. They all arrived early in the day to go through a battery of other tests: deboning fish, butterflying shrimp, preparing crab cocktails, mixing drinks, setting tables, and memorizing what they need to know about the evening's wines. Each of the waitresses and waiters is responsible for a table of six, and among the six is an examiner. The other five are expected to do little more than eat.

I sit expectantly beside our table's examiner, a Frau Giese, who joins me, Gerhard, Christina, and another couple who are friends of Gerhard. The menu that lies before us has been printed in the closest thing to old German script that a computer can pump out: "Dinner on the occasion of the Final Examination for Restaurant Industry in Summer 1997, served in the training center of the Adlerhof Casino." Gerhard has arranged it so that the food that arrives at our table—or at least three courses—will be prepared by his baby-sitter Andrea.

The mood is somber, as if we were about to participate in a sacred ritual. (One would think that such a large group of freeloaders would have more fun at their indulgence.)

If one can measure experience in the gastronomical professions by girth, our examiner Frau Giese seems to have much under her belt. She hails from eastern Germany, where she notes that restaurant jobs held higher social esteem than in unified Germany.

I tell her that I wish to experience the dinner through her eyes, through the prism of the professional tester and taster. She regards me with the stern face of someone who never seems to have truly enjoyed a meal. She refuses to share any of her impressions.

"Due to the protection of data, I am not allowed to tell you what I approve of and what I don't approve of this evening. This is a private matter between myself and the woman I am testing."

Ever since Hitler kept and misused vital statistics of every nature on his Germans, the country has had a healthy suspicion of unprotected personal information. I try to school her on the charms of a journalist's off-the-record conversations, but she'll have no part of it; her lips are sealed except for the requirement to open them for the tasting.

Gerhard winks at me from across the table. It is one of those "welcome-to-Germany" winks my friends often offer me when we together experience something we all realize would only be possible in this form in their country. He'll later tell me she's typically "Ossi," or East German. My West German friends say they travel frequently to East Germany to observe their own kind in their more natural German state, less altered by years of Americanization and Westernization.

The tester was certainly one form of "normal German"—deadly serious about her little area of responsibility. One long-term German expert in America once compared German bureaucrats of every sort to a Cambodian rice farmer: one's whole life revolves around his little plot of water-soaked rice land, every inch of which he cultivates efficiently and thoroughly. Each German bureaucrat acts in the same way with his paddy, said my friend, enforcing its borders against all outsiders. Frau Giese's rice paddy is tonight's test—we'll only get as close as she decides.

She breaks off my abortive questioning when our waitress arrives for her first task: pouring wine, which she announces is white 1996 Vollrads Sommer Riesling from the Rhine region. The waitress's hand shakes and the tip of the bottle clinks against my glass as she fills it with the rich, golden fluid. Some of the wine trickles down the side of my glass, along the stem, and onto the tablecloth. Frau Giese takes note as well. She raises a disapproving eyebrow. I hope Gerhard's Andrea is faring better in the back.

As the waitress retreats from the table to fetch the appetizer, I whisper to Frau Giese: "Does she lose points for that?"

She won't be drawn. "It's a matter of principle that I can tell you nothing about what I am thinking," she says. "Nothing."

At that moment, I hear the voice of Sergeant Schultz on *Hogan's Heroes: I hear nothing! I know nothing!*

Perhaps the greatest disincentive to being the stereotypical German is that one instantaneously becomes part of an ugly, internationally recognized cliché.

Yet Frau Giese is fiercely proud of this knowledge she may not share. It made her somehow superior to us all. She did, however, consent to provide me some general information about the program.

For the preceding three years, the waitresses and chefs had attended a course that took up an entire day each week and which complements their otherwise full-time work in a restaurant or hotel. The studies include a host of subjects, among them general economics, business, accounting, nutrition, wine, culture, a smattering of English (one semester), social studies, the theory of serving . . .

"The theory of serving?" I wonder.

"There is a science and a history to it," she says.

"Social studies?" I ask, watching this student's hand shake considerably less as she refills glasses of wine all around.

"Yes," says Frau Giese. "She must know how democracy functions to be a useful member of society." The social studies courses go on for all six of the semesters and for two of the eight hours each week.

I reflect on all the democratic knowledge that thus must reside within our waitress as she places our appetizer before us: an attractive glob of liver pâté resting on a cold pork medallion, beside a salad of sprats, tomatoes, and baby asparagus.

Our chef's first course tastes a dream.

"This is just wonderful, Frau Giese," I say, hoping to influence her grading of the baby-sitter. But I can't help but add. "Still I don't understand how all this study of democracy improves the meal."

She shrugs. "Perhaps one should cut this social studies course in half and replace it with more technical studies. But we don't want *Fachidioten* [students whose knowledge is limited to just one subject]. We want them to be able to handle themselves fully in our society."

Frau Giese nods toward the waitress. "She must learn, for example, how to defend herself when she faces injustices."

"Defend herself?" I ask.

"She needs competence in some legal and business matters. If a guest isn't happy, insulted in some way, the guest has a right to bring a legal complaint. The waiter must know about this. There is a *Gaststätten Gesetz* [restaurant law]. It regards such matters as the condition of the toilets and under what conditions one can refuse service to guests. You can't do it in a discriminatory manner. One must be able to provide justification. She must learn which justification is acceptable."

German rules and regulations, I think to myself. Those bureaucratic guests who attend every party.

"She must learn how to handle matters when a bill isn't paid. When do you call the police? When not?"

"The police?"

"There are occasions."

I wonder whether Frau Giese, like Mr. Riechl, also teaches friendliness in her own courses.

"You can't teach that," she says. "That's something people either have or they don't."

Luckily, our waitress has it. She is gaining confidence, a splendid recovery from early missteps. She and an assistant—who is a second-year student who will be tested in twelve months—whisk away the starters and bring on a cold cucumber soup. "Appropriate to the sunny weather we are experiencing," the waitress announces to the table, with a tentative smile.

Frau Giese rises to inspect the tableside work on the third of the five courses, the fish: giant scampi in a crab sauce with fennel strips and saffron rice. This is our chef's worst moment: the mountain of unnaturally yellow rice, which was molded together in its round form, is falling apart in chaotic piles. Frau Giese lets a frown slip.

I distract attention from this rice disaster to engage Gerhard in conversation about the history of the sorts of guilds that control this testing. The guilds, born in the Middle Ages, did not allow Jews inside, he tells me. So Jews drifted to less respected professions such as trade, banking, chemistry, physics, music, and the arts, areas the more prestigious guilds of craftsmen didn't control.

Gerhard complains that the chemical industry's own guild was now losing support for its dual training program. Before, he says, companies provided most of the students, particularly Berlin's largest pharmaceutical concern, Schering. Now the state had become the primary backer.

"Why should the state take on the burden for training anyway?" I ask. "If a worker wants training for a skill, he pays for it in America. Or a company runs its own training system, unattached to the state." I didn't see why the taxpayer needed to play a role here.

"We are a *Sozialstaat*," says Christina. "That is why we do it. You aren't so *sozial*. That is why you don't do it. You're accustomed to harder conditions than we are. In America, it is nothing for you to change jobs at age forty and go to another again at age forty-six. Not here."

They all agree that this is changing but insist it would be a shame if the dual system in Germany broke down. They fear they are all being dragged down into the abyss of "American conditions"—*Amerikanische Verhältnisse*. For them, this means a growing gap between rich and poor, violent ghettoes, rising crime, and a society that doesn't look after its unfortunate. The fight for profit replaces humanity, in their view.

I'm saved by the arrival of the red wine, along with the breast of chicken in cream sauce. The vegetables are firm: the menu calls them cauliflower roses, princess beans, tournierte carrots, and potatoes of the castle—slightly glazed new potatoes of perfect texture, neither under- nor overcooked.

The examiner, to my surprise, whispers some of her closely guarded intelligence in my ear. Our waitress hadn't cut the chicken with the speed or dexterity that is expected.

Sensing an opening, I ask her if she agrees with Herr Riechl that this would all be gone in a decade.

"That is a question for the politicians," she says. "Not for me."

Gerhard doesn't have the same constraints. "Companies had more social conscience when I was younger. But now the only society they care about is that of the shareholders. And what happens in Germany when people are disregarded is they turn to the right. That is a German specialty. And that is what I fear."

I look at the examiner for comment.

Not her field.

But hasn't the state interfered too much in Germany? Isn't that one of the lessons of your current economic problems? Haven't state regulations held back entrepreneurs and frightened off investment?

"I think it is good that the state interferes," says Christina. "A parent takes responsibility for his or her children. A state takes responsibility for its citizens. If a state wants to continue in its function, it must train its youth."

Gerhard, however, acknowledges that *Vaterstaat* sometimes has an ugly side. He tells the story of the problems he faced while naturalizing his adopted Peruvian child. Citizenship is far from automatic for adopted children. When Gerhard finally felt he had reached the last stage of bureaucracy at the appropriate Berlin Senate office, the bureaucrat responsible argued that Gerhard's ID card, his passport, and his birth certificate weren't enough to prove he was German. For the purposes of such an adoption, he would need to prove that his father and grandfather were both Germans.

"This civil servant, like all civil servants, acted as if he had the most important job in the Federal Republic," says Gerhard. I thought again about the Cambodian rice farmer.

Gerhard invites me over for an evening when he can show me his *Staatsbürgerurkunde*—essentially a modern-day equivalent of what Hitler practiced many years ago, proof that Gerhard was genetically clean and definitely German, as if this somehow would make it more certain that this Peruvian child would measure up to his new citizenship responsibilities.

Dessert is served.

The baby-sitter has produced an ice cream parfait with flambéed fruit. Only one problem: the alcohol won't light. After several attempts, a faint flicker is all we get. Frau Giese grimaces. We are sure the problem is a draft, and I look to close a window, but it is too late.

The ice cream arrives quite melted. Our waitress keeps her cool, sprinkling slivers of almonds in pools of expanding goo. But by now, after the melted parfait, the less-than-convincing deboning of the chicken, the hand that shook as it poured the wine, I fear the consequences.

While coffee is served, the chefs march out in parade form—the first we see of them that evening. We applaud as they stand before us in white stovepipe hats rising high off their heads and identical, unisexual white smocks over checkered pants. They looked so much happier than we, wrapping their hands around each other, providing support and solidarity: a winning team after the buzzer. The waitresses stand before them in their white blouses, black skirts, and frilly aprons.

Herr Riechl takes his place before them all: he tells them how the world will open to those who have succeeded that night. He says their profession is a passport to the world. In their jobs, he urges them to go abroad and bring back home ideas and practices from other worlds. But he reminds them to always come home to enrich Germany with their new abilities and experience.

Some minutes later, as the grades are distributed individually and privately, Andrea rushes to the table and hugs Gerhard and Christina ecstatically. She has scored three out of six points—good enough to pass, though the dry rice has taken its toll. She fills the room with her joy.

The examiner is weakening in her control of the data. She tells me that our waitress has passed as well. She wasn't excellent, but she was good enough. "I liked her manner" she said. "What she didn't do well were the small things. She didn't bend down enough when serving from the plate, and she could have spilled on you. When she removed the butter plates, she stacked them atop each other. That just isn't done. And the flambée . . . it should have been higher. It should be ten centimeters high."

"Ten centimeters?"

"Yes."

"You measure it?"

She doesn't need to. After so many years of experience, she knows a ten-centimeter flame when she sees one.

The American in me wanted to savor the extravagant flame of the amateur, that bold moment of panache for which one orders a flambéed dessert in the first place.

I then recall why I have come: to discover the normal German. Was it the examiner who guarded her rice paddy so jealously? Was it the diners who took their gastronomic outing a little too seriously? Or was it the waitress with the nervous hands and the considerable education in democratic rights? Or perhaps it was Dieter Riechl trying to teach them American friendliness without losing their German thoroughness and professionalism. And then sending them out in the world so that they could return and create a better Germany.

I look across the room to where Christina and Gerhard continue to talk and laugh with their triumphant baby-sitter. After a while, we walk outside to catch the train back into town. They wear the pride of parents who have just seen their child successfully through school. We bid a hasty farewell as I disembark at Hallensee station, the stop nearest my apartment.

"Will you play this week?" Gerhard asks as the doors are about to close between us. "We're short-handed."

"Of course," I say.

Anything for my *Verein*.

I'll play, along with the psychiatrist, the mathematician and a number of those I haven't written about: the dental surgeon, the taxi driver, the banker, the software salesman, and the printer.

Normal Germans, I suppose.

Or perhaps a basketball club is merely a basketball club.

THREE

FAMILY MATTERS

We as Americans are more open-minded. It's hard to grow close to this people. These Germans.

—JARED KOBS, MY UNCLE
WHO IMMIGRATED TO AMERICA IN 1951

My childhood in Utah was dominated by baseball, Boy Scouts, and long bicycle trips with my cousin LeRoy. When I went hiking with my father in the Wasatch Range of the Rocky Mountains that rise above Salt Lake, he spoke now and again about the similar beauty of his native Ore Mountains in Saxony. But my thoughts were more likely to drift to dreams of how I might someday play outfield like Willie Mays.

Rarely, back then, did I think about my German heritage.

And why should I?

I grew up speaking no German—a conscious effort by my mother to separate us from a nationality that could do us no good in America. And yet, one or two German words and phrases stubbornly clung to family conversation.

For example, my aunts were always *Tante.* For a time, when I was very young, I wondered why it was that all my aunts had the same first name. The other German spoken in our household was specific-use, isolated phrases. My grandmother, who arrived to baby-sit me just as my mother was tearing out the door to teach school, never failed to instruct me, *Mach das Bett!*—"Make the bed!" And at night, just before climbing back into my bed, which would invariably have been made by Grandma and not by me, I would wait for my father's low voice to bid me softly: *"Träume süss von saueren Gurken."*

I was an adolescent before I bothered to learn what he was wishing me: "Dream sweetly of sour pickles." This odd phrase always had a strangely comforting sound to it, a father's love expressed with a tone of kind humor in his native tongue. It was as different from the harsh guttural German of war movies as Oxford English is from ghetto vernacular.

Yet compared to these gentle and subtle echoes of Germany in our otherwise unremarkably American home, the house of my cousin LeRoy's parents, my uncle Jared and *Tante* Inge, was downtown Berlin. On our frequent visits there, and during my several longer stays with my cousin LeRoy, I always felt that I was on foreign ground, a place unfamiliar and exotic. I thought of them as my German relatives—my first exposure to the country and its ways.

Jared and Inge both had far thicker accents than my own parents, having arrived in America only after the war. And discipline had always been more of a serious matter to Tante Inge than to my Dr. Spock–educated mother. Still, I only remember Inge spanking me once—when I got my pants dirty in defiance of her—but it was still one more beating than my own mother had ever given me.

Their home in Sandy, Utah, a suburb of Salt Lake City, was far tidier than our own: the lawn always neatly manicured, the paint on the brick home's wood siding always fresh. Flowers rose brightly from gardens, and tomato and cucumber plants sprouted in the vegetable garden in the back. Years later, when I was in college, during my first visit to Germany, I realized to what extent Inge and Jared had married a flavor of Germany with all-American suburbia.

It seems to me that a German influence still pervades the house when I return to it years later. I am happy to see the same wooden sign hanging near the front entrance that I remembered from childhood: The Kobsens. This is their own inside joke—a German sort of inside joke. The family name is Kobs. In German, plurals of words often end with "en" and American plurals end with "s." *Kobsens* as a plural form is their own bicultural invention.

One Kobs. Two *Kobsens.*

As I step out of my rental car, Uncle Jared throws open the door and beckons me inside. The doughy, sweet smell of baking cakes blows out at me from behind him. Uncle Jared is as tall, lean, and handsome, as I remember him. I only learned later in life that he was actually a cousin, related to us through my Grandmother Schumann's line, but to us he was always a favorite uncle. His eyes sparkle with welcome and a mirth that had always made me think he was in on a joke he was keeping to himself. Though he is seventy-three years old, there has always been something ageless about him.

"So it takes a book for you to come and visit your old aunt and uncle," he says.

"No, it is your cakes," I half-lie, taking the smell into my nose. However, he can't miss my notebook.

The truth is that my venture inside my father's army footlocker has prompted my visit. All the documents my father had left had raised only more questions about my roots, about what German heritage should mean to me. I didn't know exactly what I was looking for, only that Jared would be the most likely person who could help. He was born in 1924, and his memory for the past was legendary. He didn't come to America until six years after the war, when he was already twenty-seven. I had heard bits and pieces of family stories about his time on the Russian front as a teenage German soldier during World War II. Perhaps, I thought, Jared could help me unlock some family secrets.

My parents regarded Jared as perhaps our kindest and most generous relative. He never forgets to send a birthday card, even to the most distant of relatives. The cards always include a few loving lines. He is a good churchman, a Mormon, but beyond that he is simply a good man. He was a furniture upholsterer and "shop-at-home" salesman whose customers revered his personal attention and care. He and his wife, my *Tante* Inge, were spending their autumn years traveling the world in ships, planes, and the mobile home that sat in their driveway. They doted upon their four children and seventeen grand-children—which had less to do with German habit than with Mormon predilection to multiply and replenish the earth.

Jared invites me to follow him downstairs to his study, where he has pre-pared a number of papers, documents, and family photographs.

"What would you like to know?" he says.

Why, I ask, did my mother, his first cousin, come to America in 1930, yet despite the family closeness he himself only arrived after the war?

He complains that his mother, too, had applied for an American visa in 1930, but she had been refused. The problem had been that Jared's father had a hunched back, which meant, according to the visa officers, that he wouldn't be well enough to work. By 1936, Jared's mother had divorced the father, and she applied again for a visa to the United States. This time, the Third Reich wouldn't grant permission; Hitler had decreed that all male children of Jared's age must remain in Germany, to prepare for eventual conscription.

"And that was the end of America for young Jared," my uncle states, with but a slight tone of melancholy.

Uncle Jared can look back on his life without much regret. Things had turned out all right for him. His children had done well enough in life. His life has turned out far better than that of most Germans of his generation. He also hesitates less than Germans of his generation to talk about Third Reich Germany. "I'm at the age where I can't remember what I did this morning, but I recall those early years perfectly," he says.

He recounts Hitler's election in 1933, which he had witnessed with an eight-year-old's eyes.

"The voting took place in a restaurant, a *Kneipe,* you know, a beer joint—they call it a *Kneipe.* I remember it well. Men wearing those *Plakaten* with party *Namen d'rauf . . ."*

He looks to me for a translation. "What are *Plakaten?*" he asks.

"Placards," I say, "like the fellows who walk the streets with the 'Eat at Joe's' advertisements hanging over their heads."

"Yes, that, but these men were asking you to vote for the Nazis or for the *Sozialisten . . ."*

I smiled. My aunt and uncle had developed their own brand of English, sprinkled with German words, endings, articles, and original grammatical constructions. I only came to fully understand them once I began to study German at university.

"Hitler promised people work, so they voted for him," Uncle Jared says. "Don't let anyone fool you—he was very popular with all the common people." And Jared's family was among them. "My father was in the party from the early nineteen-thirties because the party gave him work. He had been unemployed for seven years before Hitler got the *Macht.* He worked on the *Autobahn,* with a *Schaufel.* They didn't have all that equipment then."

I ask my aunt, who has delivered us glasses of soda, to join us. She is a perceptive, portly, and jolly woman, comfortable with a life well lived.

Had her family been for Hitler as well? I ask.

"It was hard in those days to find people against Hitler in our circles," she says. She recalls that she and her mother would walk from their house on the Kaiser Wilhelm Platz to Hitler's Chancellery, some forty-five minutes away, just to get a glimpse of their *Führer.* Best of all were the times when he would make a quick appearance on the balcony. She recalls how all the people outside would roar their approval. Her mother, who held young Inge on her shoulders, was among the most enthusiastic. "Because my mother had four children, we had a nice home in a duplex. Hitler rewarded women who had so many *Kinder.* When we saw him, we cheered and shouted *Heil Hitler!* You didn't think about it then. You did what the crowd did. You ask yourself now how dumb you must have been. It is true you didn't *dare* be against Hitler, but you also didn't *want* to be against him."

Inge, like Jared, speaks much more openly, with much more distance about the past than do Germans of their generation still living in Germany. It is as if their American naturalization had freed them of any guilt or responsibility for what had happened then. While Germans accompany such recollections with apologies or weak self-justification, Jared and Inge speak in a tone much more of disbelief: they don't themselves quite believe they had been part of it all.

I ask about inherited responsibility. My aunt and uncle seem to think that they had shed their Germanness at New York Harbor, yet I had strongly felt for years that my German blood, despite American citizenship and upbringing, required a different consciousness of me than if I had less-tainted origins. Had they achieved absolution through emigration?

"We have no responsibility," Inge says. "We were children. We didn't do anything."

"No," says Jared, "no one knew what Hitler had in mind. Only those closest to him. And they had to be very quiet about it or they would end up in a concentration camp themselves."

Did you see the Holocaust coming? I ask.

"I remember as a young boy, twelve or thirteen, I was," says Jared. "It was in 1937. We had a Jewish family living in our apartment house. The name was Perlmutter. I have a memory for such small things. They had a hard time getting groceries because of the restrictions on Jews. My mother was a sales clerk at a grocery store. After ten in the evening, when the apartment lights went out for the night, I had to sneak to the second floor of the *Vorderhaus*, the front part of the *Hof*, and put a bag of groceries in front of the door and then sneak back to our apartment without making a noise. Boy, that was scary."

I interrupt. Was the grocery store owned by Uncle Theo?

He said Uncle Theo's shop was one of several where his mother had worked.

Thank God for Uncle Theo.

Many families of German blood have closets abrim with skeletons. Yet whatever might lurk in our family closet, we would always have Uncle Theo. The family story was that he hid Jews and that he saved Jews. I'd heard more than once that he'd been part of some sort of underground against Hitler. But I'd never known more details than this. On those few occasions as a child when I mulled over any specific responsibility our family might share for the Holocaust, I retreated for protection to stories of Uncle Theo.

Jared apologizes that the real story isn't as good as the one I had heard. Theo hated Hitler, it is true, but he wasn't in any underground. And to the best of Jared's knowledge, he didn't hide or save Jews. His small act of heroism was that he continued to supply his Jewish customers with groceries even though they hadn't sufficient ration coupons to claim them.

I look disappointed, as if to say, *That's it?* Is there really nothing more to the man whose heroics have been part of family legend for all of this time?

"Don't underestimate him," says Jared. "One could be sent to a concentration camp for such things in those days. But he wasn't so political. These Jews were his richest customers. They were business people, and my aunt and uncle were business people, too. Business people didn't care about race—they cared about business. Uncle Theo had one special customer, a family called Wichnitzer. I remember that they left for England. The rich Jewish people, most of them, got out in time. They saw what was coming. My parents bought their bedroom set, and my aunt bought several items. They weren't allowed to take much with them."

Like so many German families, it seems, we in America had exaggerated the good deeds of our finest family member—Uncle Theo. So I wonder if we had also concealed the sins of evil family members. I recall to Jared my mother's stories about some uncle who had been a Brownshirt in Berlin—a prominent Nazi who might have had blood on his hands. Was there more bad to our family than I knew?

Nothing too bad, says Jared, looking away. He seems little interested in talking about this Brownshirt. But I'm certain he knows more than he's saying. I make a mental note to come back to the subject later. I ask him to continue his tales of Germany at its worst.

Uncle Jared says he walked the streets of Berlin as a fourteen-year-old in November 1938, the day after *Kristallnacht* when the windows of Jewish shops across the city lay in shards, their contents burned or stolen. The child Jared, however, spent the day at the theater. "I remember going to the Rose Theater on the Frankfurter Allee. They did live performances there, but I can't remember what I saw. Later it became the Stalin Allee. And then again the Karl Marx Allee, I think. That's German history for you. The systems change and the street names change, too. But at this cinema, I went to almost every show there. It cost fifty pfennigs for the *Trampelloge*."

Standing room? I ask.

"That's right," he says, "the space behind the last row. Next to the theater was a jewelry store owned by Jews. My mother bought things there. She had just given me my first *Siegelring*." He looks to me for the translation.

Signet ring, I say.

"Yes, that one. My name was engraved on it. I had to return it to adjust the ring to the size of my finger. It was too large. A beautiful, gold ring. They were nice people who ran this shop. The Jewish owner was very honest and saw to it that you got what you paid for. But when I walked by there all the windows were broken and the owners were gone." When he returned a week later, someone had boarded it up—a business and its owners had disappeared.

"Did you ask your parents what was going on?"

"Everyone wondered what happened to them, but you didn't ask many questions in those days. People were afraid. We all knew about the kah-tseds." He uses the German pronunciation for the familiar initials "K" and "Z" for *Konzentrationslager*—the concentration camps that Hitler introduced shortly after he came to power.

"Even children knew about the camps?" I ask.

"You knew even as a child if you talked too much against the government you were a candidate to go there," says Jared. "No one can say they didn't know about kah-tseds." He shudders at the memory.

And so the conversation continues. Jared recalls the closing of more shops, including one Jewish-owned business where his parents had bought his uniform for the *Deutsches Jungvolk*, a sort of Cub Scouts for the Hitler Youth for Germans of ages ten to fifteen. He also tells of a Jewish convert to his Mormon church showing up each Sunday with his yellow star—until one of the fascist members of the congregation spoke out so strongly against him that he never dared return. "We couldn't stop what happened because of the pressure on all of us not to get involved."

And he recounts how the Perlmutters, the only Jews in their apartment house, left the country one by one. The son Morris went to Israel, Jared had heard. His sister Edith ended up in England. An aunt and uncle who often visited them went to Israel via Russia. Or at least that was the talk in the neighborhood. Everybody whispered about where the Jews were going—but not loudly or with much confidence.

"We never knew what happened to the parents," Jared says. "They just disappeared. They took them by night. And then they were gone. The German people didn't know. You saw people walking around with the Jewish star on their chest and the next thing you knew they were gone."

Soon no Jews remained for Uncle Theo's qualified heroism.

My uncle Jared at age seventeen was old enough to be a soldier in 1942.

He recalls October 23 as his first day in the infantry. He was young and strong enough, in a world where German youth was quickly being depleted, so he was put into the *Führerbegleitbatallion,* a special-forces unit "just below the SS." And that meant he would go to the front. His unit was known as *Batallion Grossdeutschland* and, he says, it took only soldiers over six feet tall, who didn't wear glasses, and who, like Jared, had been trained in the *Reichsarbeitsdienst,* a sort of boot camp for those still too young to fight.

A military doctor's examination ruled Jared couldn't take the heat of Africa. He would be healthier, according to the doctor's curious ruling, on the Russian front. The first stop: Stalingrad.

My kind uncle's face transforms as he says this word, Stalingrad, as if suddenly frost-bitten. He seems to shiver. He is elsewhere, the snow blowing in windy gusts against a cattle car that is taking him as part of a fresh batch of soldiers toward Stalingrad, where German and Soviet troops had already been locked for weeks in combat.

"It was the bloodiest battle in the history of warfare," he says. "It cost the lives of two million men and women, if you include the civilians. Our leader at the time was Field Marshal Friedrich von Paulus. We hated him because he would never retreat." Jared was reading a book called *At the Gates of Hell,* that explored how von Paulus did not resist Hitler's orders that he "fight to the last man." Jared knew "the last man" could well have been him.

"We belonged to the proud German Sixth Army," says Jared, "whose men had ravaged France, driven the British at Dunkirk, and conquered Yugoslavia, but von Paulus watched as his men were torn to shreds at Stalingrad. When we arrived, it was our job to break through a corridor to his army and get them out of their misery. It was to be a relief operation."

A sad laugh. "Relief." He spits out the word in disgust.

And then he laughs hard. "Some relief operation. Let's have some cake."

We walk upstairs to the kitchen where we find *Streuselkuchen*—a German crumb cake which is my uncle's specialty and my favorite—is ready, *mit Schlag*—with fresh whipped cream. Jared also prepares a pot of decaffeinated German coffee called Pero. The Americans' Mormon religion has put him off caffeine, but the family substitute for years has been the German Pero, which they buy because it's cheaper, he insists, and not because it's German.

We settle in the living room to talk. It's full of knickknacks from their travels, many from Germany: decorated shot glasses, collectors' spoons, a few carved wooden bears with "Berlin" on them, and, of course, the Black Forest cuckoo clock that is standard outfitting in all my German-American relatives' homes.

Uncle Jared relates to me his war experiences for the rest of the afternoon. He speaks of this teenager Jared as if he is some distant stranger, a naive young man who by luck and instinct narrowly escapes death time and again. On his first night of active battle, he retreats in the frosty night to his own lines after having narrowly survived a suicide reconnaissance mission. For so having escaped death, a senior officer puts him up against a tree to be shot.

"You are still alive?" Jared remembers the officer saying. "That can only mean you didn't fight well enough, so we'd better kill you."

The officer didn't fire the gun, though. Jared chuckles that he almost died of a heart attack. Everyone laughed. It was a tough initiation.

In a matter of only a few weeks, teenage Jared grew up fast. And he learned little, awful lessons about life. He saw a buddy raise his head from a trench out of curiosity, wanting to see if he could spot the enemy. And a minute later some high-powered gun had blown his friend's head off. Jared took the lesson: he kept his head low from that point on. (Not a bad approach for life, he notes.) His only injury was a bullet hole through a helmet when he raised it out of his foxhole atop a rifle.

The recollections flow one after another. History has made it difficult for German veterans to brag; my uncle seems happy someone has come to listen.

He speaks of the sounds he can never get out of his head: the fearsome humming of a Soviet biplane—called the sewing machine—before its attack, and the blood-stopping thunder of Soviet Katyusha rockets, the Stalin organs, little more than launching pipes on the back of trucks. He often saw colleagues disappear when a shell hit, leaving only a red hole in the snow where they had once been. He remembers running in a zigzag across an open field while Soviet bullets spat dirt behind him. He still marvels at the miracle of his own survival.

"I was not a man. I was shy. I hated arguments. There were always arguments at home, and I couldn't stand them. I couldn't eat meat because I had a weak stomach. Chicken, but not meat. But in the war I became a man. I changed completely. I had to live. I did what I had to: kill, steal, survive. When

I was responsible for providing the men's food, I took it where I could [from the local people]. The chickens didn't mind that I stole them." And the locals seemed relieved when soldiers only wanted their chickens. They only panicked when they watched the teenage Jared execute that night's dinner on the spot. "You just break the chicken's neck with two fingers, like this, and it's dead." He demonstrates the simple movement, like scissors cutting paper. "I did that in front of some Russian peasants, and I was surprised how afraid they were of me after that."

He laughs again. He laughs and laughs, confronting some phantom he had long forgotten. He hardly recognizes himself in his stories.

What did he feel then? I ask. Surely he knew the war was lost at some point. Was he afraid? By way of answer, he says, "I had the order at one point to take care of the dead and bury them. My job was to write the many letters to the wives and parents that a husband or a son had died in action, to give them the place and the time he had died. I had not many feelings anymore. I was sitting on top of the whole bunch of dead, doing this job, and I ate a sandwich on top of them because I knew tomorrow it could be me, and who cares."

What kind of sandwich? He frowns at the reporter's odd question. "I don't know what kind, only that it was ice cold and frozen like all the soldiers' bodies themselves."

Did he ever think about the morality of what he was doing, of what the Germans were doing? "I had no time to think of morality," he says. "I was too busy fighting to live."

I tell him about the exhibit I had seen—the terrible photographs of atrocities—the hanging of civilians, the execution of supposed traitors by the Sixth Army during its march on Stalingrad. I had read that von Paulus's troops were among the worst in committing these atrocities. Had he seen such things himself?

The question I didn't ask was suggested: had he been involved in German atrocities?

He recalls seeing only one such event, somewhere between Russia and Poland—soldiers never knew for sure where they were. He was riding down a dirt road in a military truck with other troops. He looked outside and saw Romanian soldiers digging deep trenches along the side of the road. "I said to the *Gruppenführer.* What are they doing? He answered, 'They are digging their own graves because they are traitors. Deserters. They will be shot when the trenches are deep enough.' "

Did you think this was wrong? I ask.

"We had no time to think about what was wrong and what was right, with the Russians coming closer day-by-day." He'd also heard of a seventeen-year-old girl who other soldiers raped repeatedly and shot; such events were simply part of the horror. "But I wasn't involved" in such atrocities.

Was he sorry Germany didn't win the war? "I didn't care, I just wanted it to be over. I was sick and tired of Hitler by then, as most people were."

Was he ashamed to be German then?

Jared says he had no reason to be ashamed. He didn't know about the Holocaust until after the war. And what about the eight million Germans who died? He wonders why no one cares about them.

It is time for dinner.

I spend the entire day with my uncle and aunt, until in the evening they bring out my favorite German meal, beef *Rouladen,* thin slices of round steak wrapped like crepes around a stuffing of bacon, onions, or an assortment of vegetables. It is accompanied by the usual piles of sweet-sour *Rotkohl* (red cabbage), the sort of heavy, hearty cuisine for which their Germany was known. All my life, I had considered Jared and Inge to be the most German of my German relatives. I had come to them to learn about their Germany, but as we continue talking I discover with each sentence how little they identify with the country anymore. They had embraced American citizenship as a welcome whitewash for unwanted nationality.

I ask them why they don't feel more German, even as they dig into the red cabbage.

"It is the German mentality that allowed the Nazis to come to power," my aunt says, neatly wiping her mouth. "And it hasn't changed that much. They are too much like sheep following a master."

On a recent trip to Germany, she asked Berliners with whom she once worked, Germans who had openly made anti-Semitic remarks, how they would have felt if they had been Jews at that time of the Third Reich. "You know what they answered?" my aunt says. "They answered that if they had been Jews, they would feel they deserved to be killed. Such Germans are not Christians."

She shakes her head in dismay.

"They are followers, the Germans," she says. "And I don't know why that is. I have a *Schulfreundin* in East Germany. In what was East Germany. Not any more. You know what she says? She wishes she had the old regime back of the Communists. She wants that because she was able to follow what was there. The German is more comfortable with that. They are so *stur . . . stur . . .*" She looks to me for the American word.

"Stubborn," I say.

"Not enough," she says.

"Pig-headed?"

"Yes, that's it. Pig-headed. That's what they are. I wouldn't get along with German people anymore. I'm more flexible. Take my sister, for instance. I think she should be open-minded to everyone. But when we were in Germany we went to a café and a Turkish waiter came to our table. He was the nicest person you could find. But she treated him like dirt. I don't like the German people anymore, to be honest with you. They are always seeing what's wrong in other people without seeing what's wrong in themselves. You are always right—and the other person is never right."

Having dated German women, I smile to my aunt, I knew exactly what she meant by that.

"Oh, stay away from them," she says, not lightly.

It is a curious scene. My German-born relatives, who had served me German cakes and German decaffeinated coffee, who are now serving this German meal, and who still speak accented English with sprinkles of their native language, fire off one complaint after another about Germans, as if they have nothing to do with them.

"We as Americans are more open-minded," says Jared. "It's hard to grow close to this people. These Germans." He says even their language reinforces a stand-offish manner in them that bothers him so. "You have to call someone a doctor even though he is no better a man than you. *Herr Doktor,* you must say. And you say *Frau Doktor,* even though she isn't a doctor at all. Her husband is. But she gets the title, too. And all the time you talk with *Sie.* You know what I mean?"

I do. *Sie* is the formal voice for addressing someone—as opposed to the more familiar *du.* Jared and Inge viewed the formal *Sie* as a linguistic device that maintains distance in a country that offered little natural space between people.

I too have felt this. I have spoken English with long-time German associates so we could adopt the first-name basis and easy informality that the German language wouldn't allow us. In other European languages, familiar and formal voices complicate communication, but in German the rules of usage do in fact seem more designed to reinforce divisions.

"There is a fear of too much closeness in Germany," says Inge. "Perhaps because they all live so closely together. It's something born into the people. Maybe we are closer in America because we live further way from each other. When I worked at ZCMI (a Utah department store), I was on a first-name basis with my richest customers. They didn't act like they were better than me, the way a rich German would. We like the American atmosphere. Why do rich people have to act like rich people? In Germany, people who are more educated don't want to be with less educated people. Here people are proud to be doctors, but they don't exaggerate. You call them by their first names."

Jared's view is that Germans define themselves against others more, while Americans are more likely simply to define themselves.

"They are *Sauerkrauts*," frowns Inge.

"They are not very polite," agrees Jared.

"You know, sweetie, at first I didn't want to come to America. You talked me into it. But from the moment I came, I felt welcome and at home."

"People are always watching each other in Germany," says Inge. She says the natural proclivity to spy isn't officially exploited as it was in the era of Nazi informants or East German *Spitzel*—the State Security apparatus informants. But she still feels that everyone in her sister's apartment house is watching everyone else to make sure they are doing everything properly: emptying their garbage in the properly marked bins, taking proper care of their yard, not leaving their lights on late at night.

When I later tell some German friends about the curiously anti-German views of my aunt and uncle, they accuse them of being typically German in their quick conversion to America. If history had shown anything, it was that Germans were quickest to adjust to whatever system they happened to fall under—they were the perfect fascists, Communists, social democrats, capitalists, and even Americans. Some Germans argue that it is because over the years Germany has suffered so many wars and historic shifts: one learns to go with the flow.

Still, whatever the reasons, I couldn't imagine any other emigrant generation expressing quite so much disgust toward their own quite recent roots. I wonder out loud whether there is anything that these two relatives of mine preferred about Germany over America.

"*Gastfreundlichkeit,*" says my uncle immediately. "They treat their guests better. Look how well you are eating with us." Suddenly, he becomes German again. "With an American, if you are a visitor you are lucky if you get a glass of water. This isn't enough for the German. You'd get at least a cup of coffee and a cake whenever you come here. I'm also proud to be German because of the culture we had."

Uncle Jared seems to be contradicting himself. He distances himself from Germans when he speaks about their negative sides, yet he associates himself with their warmer nature and culture. What is his true view toward Germany?

"I suppose I think about Germany the way that you talk to a child," he says. "What you did I don't like, but I love you anyway." He and Inge consider themself a happy mixture of Germans' better sides, having benefited from the salutary effect of more than forty-five years in America.

Would they ever live in Germany again?

"No way," Jared says.

"Absolutely not," says Inge.

Why not?

"It's not Germany anymore with all those Turks," says Jared. "I wouldn't want to move back. No way. *No way!* Germany has become a foreign country. I enjoyed the culture that I was born into, but that culture is gone."

Inge agrees.

The contradictions grow. Jared dislikes Germany partly because of intolerance, but he doesn't want to go back because it is overrun by "foreigners"—some eight million of a population of some eighty million.

It is too late, however, to explore this new opening further. As I bid my uncle and aunt farewell for the evening, I remember one unfinished question from earlier in the day. "We were talking about Uncle Theo as the good German," I say to him.

"Yes, he was a good man," says Jared.

"And you mentioned there might have been a bad German in our family as well."

Jared goes back inside and returns with the address of a cousin in San Diego, California. Manfred Kramer. He is the son of my great aunt, Alma Schumann, who had been a singer at the German State Opera from 1946 to 1950. Her brother, who was my grandfather, had cut off contacts with her once she reached America after the war. The reasons had always been one of those dark family mysteries that give rise to a host of contradictory rumors—money, sex, religion, jealousy.

"Call Manfred—or visit him," Jared says. "He'd love to see you."

What's the story? I ask.

"Manfred should tell you," says Jared. "His father is the person you are looking for."

Bright stars flicker in a cloudless San Diego sky over two cousins sitting in a Jacuzzi, which bubbles beside a silent swimming pool. A family dog occasionally yaps for attention. The two men ignore him and talk over their day's work while drinking Diet Cokes from San Diego State football mugs.

It is an unlikely setting from which to consider the German past, one that my cousin Manfred has perhaps subconsciously constructed to be as far from his German past as possible. We find an easy familiarity that suggests a much longer association.

"So can you use any of the stuff I showed you?" he asks.

Manfred had opened up trunks of family history to me, showing photographs from his childhood in Berlin, when he and his brother Franz worked as extras at the State Opera while their mother sang. They earned extra money for the family in the harsh postwar years, he said, and they saved on baby-sitters. He'd also brought out volumes of my own grandfather's poetry, endless stanzas that his sister had preserved but kept hidden from our side of the family.

"I found it all fascinating," I say, expressing particular thanks for the poetry, which dripped with love for his God, his religion, and America. What my grandfather lacked in poetic skill he made up for in passion. "I particularly like the photos of you as a little girl in the straw hat." He had played this role in an opera.

We laugh. I throw a Frisbee. The dog retrieves it.

"Your mother was an attractive woman," I say. The publicity photos she'd kept from the various operas she'd performed in had been striking: her long neck, high cheekbones, the haughty look in her eyes. She was indeed a Schumann, the younger sister of my grandfather Arthur. And she had both the looks and the musical ability to show for it.

"A shame that she had such an ugly personality," Manfred says. We both know that

Alma Schumann Kramer in Die Meistersinger von Nürnberg.

it was because of that personality that our two families hadn't come together, even though my own extended family had been so tightly knit. Our every family gathering had been a cacophony of American children's laughter and elderly immigrants' German accents. Anyone even distantly related could attend.

My own maternal grandfather had come first to America in 1930, though his sister didn't follow until 1956. While my grandfather had escaped the misery that was soon to come to the Third Reich for the plenty of America, his sister had been smack in the middle of it, married to a Nazi. Her husband Erich, Manfred tells me, had been one of the earliest members of the party and of the *Sturmabteilung*, Hitler's dreaded storm troopers. He had served during the war at the eastern front in the military police. It was only after their divorce that Alma Schumann Kramer brought her family to America.

The years between their two emigrations had changed the world and their relationship; before, my grandfather had been his sister's beloved idol. Family legend had it that the two siblings fell out over an inheritance during the postwar years. And the records Manfred had shown me went far to confirm that Manfred's mother had cheated her brother. She had meticulously

Manfred Kramer in La Traviata.

catalogued the money she received from the sale of some stocks and property, and none of it ever found its way into her brother's account—though he was listed as an equal beneficiary. It hadn't been enough money to dramatically alter anyone's life, but my grandparents had led such a modest and penny-pinching life that the extra funds could have relieved them of at least a bit of the burden.

Alma hadn't only cheated her brother, she had also been insanely jealous of his wife, who by chance was also named Alma. She wrote a letter informing the bishop of their Mormon church that her sister-in-law's eldest son, Franz, was actually an illegitimate son born to a different man. The irony, I had learned that day in the records, was that her own first child had also been conceived out of wedlock and was born only twenty days after her marriage to the Nazi Erich Kramer.

"She could be a vindictive woman," says Manfred. "I wouldn't put anything past her." He tells stories of how on frequent occasions she tried to sour his own marriage to Delores, his delightful if thoroughly American wife. In marrying her, as in his choosing life as a California furniture merchant, he seems to have tried to drift as far from Germany and his mother as possible. After finishing his U.S. military service, which included a stint in Germany, he never returned to his original homeland. And he never again saw his estranged father before his death in 1983.

I ask cautiously whether he doesn't think that part of his mother's bitterness might have to do with the nature of the man she married. Manfred shrugs that it's possible. It seems clear, he says, that her pregnancy prompted the marriage, and that she had been in love with someone else at the same time, an officer in the navy about whom she spoke wistfully until her death. "I'm not sure she ever loved my father."

A part of him probably hoped that she didn't.

Manfred's father had been a true believer, having joined the SA

Brownshirts back in 1928, after he'd been laid off as an underground construction worker, joining the growing ranks of unemployed who were ripe
picking for the Nazis. Manfred tells me that his father appeared in a biography of Horst Wessel, one of the SA neighborhood leaders. Wessel became
a martyr, and a song that he wrote became one of the Nazis' fighting ballads.

Goebbels, the Nazi propaganda chief, knew and liked Manfred's father
as well. At one point, Erich had lost his Nazi party membership because he'd
been on the wrong side of an internal power struggle. The talk in the family was that it was Goebbels who had Erich's membership reinstated.

"Nice list of friends," I say.

Manfred says he had not known his father well. Born in 1939, he was an
infant when his father went off to join the war's very first day in Poland. He
only came back on occasional leave until he returned from Soviet prison
camp in December 1949 for good. And then, almost immediately, began the
fights between his mother and father, with violent beatings. His father began
to beat Manfred's older brother Fritz; and the worst moment came when
Fritz tried to defend his mother against his father's blows.

Manfred recalls in vague details a flight by the family from East Berlin
to West Berlin shortly thereafter. They had been but a step ahead of
Communist arrest. But several months later, his father was arrested anyway,
in the West, and charged with "crimes against humanity."

So, I think, now we are getting to the point at last. That was the charge
at Nuremberg that had led to so many executions, I say to Manfred.

"They held him for a year, but then they let him go. He always told us
that it was because of 'lack of evidence.' But I don't know."

"You think he did it—that maybe he killed Jews?"

"I wouldn't put it past him."

Manfred recalls when his father came home in the last months of the war,
before he was arrested by the Soviets at the front. He was accompanied by a
Polish volunteer, who was acting as his valet. He talked as if he would never
return; he seemed to know that any capture would mean his death. He wanted
his wife to be able to protect herself and their children, so he left her a pistol and his German shepherd, Nero.

"What a loving gift," I say.

Manfred can't think of anything that could have been more useful at the time. Manfred's father told his family how often the dog had saved his life in the past, sniffing out potential enemies hidden in the woods. "All you had to do was tell the dog, *'Greif Bolsheviki'* [Attack Bolsheviks]—and he'd attack."

Manfred smiles sadly. Perhaps he's better off knowing so little about his father. He doesn't much want to return to Germany, though he informs me of a new inheritance of property in Berlin that might also be partially mine. This time, he's making sure that his side of the family approaches the matter fairly.

His wife Delores arrives with fresh towels. She invites us back inside for some dessert before going to bed.

"When I return to Germany," I tell Manfred, "I'd like to look into your father's story a bit more, if you don't mind."

"Fine by me," he says. Manfred suggests I look up his older brother in northern Germany. He had stayed behind in Germany with Manfred's father when Manfred and his mother had come to America in 1956.

"Why was that?" I ask.

"He was in prison," Manfred says.

Nice family, I think to myself. "What did he do?"

"I'd rather leave it to Franz to tell you. He also knows a lot more about father. They grew closer after the war. I don't know how much he'll tell you, but he knows a lot."

For bedtime reading, Manfred lends me the Horst Wessel biography. In it I discover that my great-uncle met his first wife while guarding Horst Wessel's grave site. He wooed her away from a buddy whom she had intended to visit.

As I doze off, it strikes me that I am treading on that unsafe territory where so many Germans before me had ventured—that of family history. For better or worse, the line that fate had arbitrarily drawn between my Americanness and my German family was beginning to blur.

FOUR

FORWARD MARCH

The Germans have a past, but they have to get over it. There is too much present to deal with.
—MAJOR GENERAL YVES LE CHATELIER,
  FRENCH COMMANDER OF GERMAN TROOPS
  IN BOSNIA-HERZEGOVINA

The dark sides of German history and these new, bright sides belong together. Some of our success in the postwar years can only be explained because we've seen the depths of hell.
—VOLKER RÜHE, DEFENSE MINISTER,
  IN SARAJEVO

The acne-pocked, moon-faced German private at the checkpoint demands our documents with a guttural bark. His small frame carries his full battle gear badly. He inflates his inadequate chest behind a bullet-proof vest.

"Ah, c'mon, Schneider," says my accompanying officer, Captain Alexander Reinhardt. He's been through this before, it seems. "I'm with an American reporter and he's just arrived in-country." He nods toward me. "No way could he have his papers yet."

"Rules are rules," barks the soldier, uncowed before his superior. In the German army, regulations outrank everyone. And this, after all, is for all of them the first month on the most important mission of Germany's postwar military history, and Good Soldier Schneider is determined to get it right. "If you want to pass, Captain, you'll step down and fill out the appropriate forms."

Reinhardt sneers as he carries my passport and press pass to the guardhouse and writes my name into a log. Several minutes later, Schneider lifts the heavy steel bar. We drive past his self-satisfied smile.

"Ass," Reinhardt grumbles as we turn away from the gatehouse. "I'm sorry, but sometimes some Germans still are a little bit too much German."

The setting is Rajovice, a former Yugoslav Army Air Force base where German troops have joined French and Ukrainian soldiers for their first combat mission abroad since World War II. But for all the novelty of the mission, the Germans have settled in like old pros.

By the time of my arrival—during the second week of their deployment—they had set up cozy heated and air-conditioned living containers. They'd parked the newest and best tanks and APCs "in theater" on the combined forces lot—freshly painted and unscarred by action, in contrast to the weathered and worn French materiel. And they were standing about in uniforms a bit too clean and neatly pressed, befitting the jittery debutante.

At first glance, German troops in Bosnia reinforce old stereotypes. There is a press officer who advises me I must clear with him anything I quote from any soldiers with whom I speak. (He's later overruled by cooler heads.) There is the Colonel Klink look-alike who corners me for an hour and tells me in the most obsequious possible tones about every American officer he has ever met; he reminds me repeatedly that he is on the record—"here's my card with the spelling of my name."

And there are the German officers who strut about with the pumped-up pride of children whose father has given them their first real cap gun in a leather holster.

Yet Bosnia is more about exploding German stereotypes than it is about confirming them. It may have been hell for Bosnians, but for Germans, the

Bosnian conflict is a godsend. It is a way of demonstrating to the world that Germany's military is a force for good, a message that also isn't lost on the country's legions of left-wing pacifists. Bosnia is playing the role of a reverse Vietnam for Germany: restoring faith in a military's ability to do right among a population where pacifism for many had been the lesson of World War II.

Bosnia is about soldiers like my accompanying officer, Alexander "Sasha" Reinhardt, a former keyboard player in a rock band who was one of the 7,400 Germans who landed in early 1997. His father, an intellectual general still serving as chief of the German army command, had thought his son too soft for the military and advised him against joining. Captain Reinhardt recites his life story as he escorts me to the football stadium-sized mess. We join French soldiers in line, who look dubiously upon the sausage, mashed potatoes, and sauerkraut that newly arrived German cooks slop onto our trays.

Sasha came into the military through his father's former unit, the Mountain Infantry Batallion 222, which still practices James Bond–like winter maneuvers in the Bavarian Alps. For his smarts and quiet thoughtfulness, his superiors eventually hand-picked him to be one of a hundred *Bundeswehr* youth officers whose mission is to educate the skeptical German young on the role of a military in a democratic society. In Bosnia, he's an escort officer for reporters like myself.

"You once faced social ostracism when you joined the army," he says, fixing his thoughtful, clear blue eyes on me through gold-rimmed, round glasses. His demeanor is more that of the law student than the junior officer. Sasha recalls how his high-school history teacher—history had always been his favorite subject—took him to the side when she learned he was taking the examination for acceptance into officer training. "How can you throw away your talents like this?" he remembers her saying. "You have so many other possibilities." Sasha says the woman he married "was one of the few girls I ever met who could be proud of me when I put on a uniform."

"One of the best things about Bosnia is that this anti-*Bundeswehr* attitude is starting to change." Captain Reinhardt volunteered for this mission, as must any German who served in Bosnia. "You get a lot of respect for coming here, even from people who are against armed forces in general."

As we talk, some French soldiers who have joined our long table speak of how the German military is actually much more humane than their own.

The housing is better, they say—they were stuck in tents throughout the winter—and the officers treat the lower ranks with more respect. One of them jokes that he is thinking of changing his citizenship—he has a German relative—and his army.

Reinhardt smiles, but as we walk back to his quarters, he tells me that he hasn't any intention of a military career. "I want to get a job in public relations once I'm finished here," he says. "It's going to look very good on my resumé to have been in Bosnia. I've been in the military for twelve years, and I need to do something new. The army is just too hierarchical for me."

Perhaps, he muses, he might find something in the music business. He tells me of his plan to bring a hot German rock-and-roll group called Tic-Tac-Toe to perform in one of the air force hangars to promote the band's new CD and to raise money for Bosnian relief. His local superiors are cool to the idea, but his father the general has cleared the way. He figures it's time to update the military's image.

Sasha's father, however, had some misgivings after he went on a rock radio show in Germany to promote his son's unusual event. After taking some Q & A, the General was treated to some of the group's better-known tunes: "I Think You're Shit" and "Piss Off." But if Germany was to rewrite history, perhaps one needed some irreverent theme music.

I tell Sasha I need to locate the best place to visit in Bosnia from which I can contrast past and present. He doesn't hesitate: he insists on sending me to the Serb town of Foča on the banks of the River Drina. There, he says, I will find a bridge that had recently been constructed by German troops. It stands on the same site where, after World War II, German prisoners-of-war—soldiers from a Third Reich army that had lined up Serb menfolk and shot them in retribution for partisan attacks—had put up an earlier bridge.

The new bridge is only a temporary structure of one lane, formed by planks of steel held together with welding, rivets, and a modest superstructure. I look down. There, in the river running powerfully by, I can see the ruins of the former German bridge, eroding there since September 7, 1995, when it was destroyed by Allied planes in their successful attempt to force a peace on the region.

My escort officer proudly shoots snapshots of the bridge from every angle. It is a happy contrast to the controversial exhibit on *Wehrmacht* atrocities that I had just seen in Germany, made up largely of soldier snapshots from another era—of hangings, summary executions, atrocities. The German soldiers are back, with newer Leicas, this time recording a more positive history.

"These are documents of change," he enthuses as if scripted. "It's almost as if the fifty years before this were static. Now everything shifts so quickly, so all at once. When I joined the military in 1962, we were preparing to defend our own borders against the Soviets. We never expected to serve anywhere else—that was for the Americans and the French."

But, I say, it is clear now that Germany's influence on the world stage will grow. Bosnia is merely a beginning.

The officer frowns. "The art that is demanded of us is to take on our new role with all seriousness but also with restraint and humility." He notes that Germans aren't always the best at humility. "We have to win back the trust of our neighbors. That's what this is about."

The stage was appropriate. Hitler attacked monarchist Yugoslavia on April 6, 1941, after the Serb-dominated Yugoslav army had staged a coup d'état in response to the country's decision to join the fascist Tripartite Pact with Germany, Italy, and Japan. The country, torn by ethnic rivalries, didn't put up much of a fight; the *Wehrmacht* declared victory after only eleven days. Hitler established a fascist puppet state in Croatia, to which he gave all of Bosnia-Herzegovina, and a military regime in Serbia, and the Drina formed the border between them.

In the war years that followed, the ultra-nationalist Croat Ustashe slaughtered tens of thousands as they tried to expunge the Serbs from the areas they controlled, while the Serbian nationalist forces, the Chetniks, put up military resistance not only to the German occupiers but to the Croats as well. The Germans meted out savage reprisals, flattening villages that hid partisans and executing as many as a hundred locals for every soldier killed. Serbs still speak of the notorious German slaughter in the autumn of 1941 of more than two thousand people in the Serb town of Kragujevac for the killing of ten soldiers nearby.

Standing at the entrance to the bridge, I scan passers-by for faces old enough to have experienced German atrocities. I want to know what they think of the German return.

I stop an old man who introduces himself as a seventy-six-year-old former construction worker. Tomo Antunovic tells me how he fought the Swabians, as he calls the Germans, as a partisan in World War II. He scratches the gray bristle of his beard and buttons up his soiled, suede leather coat with a fur collar.

For the life of me, I can't get him to say anything negative about Germans. The war, he says, was so many battles ago. Who can think of them as the enemy anymore? One has so many new enemies.

But what does he remember from his partisan struggles, I ask. Did he witness executions?

"At some stage, Germans did bad things to people here," he says.

That's as far as he will go. And how does he view the new Germans?

"There are different opinions."

And his?

Germany the enemy, he says, is now German the country that is most likely to provide economic support to rebuild Serbian Bosnia.

He talks of the local construction company that the Germans employed when they rebuilt the bridge. He enthuses about the salaries they paid, higher than anyone in Fôca had ever seen before. He also has friends whose children work in Germany. They send significant sums of money home to their parents. The Germans, he says, taught these Serbs how to work and how to earn.

To his mind, America and Clinton are the Serbs' enemies. Not the Germans. Germans built the bridge. Germany pays big salaries. Serbs live in Germany, and do just fine. The bottom line: Germany's atrocities are a faded postcard compared to the Technicolor war that has just ended.

Unable to find any anti-German sentiment on the road by the bridge, I march off in search of the town mayor, a man who had gone on German television in opposition to the German troops' arrival. *Hadn't Germany done enough harm to his country,* he had said.

It's Saturday, so it takes some time to track down Mayor Petko Cancar, who had been out that morning boar-hunting. He agrees to meet me at city hall, where he unlocks the doors and lets us in to his small office. He wears the soiled, checked, flannel shirt and heavy trousers he had on the hunt. His manner is that of the old Communist leaders I know so well from Eastern Europe: gray and suspicious. His dull eyes send out a fog of distrust.

As I pull out my notebook, he takes his own thick desk diary out of the desk. As we talk, he jots down each of my questions and each of his answers—to ensure that he's properly quoted. He writes slowly. I can see this interview will take some time.

Why didn't he want the Germans in town? I ask.

He writes down the question. Each word, every letter. And then he looks up.

He concedes his initial instinct was to oppose the German arrival. But in the end they built a strong bridge, and they behaved themselves well, he says. They stayed out of town entirely—commander's orders. He was so happy with their fast and efficient work, he says, that he arranged a celebration for the day they were due to finish, in October 1996.

He then turns away and writes down notes of what he's told me. I wait.

"So you changed your mind about the Germans?" I ask.

Work on the bridge was running late, and on the day it was due to open, the mayor invited the officers to a local café overlooking the river. He toasted their accomplishment by offering up straight shots of plum brandy—"a very good one," he says. "And I remember what I said to them at the time: I know you are bothered that you are late, because you are German. But you are here to enjoy our habits a little, so have a drink." And then he told them all, as best as he can recollect, "Whoever calls up the ghosts from the past loses the future . . . German construction soldiers have saved the honor of the armies whose airplanes destroyed the bridges. We have both paid a lot of bills over the years," he said, "and now we are even."

The mayor doesn't want to talk about his initial TV comments about the Germans. He had had a bad day when the Germans first arrived. His wife's brother had died in the fighting. He speaks about "new feelings" for Germans now.

"A lot of German tourists came here. They canoed on our river, they hunted in our woods. We want them back. We have a women's stocking company that exports to the Germans, a fur company as well that sells most of its products to them. All the technology and equipment for our forest industry is from Germany. Now that the war is over, we are getting spare parts again. And all of the families who have lived in Germany after the war came back much better off. They made friends—many intermarriages. They learned European standards of work and they brought them back. We have a new history. The thing that happened fifty or eighty years ago, that's gone."

"The thing?" I ask.

He's not writing down my questions or his answers any more. "These are a genius people, the Germans. Always geniuses, but some historic periods were oriented in the wrong way. They work hard and are disciplined. When our people came back from working in Germany, they said that if we worked as hard as the Germans we would have a rich country."

It is a story I hear in one form or another throughout Eastern Europe, where the fighting was worst and the Holocaust most bloodthirsty. Eastern Europeans know history, but they are also closer to present-day Germany. And they are more dependent on its trade and investment. Curiously, the closer one lives to the new Germans, the more one accepts them and sets aside the past in the face of new opportunity.

You don't fear Germans any longer? I ask the mayor.

"Everyone is afraid of everyone a little. The mouse is afraid of the cat, the cat of the dog, the dog of the wolf and the wolf of the bear, the bear of the human. But is it the German we should fear? No, we fear the Muslims and the Croats. Our war with them destroyed in a year what we built in ten years or more. Economic reconstruction is what we need now. Germany is what we need now."

After we finish, I walk over the bridge to the waiting *Bundeswehr* Jeep. A plaque rests at the front of the span: *Construction by German Pioneers, October 1996.* The ruins of the previous bridge, built by German POWs, slowly dissolves in the rushing waters below. Bits of history disappear into the Drina. And new history hovers above.

Back in Sarajevo, I've got a date for dinner with General Klaus Frühhaber at the best local restaurant. He brings along a half-dozen other officers—who will all sup on my tab.

The officers strut heavily into the restaurant in full camouflage dress and combat boots. A table is ready. I'm uneasy with our brash entrance. I look around and see the restaurant is peopled by businessmen in suits, and a few older men with women too young to be their wives.

None share my discomfort with our military invasion. They've seen so much military in past months. What difference do a few new Germans make?

General Frühhaber was born at a time of war, he tells me, in 1939. His first day of school wasn't until the fighting had ended. Although he was a war child, he was reared "as a humanist" by a father who was a Protestant pastor, a man who had been spared from combat by the fact that he was born with only two fingers on his left hand.

The general recalls that his mother, who decided most matters in the family, listened secretly to the BBC during the war—a punishable crime. Whenever the occasion called for the stiff-armed Hitler salute, General Frühhaber's mother would bend over and tie her little boy's shoelaces.

Her husband's brother, a true Nazi, wanted to turn her in at one point for her disloyalty to the Reich, but General Frühhaber's father threatened to kill him if he did. The point the general wants to make is that he isn't a typical military man: his education about the Nazi period came from his mother. And his hero is Count Claus von Stauffenberg, the colonel who tried to kill Hitler on July 20, 1944.

As he tells me this story, I think about how many military men that week had voluntarily provided me their personal backgrounds, in most cases to show how "atypical" they were. They all sought Stauffenberg-like pieces of German history that they could cling to like rock outcroppings as an avalanche of stones passes by. For the conformity of it all, I almost yearn to break the mold: *"That Hermann Göring, what a genius he was. And Eichmann, now there's a lad . . ."*

"At ages fifteen to sixteen, one needs role models," says General Frühhaber. "And that isn't always easy in Germany. But Graf Stauffenberg was a true hero."

After Frühhaber graduated from high school in 1958, he decided he wanted to join the military despite his "humanistic," anti-military mother. What inspired him to do so was the Soviet crackdown on Hungary in 1956. "I can still hear it on radio, the first one we bought, in 1951. I remember the voice of Imre Nagy. 'Help us or we'll go under,' he said. I was a teenager then, and I was moved to tears. So I mixed my early ideals with the idea of becoming a military officer. It was a curious combination at the time."

His pacifist mother, whose approval was necessary for him to enlist, as he was still a minor, refused to sign the required papers. She urged him to go to university and study something "useful." But the young Frühhaber was stubborn; he worked at odd jobs and sold goods on the black market to make ends meet until he was twenty-one and could join up, without his mother's blessing.

The next major influence on young Frühhaber was the 1968 student revolution, when he was a twenty-nine-year-old officer with a promising military career. It was also the year that he married a professional singer, at a time when no one could understand why such an educated and artistic woman would wed a soldier.

"I saw how these sixty-eighters overturned street cars. I saw with what sort of resolve these young people fought. I was impressed by their personal commitment to a cause. My soldiers weren't as brave as they were."

Frühhaber had a crisis of confidence. "I asked myself whether I could stay in the army or not." What kept him, he says, was the logic of deterrence and the horrifying reality that Germany probably would be the first country to go up in a nuclear mushroom cloud. He learned how much one needed America as well, for it was clear Germany would never have its own nuclear weapons. "We will never be that normal." For that reason, he argues, America will be Germany's critical partner for the future.

And the French? I ask. They also have a nuclear deterrent.

The officers around the table chortle. They find the idea of the French protecting them an amusing one. One mumbles, "Some things the French will never share."

They all nod in agreement.

That said, Americans aren't always sensitive enough to Germany, says Frühhaber. When he was part of the nuclear planning group in Brussels, he discovered the American strategic planners had picked his home town of Weiden as ground zero for atomic weapons use during one exercise.

"Jim"—he remembers telling a lower-ranking American colleague—

"that place where you just dropped your kiloton of bombs is where I was born and raised."

"Gee, sir, I'm sorry. I'll choose another target."

"That's not my point. Where's home for you, Jim?"

"New Hampshire, sir."

"Out of cooperative reasons, why don't we plan the nuclear attack on New Hampshire next time."

Jim's face turned white. "I hadn't thought about it that way, sir."

"Please do. Please remember that your *Schlachtfeld*"—the German word for battle ground, which literally translates as "slaughtering field"—"is my homeland."

"It was that knowledge that defined everything in the postwar years," he says. "It defined NATO, Germany's friendship with America, Germany's division, German fears."

"And your career," I say.

"And that's what's gone now, this fear. Do you have any idea how important that change is? We are no longer the *Schlachtfeld.*"

The men around the table hang on his every word. "It was one of history's lucky breaks," he says, "that we were united. Our Fatherland was united. Without a single shot."

He talks as if about a miracle that everyone has seen but no one has properly understood. Such an improbable outcome to the German story—and now this. Now this Bosnian opportunity to make amends for history!

"With this liberation comes obligation. We have an obligation not just to take care of ourselves. We can't let others risk their soldiers' lives for us, as we did when Saddam invaded Kuwait, while we just provided some money to finance the mission. Others have risked their lives for us—among them you Americans—and now we must take some risks ourselves for others."

For that, General Frühhaber has been busy helping to change the operational thinking of an entire army, from one of national defense to one of rapid-response for allied missions. "We had to change our doctrine and thinking. How do we do out-of-area operations? It was something we never thought about before."

He says his country's great disadvantage is an inflexible bureaucratic thinking that seems contradictory to the very idea of rapid, mobile response. "I need to justify every soldier I have down here. And each request for one new body requires two pages of explanation. Do we need 2,401 troops, or 2,430? My French colleague gets what he needs overnight. But we have discussions about each and every enlisted man or major."

And the German strengths?

"In the field, we are more flexible in our thinking and execution than the French. We are mission-oriented."

Every German officer talks about the fabled *Innere-Führung*—a concept that translates as "inner leadership" and dates back to Field Marshal Helmut von Moltke in 1870. The idea is that each officer in the field must make independent decisions about how to implement general orders from on high. The German lower-ranking officer has a lot more latitude for decision-making than his French equivalent.

"I don't tell officers how to do it," says Frühhaber. "I say this is your objective and you tell me how you'll get there. Oh, yes, we also have another advantage. We are the perfect organizers. No muddling through. It is an inbred characteristic of the Germans to be organized. We learn it with our mother's milk."

Another German characteristic, much more recent in origin, is the willingness to take orders from others. Though German troops in Bosnia outnumbered the French, the Germans were happy to leave overall command in French hands. "It is because of our history that we are the most loyal—and sometimes the most naive—representatives of the alliance. It's in our blood. We've gone it alone in history only at great expense. We've learned some tough lessons. It could be that my children will think differently. In ten or twenty years perhaps they will ask: why should we take orders from our allies? We're strong. We're healthy. We should give the orders. But for now that isn't the case. We arrived in Bosnia with history in our rucksacks."

The floor manager comes by with the bill and free drinks of slivovitz. She thanks the Germans for coming to the restaurant—and to Sarajevo. She chokes back tears. She is grateful for these soldiers. These *German soldiers.* She says they conduct themselves far more correctly than some other of the Western soldiers, and because of that they are always welcome.

General Frühhaber raises two toasts:

"We want to show that the World War II history is finally the past through this Bosnian engagement."

We all drink.

"I want to send my 2,400 men home safely. That is the only question that I ask myself every day—how can I do that?"

She refills our glasses. We all drink again.

On the drive back to the base, I ask General Frühhaber what he thinks when he closes his eyes and pictures Germany. With lids tightly shut, he tells me in soft tones that he thinks of Brahms's *Oratorio*, Handel's *Messiah*. "I hear a hundred concerts in a hundred concert halls." He wants the world to hear music when it thinks of Germany—maybe Bosnia will help.

Volker Rühe carries himself in a way befitting the new German military—unthreateningly. As I watch him review his troops in Bosnia, I see that he doesn't march in front of them. He shuffles, almost apologetically, hardly lifting his feet from the ground as he moves forward. His shoulders slump, head hanging forward, more like the high-school teacher he once was than the defense minister that he had become.

It's soon apparent this Sarajevo trip is as much a photo-op as it is a chance to rally his troops. The camera teams follow him about: Rühe in front of the hangar. Rühe in front of the tank. Rühe beside the local boys in their battle dress and black-streaked combat faces. So abnormally normal.

And he's brought along representatives of all the major parties to join him in frame: even the Greens, to show the ranks the consensus that he has been able to rally behind them. Even though he, too, would leave office after the election of 1998, when the history of unified Germany's first years are written, Volker Rühe will get a good deal of the credit for two of the country's most positive first moves: he forged the domestic consensus that allowed German combat troops to join United Nations and allied missions abroad for the first time, and he led the diplomatic efforts to expand NATO eastward.

Rühe was the first Western politician to publicly support the concept of NATO expansion, and did it forcefully in March 1993 in his Alastair Buchan Memorial Lecture at the International Institute for Strategic Studies in

London—at a time when the American president and his Pentagon remained either against NATO expansion or neutral on the issue.

And he most articulately defined the most important element of this expansion: the German-Polish rapprochement. That bilateral relationship could do as much to define Germany's success in the twenty-first century, he says, as its improved relationship with France defined it in the last half of the twentieth. Hitler's vision began with Polish invasion: a new German vision begins by embracing Poland.

With frequent help from an impressive group of aides—including the savvy advisor and policy architect Vice Admiral Ulrich Weisser—he devised a plan by which Germany could make the transition from being a security consumer, which it had been for the previous half-century, to being a security exporter.

Mr. Rühe was well suited to the task. He had a long history of independent thinking, even when it upset party or ministry allies. I first ran across him in the early 1980s when he angered the White House with his opposition to a new generation of short-range nuclear weapons, which were to be based in Germany. "The shorter the weapons, the deader the Germans," he said famously, calling the American policy into question.

It was with Mr. Rühe that I had flown to Bosnia, riding to the front in a plush government jet, where he sat in his private compartment reviewing reports and preparing for his day's rounds. As an air force steward handed me stereo headphones, I thought of how differently my uncle Jared traveled to Germany's last foreign engagement—in cattle cars bound for the Russian front and the siege of Stalingrad.

Mr. Rühe talks about one of the key goals of his push to expand NATO eastward, the effort to bind Poland and Germany together. In November 1996, according to Mr. Rühe's plan, Polish and German construction brigades met on the once-disputed Oder-Neisse border and built a bridge that would join the two countries. "The German part of the bridge was very modern. The Polish part was quite different, of an older style. Normally the two wouldn't fit together, but in the middle they jerry-rigged a small segment of about ten meters that could merge the two types. This bridge was symbolic in many ways."

Yet Rühe knew the Germans must overcome deep prejudices to truly

close the German-Polish gap. "It won't be as easy as the German-French relationship after the war because the Germans admire the French. The
Germans do not admire the Poles, to put it mildly. The first Poles loved and
admired by the Germans were the Solidarity members. For the young generation, this has made a big difference in perceptions. You still find so many
prejudices from the past."

The term "Polish economy" was until recently a favorite oxymoron.
German workers near the Polish border resent the Poles most, blaming them
for stealing their cars and their jobs.

Rühe took the first concrete measure to add substance to NATO expansion by creating a joint Danish-German-Polish corps that would have its
headquarters in Szczecin. Polish troops were already led by a German-
speaking general who had been trained at the Hamburg *Führungsakademie*—
command school. At the same time, Germany was sending some of its
officers to Polish training. Rühe attended the first year's graduation in 1997
when a German finished first in the class and thus gave the graduation
speech—in Polish.

"This is unheard of," he says. First, never before would the Poles have invited a German officer to attend, not even an eastern German despite all the
Soviet propaganda about socialist brothers. But even if they had, he says, they
would have made sure that a Pole placed first.

I'd known Rühe for years, but I'd seldom seen him grow as animated as
he does when he talks about the improving relationship with Poland. "This
is a big change in Central Europe. *The* big change."

The critics of such Rühe moves are legion, and many of them are in
France. They feel that he is fulfilling the dread fear of Germany moving
east—the *Drang nach Osten*—and away from its Western underpinning to pursue its own ambitions.

Yet Rühe notes that his military has been so absorbed by the West that
it doesn't even have its own general staff to go it alone. "I always thought
those fears [about *Drang nach Osten*] were a whole lot of nonsense. We don't
move east—the whole of Europe moves west. The Poles certainly don't want
Germany to move east. They want Germany to help them move west."

East European expansion is also a matter of principle for Mr. Rühe.
Germany has a moral duty to back Poland's entry into NATO. "I had the

feeling, and I still have, that we owe a lot to Poland," he says. "We owe them in a negative sense for what we did to them during the war. And we owe them in a positive sense for their courage in the 1970s and the 1980s. Their liberating themselves was really the key to overcoming the division of Europe. We need to understand that there would have been no Leipzig without Gdansk."

With that, he draws a direct connection between the rise of Solidarity against its oppressors in 1980—the first massive democratic movement in postwar Eastern Europe—and the Monday demonstrations in Leipzig nine years later that sped the fall of the Berlin Wall.

I knew few Germans who were willing to give the Poles as much credit for German unification. Germany's historic feeling of superiority over the Poles wouldn't allow it. Many Germans would rather credit Mikhail Gorbachev, a Soviet who accompanied Soviet decline, rather than the Poles who did so much to stand up to oppression and start the pro-democratic domino effect.

Mr. Rühe's outlook has virtue in that it is logical, but it is also moral, healing, and visionary. It addresses an oft-times almost racist German feeling of superiority over the Polish neighbors by correctly crediting the Poles for being far more courageous in fighting for democracy than modern-day Germans have ever been. It links German unification to Polish courage, and it recognizes a moral aspect of German policy toward Poland that goes beyond merely the burden of Germany's bad history to the obligation to modern-day Polish heroes.

It represents the new Germany I hoped for.

On NATO expansion, it took many months before the U.S. government position caught up to that of Mr. Rühe. Weisser, his deputy, remembers helping to lay out the strategy in September 1992 as something that would not only set the tone for a new Germany but also provide Mr. Rühe with a long-term, attention-getting policy that would show that he was the stuff of national leadership. He could be the founding father and continuous promoter of a change that would redraw Europe's political map.

"This was the first time this idea was publicly presented, and it was invented by us," says Weisser. And the audience received it with an ice-cold reaction, he recalls. Some said this was the dumbest idea they'd ever heard of, ruining the good, old NATO that had been created by such a long and difficult process. "But we knew better than any country in the world how much the map had changed and that we needed to come to terms with it."

Mr. Rühe believes in the power of symbols. And nothing could have been more symbolic than a secret meeting of defense ministers from England, France, the United States, and Germany at Versailles during one of the most critical periods of negotiations to expand NATO.

This was the same location where Western allies had met to decide Germany's fate after World War I, nailing the country into a humiliating and financially costly position from which it ultimately broke out with Hitler and fascism. This time Germany was playing the role of co-architect for a new European construct that would be highly favorable to it.

Much of the approach to the Russians that then followed, particularly regarding how to handle conventional forces in the case of expansion, grew out of a German position offered in Versailles—one of several secret meetings among the four key allies during that period.

Critics say the Germans were far too ready to allow the Poles and others to become second-class members of the alliance. They were said to be making deals with Russia under which the Poles would be banned from having nuclear weapons or large contingents of foreign troops based on their soil. What's true is that Rühe and others didn't see any logic to nuclear deployment in Poland or the basing of major formations on Polish soil. The Germans preferred unilateral declarations that said as much, rather than ceding these points in negotiations with Moscow. They feared such an outcome would have set the precedent of giving the Russians a veto and right of co-decision regarding NATO policy.

"There we were in Versailles, the place where all the things went wrong in establishing a postwar order," says Mr. Rühe. "And we were trying to make sure all things went right. This was the third attempt in this century to establish a peace order in Europe. The first was at Versailles, and that went completely wrong and laid the seeds for the next war. The second was after World War II—everything was right in the West but the East was kept out. Now we knew we had the chance to do the right thing for all of Europe—and the place was Versailles—four defense ministers with their aides in a very small room."

And the Germans, who had nearly destroyed Europe twice this century, could set matters right.

Rühe continued to push from behind the scenes for expansion, even when public differences with his foreign minister and a reluctant chancellor (who wasn't yet ready to back him) forced him to retreat publicly. By the time it was finally blessed by NATO in mid-1997, Rühe had already given seven hundred speeches in Germany and abroad on the issue.

"He was a wandering priest," smiles Weisser.

"My whole approach to the job from the beginning was that the biggest risk is not to take risks," says Mr. Rühe, not with braggadocio but, rather, fatality. "You have to lead from the front. If you want stability, you either export it or you import instability."

And out of that has grown a policy for a new Germany—leading from the front, as it has never done since World War II, and exporting stability—which it perhaps never has done. And the policy, as Mr. Rühe made clear, grew out of a moral imperative born of Germany's history, its size, and its geographical position.

And that's where Bosnia came in. Rühe's politics was to make parliament accept that Germany couldn't be a part-time ally, but must participate in missions whenever and wherever it and its allies see purpose. Beyond that, however, he made it a point to slowly shift public opinion, to show that pacifism in the face of world tyrants was an immoral policy that Germany's very history of tyranny prohibited.

In seven short years during Mr. Rühe's reign at the defense ministry, Germany moved from being an object of allied military concerns to being a player in addressing new European security problems. "The dark sides of German history and these new, bright sides belong together," he says. "Some of our success in the postwar years can only be explained because we've seen the depths of hell. I don't think Germany would be this kind of country playing this sort of healthy role now if it weren't for the dark chapters."

Mr. Rühe's first campaign to redefine post-unification Germany's security mission came one week after taking office. He decided, against the counsel of his top advisors, to fight for parliamentary approval to send German medical troops to Cambodia as part of a U.N. mission. His advisors felt such a move, even if Mr. Rühe at some point might want to take it, was too great a risk for a new defense minister.

"I asked myself, what was the risk and what was the opportunity? I knew it had to be done at some point, and I knew how to handle the risk. I could summon public support for those medical units."

He won the first skirmish, and the first German military doctors were off for Cambodia. When the issue shifted from Cambodia to Somalia, the greater dangers called for larger numbers of non-combatant troops as well as signal units. The Bundestag went along, but the Social Democrats' foreign policy expert, Norbert Gansel, told Rühe that he'd withdraw support if one German soldier was killed—or if a German soldier killed a single Somali.

"Robert Frost said that freedom consists in being bold," says Rühe, who quoted the poet at the beginning of his historic speech on behalf of NATO expansion. "My whole approach is that we couldn't just sit there and wait for things to happen. If you feel something is right, you have to do it. I've done that again and again, and I'll continue acting in this manner."

No German died in Somalia. Rühe was ready for the next step.

For Mr. Rühe, the Rubicon to cross in the debate about sending German troops out-of-area came when NATO began to prepare for bombing missions over Bosnia by sending up AWACS reconnaissance planes. Those planes, when on training missions, included Germans as pilots and crew. However, his own coalition partner, the Free Democrats, asked him to pull Germans from the planes once it was clear that they would be guiding allied planes to real-life targets.

It was at that point that he stood up to the foreign minister, Klaus Kinkel, the leading Free Democrat in the cabinet, who said Rühe would be violating the constitution by keeping pilots in the planes. Rühe insisted Germans stay aboard, and took the decision to Germany's highest court.

Until that point, the accepted interpretation of Germany's constitution was that the country could not participate in any combat mission not aimed at the defense of its own territory. It was this interpretation that Mr. Rühe sought to overturn. Chancellor Kohl, at the time, was more concerned about holding his coalition together than fighting this issue, but Mr. Rühe wouldn't budge. He was concerned about the idea of withdrawing German soldiers just when the going gets a little tougher for the alliance. Rühe traveled to Karlsruhe to brief the judges, carrying the same message that he argued at the cabinet and before parliamentarians. AWACS, he argued, symbolized the new Europe and transatlantic cooperation: twelve countries were represented on board. He feared that to pull out at such a critical moment in Europe, when issues of war and peace were in the balance, would continue to marginalize and singularize Germany, just as had been the case before unification.

"People accused me of ruining the coalition," he says. "They said: why can't you be more pragmatic on such subjects? I said if we don't do this we'll see a renationalization of military history in Europe. I saw this plane as a symbol of the progress of the new Europe after the Second World War. You don't have classical alliances as in the nineteenth century, but you integrate your armaments. When you abandon such a symbol, you destroy this idea of cooperation."

More to the point, Rühe knew, if Germany didn't participate in such missions it would have far less voice on any European political-military issues, from Bosnia to eastward expansion of NATO. And these were the sorts of issues by which a new Germany would define itself.

What others saw as a risk, Rühe viewed as an irresistible opportunity. The AWACS challenge, he reckons, was the right time and the right issue over which to challenge the interpretation of the constitutional restraints on German military missions abroad.

In the end, the high court sided with Rühe, and the Bosnia engagement was the final outcome—Germany was finally free to take the proper lesson of World War II: it could use its military to stand against new tyranny. It only grew clear how much German thinking had shifted, however, when the new Red-Green government endorsed the Rühe approach in one of the first Bundestag debates following the elections. Even the Green members of the coalition voted by a large majority to allow German fighter planes to operate over Kosovo in an allied effort to stop Serb attacks on their Albanian minority and even fire upon Serbian targets if the alliance considered it necessary. Rühe warns me not to make too much of it. This isn't the beginning of Pax Deutschland in Eastern Europe, nor would a do-gooding Germany put its troops on the road to join the global battle for freedom and democracy.

"We are not Americans," he says. "We can't be missionaries, you know, bringing a message to other countries and peoples. But what's new is that we have to understand that what we do or don't do has an impact on everybody else in Europe. And that brings us back to the *Bundeswehr*. If we think we shouldn't send our troops somewhere abroad because it might have an effect on others, we must also realize that *not* sending them also has its impact. There's nothing really anymore that Germany does or doesn't do in Europe without impact."

Indeed, where unified Germany goes, Germany is noticed.

Anyone who doubts that need only visit the commander of the Germans in Bosnia-Herzegovina, French Major General Yves Le Chatelier, who has scrutinized every detail of the German deployment. We sit in his office in the dusty multinational headquarters just outside Mostar, where he acts as chaperone to a historic coming-out party. General Le Chatelier speaks with the wisdom of a man who has seen conflicts on more than one continent. He is gray, lean, and calm and only a few months from retirement. He speaks German to me, an exceptional trait for a French general. He was deputy to the commander of the French forces in Germany from 1991 to 1993, so he knows the German army well. In a show of respect for Mr Rühe, he speaks German at a press conference he co-hosts with him.

French troops, he says, came to the region in a hurry and lived for many months in the discomfort of tents before anyone offered them bungalows. Some still slept in tents, little protected from the elements. German troops, by contrast, arrived weeks after their logistical teams had meticulously planned the placement of every heated and air-conditioned container and enclosed toilet. The facilities arrived long before the soldiers. Every space was regulated by federal law.

The French soldier improvises, says Le Chatelier, but the German soldier is an obsessive planner. The French soldier is tough and hardened by his officers, he says, while the German is pampered and softer.

Most striking, he says, is how German officers lower themselves by dining and mixing with the common soldiers. They even stand in the same mess lines! A French general would never think of such a thing—he dines in a well-appointed officer's canteen. The French issue orders from on high, and the troops carry them out unquestioningly. But the German soldier has this curious thing called "inner leadership." Who needs such a thing when one has outer leadership one can rely upon?

It isn't that General Le Chatelier isn't happy to have the Germans—they have brought some of the best equipment, new and sophisticated, that allied forces have in Bosnia.

Yet all this fine good equipment, the close officer-troop relationship, and the cozy quarters and toilets are causing him some morale problems with his own troops. "When the French arrived in April of 1994—three years ago—we just lived the best we could. The French way is to set up quickly and establish the organization later. We improve the conditions only slowly and over some time. After even more time, we buy bungalows for our men, but we get them as cheap as possible and if at all possible get someone else [the host country] to pay. The German approach, on the contrary, is first the thinking, then the organization, then the buying, then finding a good military position. The living quarters first, the men afterward."

He shakes his head at this military heresy. *Hardly a way to go to war.* He worries that perhaps the Germans, the military that once so terrorized Europe, have grown soft with the years. "We French can demand more from our soldiers," he says. "Our discipline is more formal. At its very basis, the German army was created differently. One has to have a greater fear as a German officer not to violate the rights of the soldiers. Perhaps it sometimes goes a little too far, though I understand the historical reasons."

So what he's saying, I interrupt, is that the German military is more democratic than his own?

"*Mais oui,* it wouldn't be wrong to write that," shrugs the general.

"The *Bundeswehr* is extremely conditioned by its past," he says afterward. "Let me correct that: the *Bundeswehr* has no past. The big difference between us is that we French don't have any problems with our history. You can read the history of all our battles on our flags and in the medals that hang from our uniforms. We are proud of that. The history of our units runs without gaps through today.

"But German traditions belong to the past. Most of their battalions don't have any traditions that predate World War II. I think that causes them problems in creating morale. I always lived with units with traditions. It is a good way to motivate the simple soldier. He responds to these traditions. He goes into the Hall of Honor to read the history and see the uniforms. It is a tool for the cohesion of the regiment, a tool for patriotism, national feelings."

So he wants Germany to have such national feelings again? I ask. He wants them to be as nationalist as the French?

He smiles. I've got him there. "Of course I don't want that."

No one does—including most Germans.

He talks about how his wife's family lost their chateau to invading German troops during World War II. She still shivers when she attends the torchlight parades the German troops often stage for changing command, one of the small bits of tradition Germans here have kept—but too much for Madame Chatelier.

"There is a special problem for Germany," says the French general. "Germany has been declared guilty for the two wars of the twentieth century. Perhaps Napoleon was guilty earlier as well of many things, but we look at things differently in our modern era."

Napoleon didn't have to deal with the media or Hollywood, he says.

Still, Le Chatelier believes Germany must shed its fear of the past to take on such assignments as Bosnia. He opposed the German policy to keep its troops out of Serb-held territories. He resisted basing arrangements that, for security's sake, left Germans together in large contingents, instead of scattering them where they were most needed.

"I've told them that this was an operational and psychological mistake. One sees that they came here with some fear—they wanted to make sure above all that nothing went wrong this first time."

A siege mentality of a sort, I say.

He nods. "No other country here sets such sorts of limits for themselves. This self-containment is primarily in their heads, and it is a big disadvantage to me. I want the Germans to be deployable everywhere. I know there is a past, but they have to get over it. There is too much present to deal with.

"It is an important moment in German history. Maybe with this they can put away some of their historic guilt complexes. I hope for Germany that this is true. What better way to come to terms with the past than by tackling a completely different mission in a place where the ghosts of the past still hide. Many French and their allies thought it wasn't moral that the Germans weren't here. If Germany wants to play an important role in the world, as France already has for many years, then the Germans must pay the price."

And the Serbs? Don't they have a problem with German troop presence after all that ugly history? Doesn't he fear attacks, perhaps of a terrorist nature, based on that?

"There are few Serbs who are thinking about the German past. Since that time, they have had years of Communism and then a terrible civil war. World War II is further away for these people than it was for most others in the world."

He does have a little advice, however, for his arriving Germans. Considering how little time they've spent on such missions abroad, they've arrived with too little modesty. They also lack an ability to mix easily with the local populations—too cool and distant for that.

"They shouldn't show too much self-confidence. And they should show humility for the civilian population and other soldiers. The Germans have an image here already of doing everything quite seriously and with great pride. My advice would be that they should be a little less proud."

And a little less serious?

"*Exactement.*"

I retreat to the bar on the base that the Germans set up when they arrived. It has become the most popular watering hole for the French, Spanish, and Moroccan soldiers who share the camp. Its comfort can only be described by the German word *gemütlich*, or cozy.

It is a solid structure, built of canvas over wooden beams. Sandbags run up the sides to above head level. It is a cross between a small Bavarian beer tent and a military bunker, sandbags running up all the walls inside as well to chest level. Solid wooden tables await heavy glass mugs of beer. Colored lights hang from string over a wooden bar. A German GI serves local beer from tap or, at a premium price, good German brew that's shipped in as one of the staples.

I'm early for the evening crowd, which has just begun to collect. I over-

hear the conversation of a handful of young German soldiers, the first to arrive, who I later find have been in Bosnia for less than a month. They wear
the brash certainty of newcomers. They are shocked about the destruction
they've seen—worse than any of them expected: houses in ruins, whole villages burned, entire ethnic groups murdered or forced out. They are shocked
at how quickly they have grown accustomed to it.

"These are such vicious people," says a baby-faced senior corporal who
introduces himself as Alexander Lotz. "My grandfather was here in the war.
He told me to stay away from here—he said that these are vicious people."

Speaking of vicious, I wanted to ask what his grandfather had done in
Yugoslavia. Did he take part in atrocities? Did he execute partisans? See off
transports to concentration camps? But I was just joining their conversation.

"So what did you say to him?" I ask.

"I told him that this mission was about bringing peace and not war. But
he still told me not to come."

"Your grandfather's Germans weren't exactly angels here," I venture.

"As bad as Germans ever got in the Second World War, I can't imagine it
was ever as bad as here," Lotz says. "We didn't fight in a civil war. It was of
different dimensions. There were rules."

Nothing was more regulated than the Holocaust, I thought to myself. But
I stood back to buy the boys a round. I listen to them talk for a while—about
their hometowns, about their girlfriends, about their plans when they get
home. About how they like the easy-going Spanish, Italian, and Moroccan
troops they deal with better than they like the standoffish French. They then
talk about their training—anti-terrorist stuff, mine-clearing stuff.

So what could they tell me about Germany's history here during World
War II?

A little silence. Don't really know much. There had been something
taught in training camp. Can't remember the lessons very well. They remember far better the instruction about security and how to work the weapons.
They needed that.

Ah, c'mon, I say. You must remember something.

One offers that the Germans sided with one of the parties, but he can't
remember which. Another has heard that there is a problem with the Serbs
now because of that history, but he isn't exactly sure why.

Atrocities? Had they heard about those?

Well, those always happen in war, don't they? On all sides.

Had any of them been issued any special instructions about how to act toward any of the local parties because of history?

Nope. They're all sure of that.

Lotz sounds up again. "We Germans don't need to act any differently because of our history. I'm a soldier, like the English, the Americans, and the French. I have friends in Germany who come from Yugoslavia. They are just young people like I am. Serbs, Croats, and Germans. All young people. History—that doesn't affect me."

The beer has bought me a place in the group. We continue to chat as the bar fills up with other soldiers of the multinational group: Spaniards, Moroccans, French, and Italians. The Germans are the only non-Latins, but they make friends more easily than the French because they do better in the broken English that serves as the common language. Only the French insist on their own language.

Peter Schwall, a twenty-four-year-old staff sergeant, thinks that I'm wrong that they should know more about the German past in this historical minefield. "As Germans, we are of a different generation. We should have a critical look at our history, but I reject any notion that we have a special responsibility or guilt because of it. I don't think it would be good for us to feel that way. At some point, you have to close the door on it. Our deployment here hasn't anything to do with that history."

Michael Lahr, a satellite communications technician, frowns. "You just look at what they've done to each other and you see how different you are. It's shocking. I didn't know it would be this bad."

Two other soldiers walk up, tall and lean. One, Andrzej Wohlgemuth, explains that he extended his contractual time in the military because of this deployment—he wanted the chance to do something exciting. "And the job market doesn't look so hot back home, either," he says. After some more experience with communications, he hopes the telecom explosion at home will provide him work.

One of the soldiers briefs him on our discussion of history.

"That's yesterday's meal," he says. "The federal republic has paid enough reparations, done enough reconciliation. We've shown that nothing more bad is going to happen from our side. At some point you've got to put this to rest. We've got it together, our Germany."

The lower the ranks, I find during my time in Bosnia, the greater the willingness to express national pride. There is a rough correlation between the age of the soldier and the extent to which he feels he must apologize for the past. Says Lahr, the satellite technician, "I am proud of my country and everything we've achieved—why shouldn't I be?"

Staff Sergeant Schwall leans his head toward me, takes a gulp of beer, and says calmly. "After the Second World War, you couldn't be proud of being German, of being associated to that Germany. But look what the Germans have built up and become. It is not natural that we aren't allowed to be proud of that. But if you say you are proud to be German, back home your friends immediately put you in a right-wing category."

And if the Germans are so bad, they all say, why is it that all the French soldiers want to join their army? They want their housing, their pay, and their less abusive officers. They even use their toilets in heated containers instead of the French outdoor latrines.

As time passes, some of the higher ranks begin to join their troops at the bar. But only German officers. The French officers socialize among themselves. I'm introduced to Lt. Volker Fritze, who hands me a card that says he is the deputy chief of one of the ten headquarter departments, G-3, which he tells me is the most important: training, organization, operational execution, and planning. His boss is an Italian.

Another officer whispers into my ear: "You know who is really running things if an Italian and German are the two chiefs of organization and planning . . ." The point: Germans could never accept that Italians have their planning talents.

Fritze overhears and disagrees. The Italian has had far more experience in such multinational engagements abroad. Of the ten headquarter departments, a German leads only one and Germans are deputies in four others, he says. Fritze says this secondary role is intentional—the Germans are on their first such mission and they must learn leadership.

"We aren't fighting to be the chiefs of any of the departments," he says. "We have consciously taken a secondary role. You make fewer mistakes as deputy, and this is just the beginning for us. We will make our influence clear without having our people out front. We can't come here and say what needs to be done. The others have been here since 1991. The French were here when there was fighting in the trenches around the Jewish cemetery."

Fritze comes to embody the German situation for me. He is willing to deal with his colleagues in whatever language they choose, and it is rarely German. His English and French are fluent, his Italian and Spanish aren't bad.

Fritze says Germans share information better than the French—and he thus also engages in more brainstorming sessions with other departments.

"A French person thinks first of the French," he says. "And I think first that I have to keep everyone informed so that I won't upset any of the foreigners with whom I work. For the French, information is power that should be tightly controlled—to show that one is better or smarter than the other. The German thinks: every department involved should know what I know so that there are no misunderstandings."

Yet Fritze also understands the French well enough to sell them his views. "The personal relationship is the key to getting what you want from the French." He says a meeting might go disastrously, but that only means that one needs to go out for a meal and a bottle of wine. "You need access to the personality if you want to change something. The Germans must learn this. And if you know of a more efficient NATO procedure you want to introduce, call it something else. If you say it is from NATO, and it is better than what the French do, you are injuring their pride." For the French, he notes, NATO is too American, a command structure in which they still aren't fully integrated.

Fritze says part of the mission here is to keep the Bosnian peace, but part of it is to undo the German stereotype. "We try our hardest not to become the cliché—spiked helmet, goose step, heels clicking together. When we do that, we are finished. Sometimes it isn't as much a question of what needs to be done as what needs to be avoided."

I tell him about my conversation with the enlisted men at the bar—the fact that they didn't know their history and didn't feel they needed to do so.

They have history lessons in their preparation for Bosnia, he says, but "eighty percent sleep during the lessons and the other twenty percent have already heard it before. When soldiers pay attention is when they are trained how to protect themselves, how to deal with terrorist threats, how to remove mines and disarm enemies. The German soldier will get a medal for coming here, and that's what's important to him." That and the fact that he'll be able to tell all of his friends he was in Bosnia. The officers' attitude: why fill him with guilt for the past when you can inject him with pride for the present?

Still, it bothers me. Shouldn't they know more about Germany's horrific occupation here?

"The officers need to know if they are going to a village where people have been lined up against the wall and shot by Germans," says Fritze. "But the soldiers don't need to know this. They need to know that there is danger, but not about history."

So how are the Germans getting on with the French?

A handful of junior officers gather around to brief me. Most of the problems, in their estimation, are based on jealousy. When the German bar was first established, for example, it was hooked up to the closest energy source, a giant French generator. When the Germans' own generator arrived, the French wanted them to switch the bar to that source. But the Germans had considered the one coming in as a reserve.

"They fought us on this because they don't keep reserves," says Peter Tschiporikov, a twenty-eight-year-old staff clerk. "We have the most efficient, comfortable bar in the camp. It's the only place where all the ranks and nationalities gather and mix comfortably. They all walk up to us and say, 'You have so much money.' But partly it's because we just treat equipment better. The Frenchman gets in his car and leaks oil all over the place. We fix the oil leak. When they go out on patrol, they are in trouble if someone is injured. But we send members of the medical corps along all the time just in case something happens."

In short, the junior officers agree, they simply perform each task a little more perfectly.

A German tank commander has overheard our conversation. He sits down with a flourish, his handlebar moustache the visible expression of his flamboyant personality. He speaks French fluently and has worked with the Gauls as part of a Eurocorps intelligence group. "The French soldier feels much more a part of his society, his country, his history. We are less confident of our role in society as Germans."

He worked with a French battalion whose gold and white flag and symbols dated back to 1682. "The German officer is perhaps too modern. Curiously, that's because he knows the history of his country a little too well. A soldier is by nature conservative. He protects the state, the status quo. He has to have something he believes in, which he will protect against all enemies. You have to believe in Germany to protect it properly."

Back in Sarajevo, Sasha Reinhardt is waiting for me with a bullet-proof vest, combat boots, and a helmet. I am to accompany one of the first German armored cavalry patrols on its rounds in Croatian-held Bosnia-Herzegovina. As this is one of the first such German missions, the French provide the escort and the training—they are teaching the Germans the ropes. I ride in the back of the command jeep. Up front in the passenger seat sits a tall, weathered French officer. He provides instruction to his younger, enthusiastic German colleague. It is the old pro, comfortable in these alien surroundings, coolly providing tips to the promising but somewhat jumpy amateur.

The French officer is Captain Michael Casaque of the marine infantry. He's thirty-six years old and has served in Djibouti, Gabon, Chad, and Somalia. His German student is Hauptmann Markus Kreitmeyer, who at age twenty-nine has served only within German borders. His battles have all been simulated.

"You see the difference between us?" shrugs Kreitmeyer modestly.

As we drive down village roads, the German eyes dart around the landscape for dangers. The French officer scans the environment calmly, providing occasional hints and assessments.

He stops the jeep beside what looks like a construction truck, but it has a seal on its side door that the French officer points to. "These are bad guys. Very bad guys. They are the Croatian special forces who have become civilian police. They are called HOVO. Two nights ago, they went in and shot a man in a bar down the street. I'll show you the bar."

The German listens closely to every word, spoken in simple, military English. The German speaks no French, for which he apologizes, and the Frenchman privately tells me that he hasn't any desire to speak German.

As we drive further on, Casaque provides Kreitmeyer some local history: the areas where troubles have occurred before, the neighborhoods where tensions still exist, the hangouts where the local bosses do their business. He also complains to me, like so many Frenchmen, about how easy the German newcomers have it. "My soldiers spent many months outside in the cold without much in the way of supplies," he says, proudly.

The German responds. "Our society and its politicians want to show they are taking good care of their soldiers. The Bundestag requires it."

The Frenchman snorts. He explains to the German how best to run an anti-sniper mission. He points out the cafés where it is safe for an officer to eat, to drink.

We reach a weapons warehouse which allied troops monitor under the Dayton agreement. The Croats open up their doors regularly for inspection and inventory checks. If any weaponry is missing, the allied officer must conclude it has been deployed and hence the Croats would be in violation of the treaty.

Yet the Frenchman counsels the German not to grow too enthusiastic about confronting the locals over minor matters. "Don't forget, you are not in a situation of war. The mission is different now. You do what you can do. But not too much. Always act to lower tensions between factions. With these people, you must be strong but not aggressive. We say it this way: fair, firm, and friendly. Respect them, respect their officers, but above all they must respect us."

The German listens and nods, recording the advice in some memory bank.

"Don't forget," says the Frenchman, "a small incident here could be a big political event. That's why we have to be so careful with all matters concerning weapons."

They go inside, opting to leave me in the cold outside, fearful that the Croats would view the arrival of an unannounced journalist as a provocation. So I share a slivovitz with one of the locals in a shack that acts as a guardhouse outside. He tells me how he wishes the Germans would leave. I assume he's making some statement about history and politics. Is it because of bad memories in the region about Germans? I ask.

No, he smiles, it is because he wants his Croats to finish wiping out the Muslims and then create their own, independent region that can be linked to Croatia. For that matter, he'd like to teach the Serbs a lesson, too. "The

Germans and others should go so that we can finish what we started," he says. "Otherwise, we bear them no ill will."

On the drive back, the two officers tell me that they found everything at the warehouse to be in order. All boxes of weapons were in place, though they didn't open any of them. Most important, the German tells me, was to confirm that none of the heavy weaponry was gone. Clearly, one can't count every gun and bullet, but rocket launchers are another matter.

He's learning quickly. The Frenchman nods his approval.

So how does he view this mission? I note that only a few months earlier Volker Rühe had said Germans would never set foot in a place where the *Wehrmacht* had operated before. All that now seems forgotten.

"We are writing a bit of history today," he says. "I don't think about it much, though, except when you mention it. And that's good. Our situation as a country is almost completely normalized. We are accepting our responsibilities in all areas, and also now here."

And the Frenchman: how does he view his mission? I tell him that his commander sees the French role to be that of chaperone to the Germans for their coming-out. He seems to serve as ground-level guide for the newcomers.

"Both of my grandfathers were killed by German soldiers in World War II, and that is a problem for me." He glances at his German colleague, who looks away. The Frenchman slaps his hand on Kreitmeyer's shoulder. "But we are professional soldiers, *oui?* And with professional soldiers, you can be enemies today and friends tomorrow."

I ask how he considers himself different from the Germans.

"Are we so different?" We drive by a pretty woman and they both look back at her. She smiles. "You see, everyone looks at the same woman and considers her beautiful. We are just the same."

So he has no trouble with Germany taking on a larger military role in the world?

"Yes, it's a problem for me when I think about it. But it is my job to help them learn how to do it. And I do my job as a professional soldier."

You don't really think you could be enemies again, do you?

Casaque shrugs. "Who knows? These aren't questions for the soldier. The professional soldier asks only where he will eat and where he will sleep."

Kreitmeyer frowns. He knows the Germans carry their historical baggage with them wherever they go. "Germans ask themselves this question all the time. Can I be proud to be German? Am I allowed? I answer yes. I am proud." Thanks to Bosnia, he no longer has to apologize at home for being a soldier. And thanks to his country's postwar performance, he doesn't bow his head before foreigners.

"I am proud of our country. People showed they could put themselves back on their feet. They achieved something fully new—they learned democracy. To change this much is remarkable. They have integrated in the world community without being arrogant. They have done it with modesty. And yet we still have our hugely individual culture. Yes, one can be proud as a German."

Captain Casaque's expression doesn't change during Kreitmeyer's short speech. He's not impressed. He doesn't want to comment on Germany, and he hasn't much to say about France.

"We are more like our fathers or grandfathers than the Germans. We haven't experienced the same emotional break. France is in our hearts. If the French president says this man is the chief and he gives the orders, we obey the orders. That's simply the way it is."

"We obeyed too many orders in the past, perhaps, to think that way," says Kreitmeyer.

So often when I grow more confident of Germany, events ambush me. I had barely returned home to Berlin from seeing the Germans at their best—the military mission to Bosnia—when a series of stories challenged my optimism.

A national television station aired a horrifying film. Soldiers based in Hammelberg, Germany, training for the Bosnia mission, found themselves some free time and a camera. They used it to stage gruesome theater: the execution of hostages and the raping and torturing of locals.

The public shock of the first incident had barely passed when German TV showed a second video. This time soldiers of the *Gebirgsjaeger Bataillons 571* in the federal state of Thuringen charged forward shouting Nazi slogans and anti-Semitic and anti-foreigner curses.

Then news leaks out that a notorious neo-Nazi, Manfred Röder, who had been convicted of right-wing terrorism, had spoken in 1995 at an officers' academy in Hamburg. He then joined a banquet with thirty officers who feted him.

In Dresden, such news tidbits continued through 1997: two Panzer grenadiers tried to burn down a refugee's home, feeding a general concern about anti-foreigner attitudes of the enlisted men that had started the year earlier when soldiers with baseball bats went on a drunken rampage against Turks in Detmold.

The military then shuts down an exhibition in the Eifel region of Germany which was showing off decorations and medals that the German air force, the Luftwaffe, had awarded during World War II to the local *Jagdgeschwader* 52. A pamphlet from the exhibit said: "With more than 10,000 victories in air battles over the French battlefield, the Battle of Britain, in the Balkans and Russia," fighter squadron 52 was "the most successful fighter group in the world."

And there were a series of small incidents. A court in Verden fined two twenty-one-year-old soldiers 1,750 marks each because, at a party in their barracks, they sang the racist songs of neo-Nazi rock groups and raised their arms in Hitleresque salutes.

The events were so numerous that even friends of mine in the Bundeswehr expressed concern, men who always before had said such incidents were one-off aberrations. The statistics were troubling. According to the defense ministry, extraordinary incidents of the right-wing kind numbered 160 in 1997, the year I was in Bosnia, compared to only 44 the year before. The events are suddenly so numerous that even friends of mine in the Bundeswehr begin to express concern. After my trip to Bosnia, I find it only curiously anecdotal within all these more telling stories to hear that my Captain Reinhardt's Tic-Tac-Toe concert in Bosnia won't come off.

The first problems arose when he learned some members of the group had lied about their age and weren't really over eighteen years of age, which posed problems in booking a military flight for them. Not insuperable, but what sorts of kids would lie about their age? Then *Bild Zeitung*, Germany's giant boulevard tabloid, revealed that the lead singer had been a prostitute. The situation was uglier, but the concert was still on. Then *Bild* carried a story about her husband's death—he was found mummified and hanging from a hook in an abandoned house.

In the midst of the scandal, the army counted itself as lucky when Tic-Tac-Toe's agent called to cancel the engagement. Captain Reinhardt's father, the army commander, proposed to replace the popular rock group with the Federal Army band—an offer his son turned down.

But as sexy as the story was, the military and the defense minister had more pressing problems with mounting military scandals. Parliament launched an inquiry that within months produced a long report.

Mr. Rühe summed up the emotion of the report weeks earlier when he said the problem wasn't so much in the military but rather in the society that produced the soldiers. (He easily survived efforts by a radical few parliament members to gain his resignation when the scandal first broke.) Rühe seemed to be saying that it wasn't military officers or the defense minister who should step down, but mothers and fathers across Germany who had inadequately raised their children.

And who will replace them, I wonder.

FIVE

THE KOHL GENERATION

They are a better lot of Germans. They travel the world. They speak languages more than we ever did. They live in a more multicultural society. There is no doubt that they are more enlightened than their parents or their grandparents.
—INGE DEUTSCHKRON, AGE 80,
HOLOCAUST SURVIVOR

What better judge of German youth could there be than a Holocaust survivor, one who narrowly escaped death at the hands of an elder German generation? To make the judge all the more appropriate, this particular survivor opts to spend a good portion of her remaining life telling German high-school students her story. She sees them as the country's source of hope, but only if they get a little help from outsiders like herself.

Inge Deutschkron marches purposefully by me into the second-floor conference room of the Wannsee Villa, the lakeside mansion near Berlin where Hitler's lieutenants hatched the Holocaust. Her red hair is as incendiary as her personality. She wears that effervescence that one often finds in survivors—as if they know that every minute of their lives is an unexpected gift. She seems only now, at age eighty, to have ignited life's booster rockets.

In a few minutes she'll tell a crowd of high-school students how she survived the war in Berlin by living underground, protected by twenty different German families. But as they wait, she explains to me why she takes so much time with this generation of Germans, the best vintage she believes the country has ever had. "They are a better lot," she says. "They travel the world. They speak more languages than we ever did. They live in a more multicultural society. There is no doubt that they are more enlightened" than their elders.

The students fill every seat to listen to her dramatic tale of survival, though many of them already know it from her book, *I Carried the Yellow Star,* which has been part of their coursework. The class had made an evening outing to a performance of the play that was adapted from it: *From Today, My Name is Sarah.* The Grips Theater in Berlin has been performing the story of Inge Deutschkron's young life for one German school class after another since its opening in 1989. Learning their country's sins is a multi-media rite of passage for most German youth.

It was the staging of her play that brought Inge Deutschkron back to her birthplace of Berlin from Israel, the home she adopted after the war. Invitations from school groups followed, and over time she became a star attraction of a curious sort, the last chance of a new German generation to have human contact with their grandparents' victims. They'd seen enough documentaries and the movie *Schindler's List.* And it was young Germans who put Daniel Goldhagen on bestseller lists with his book *Hitler's Willing Executioners,* a text that did more to condemn an entire generation of "ordinary Germans" than any book that had come before it.

But Deutschkron is unique: a living, breathing witness, someone who lived through their country's worst moments and can tell them about it. The students buzz among themselves as they wait for the session to begin ("She can't be that old . . . she's quite pretty . . . I want to ask her about what my grandfather told me").

Frau Deutschkron rarely turns down an invitation from student groups, and she never accepts the many she receives from senior citizens' organizations. To her, the pensioners are the enemy. The allies stopped them, but they'd never be able to rewire them. German youth is the opportunity.

"My job is to build up the young," she says. "I want to give them the civil courage that was so lacking in an older German generation. My job isn't to go to old-age clubs and wipe away these people's tears. I can see their consciences laid bare before my eyes. I don't spend my holidays in Germany because I don't want to meet these people. They are the ones who are guilty. I don't talk to them unless I know them extremely well—unless I know exactly what they've done in those years. When I walk down the street, I won't meet their eyes. They don't exist for me."

For Inge Deutschkron, two Germanies exist. One of them is dying out a little more with each year, and good riddance. The other is emerging, and for it she has a good deal of hope. Seldom, in her view, has there been such an improvement in humanity between grandparent and grandchild.

The older generation remains the greatest danger—she blames them for new outbreaks of neo-Nazism, attacks on asylum homes, and the surprising election result that gave the right-wing Deutsche Volksunion some 20 percent of the vote in the eastern German state of Sachsen-Anhalt in 1998. "But," I protest, "these problems you cite all have their roots within the German young—particularly the East German young." "True," she frowns. "But those who are involved have merely been poisoned by parents and grandparents who pass on their habits of intolerance."

One of the positive outcomes of the Holocaust, she reckons, is how it has forced most of the oldest generation to remain silent so that the young can form views independently and with the help of their sixty-eighter parents and instructors like Frau Deutschkron. The reason eastern German youth is less enlightened is because it was raised by less progressive parents and told by an unenlightened regime that Communist East Germany was a creation of World War II victims and hence its citizens needn't feel any special responsibility for Nazi crimes.

But, in general, she believes each successive German generation is growing more open, more tolerant. "When I first was asked to start going into schools in the early 1980s, only a few teachers wanted me. And the questions that came from the students! They wanted to know why Israelis were so bad. Why were they so hard on the Palestinians. They didn't understand why this poor, sick old man Rudolf Hess [the former Third Reich leader) had to be held in prison. Finally I couldn't take it any more. I told them: I don't care a shit about Rudolf Hess."

For a time, she stopped visiting German schools. Germany wasn't ready to listen to her yet. But when she returned after unification, she found a significant shift in attitude among the young—and their teachers.

"This generation is so different, so open, so curious, so uninhibited in their speech." She wishes Americans and other Europeans would more openly recognize this German transformation. By continuing to point the finger at young Germans, one threatens to alienate them. A struggle is still on between a minority of right-wing retrogrades and the more positive majority that she sees each day.

She particularly condemns American Jews for holding to outdated views of Germans. She complains that American Jewish groups refuse to stage her play because it highlights "good Germans" who saved and protected her. "They tell me they don't believe my story," she says. "You can't speak to American Jews about good Germans. They don't want to hear about it. Israel doesn't interest young American Jews, nor does the synagogue. What binds them together is the Holocaust. They can't be Good Jews without Bad Germans. It's an identity thing."

She sighs.

But for a new German generation she regards the story of her "good Germans" as the oxygen they need to breathe. They need to see that role models, however few, also existed in Third Reich Germany. She tells her tale as often as possible to as many young Germans as will hear it. "I feel for these kids. They are not to blame. The only responsibility they have is to know what happened. No more than that. They travel abroad and simply want to have fun with other young people from other countries and not be called Nazis. I have a good friend whose father was hanged at Nuremberg. She keeps going on about it. I finally had to say to her, 'Stop feeling guilty. You will influence your son with that guilt.' You can't make young people who have nothing to do with it feel guilty. It doesn't help them."

The students sit forward in their chairs as Inge Deutschkron stands before them. She scans their faces, and they look up at her, a chance to grow accustomed to each other. She smiles warmly, acceptingly. A few of them return a sheepish grin or nod of head.

This isn't one of the dead Jews they'd studied. This is a woman who somehow triumphed over all that. She tells them how it all started: the Nuremberg laws that brought with them "two thousand" regulations against the Jews—the mind-numbing German efficiency of it all. She relates details that make it real to them: how laws prevented her from having her hair cut in public, how her family was banned from buying irons to press the wrinkles out of her dress or purchase radios to listen to the news. These were little matters, but I can see she is reaching her young listeners with these small details of daily life.

Jews couldn't walk in the forest on Sundays with other Germans, she says, and they weren't allowed on public transport unless they needed to travel more than seven kilometers to work. *And then they were forced to stand.* "There was an indescribable amount of regulations," she says.

"Well, at least that hasn't changed," sneers a boy in the audience.

They all chuckle nervously.

"Yes, some aspects of German personality remain the same," she frowns.

She tells them how Jews lost access to ration cards, so they were forced to break laws to get food. And then she talks of the families who risked everything to conceal and protect her. She tells them more about one of the stars of her play, the owner of a workshop for the blind, who had been particularly heroic in employing and then protecting Jews.

And she talks of the gathering points from which family friends were shipped to their deaths, real people with real names. She mentions street names and city districts they all know. Her audience is barely breathing as she speaks with a witness's passion.

She says the horror didn't start with her family being Jewish, but rather first with the fact that her father was an enemy of the Nazis as a prominent Social Democrat. "In the 1920s, as a little child, I didn't know what Jewish was. We had a Christmas tree, and I looked for Easter eggs. My parents were socialist and didn't think much about religion. What I remember were the fights among political parties." It wasn't until the 1935 Nuremberg Race Laws, she says, that she figured out that it was something different to be Jewish.

She speaks of September 15, 1941, when she was first forced to wear her yellow star. She remembers a German bureaucrat sticking a pencil under it and then ordering her to sew the star more firmly into the material. "German efficiency."

A nervous titter in the room.

"Others were imprisoned for this lapse," she says. "I was lucky that I was not punished. The star had the impact that everyone looked at us, but most would look through us. Some looked at you with hatred. But once in a while someone would slip you an apple or a coupon for meat. Those were wonderful moments."

Her message to them is clear: there were good Germans during the war who dared to take noble actions. Even if the majority were cowards, a handful showed moral courage. It *was* possible.

Inge Deutschkron's message is one for the future—she doesn't want the young to wallow in the past but rather to search it for sources of inspiration. "Twenty Berlin families over this period of time risked their heads for us," she says. "These were people who were willing to do big and small things that were good. For two years and four months, we lived in hiding, we lived on the run. I remember hearing Russian tanks roll through on April 22, 1945. That was for me like the music of Beethoven."

She finishes. A collective outtake of breath. The questions follow after a few moments of shy reluctance.

"Do you still hate the Germans?" asks a young girl with an uncertain voice.

She utters the word *Germans* as if it is a race to which she only reluctantly belongs.

"I never had hatred, not even then. Perhaps it was because there were also Germans who helped us. You can't generalize about a race, and hate doesn't help you."

Then she corrects herself. She had felt some bitterness when she came back to Germany after the war as an Israeli journalist, working in Bonn, and found many former Nazis in leading political and business positions. "No one was guilty then. No one was a Nazi. No one would 'fess up to what he had been. I found that reprehensible. In the first years, not enough was done to come to terms with the past. Your generation is far better."

"Are you comfortable living in Germany now?"

"Now," she smiles. "But not at first." She tells how she almost left for good back in 1990 and 1991, after receiving hate mail and telephone threats. "Frightening letters called me a Jewish pig who had to be slaughtered. One arrived in the post with a drawing on the envelope of a fat sow with a star on its chest, a huge nose and fat lips. It was the old story all over again. I asked myself what I was doing here."

And then a local newspaper ran an article about her problems, and hundreds of letters followed, begging her to stay. "The Nazis are dumb and powerless," said a typical one. "Don't let them get to you."

This demonstration of support prompted her to remain, she says, and she now divides her time between Israel and Germany. She, like so many others, learned quickly that Germany remains divided between evil habits of the past and new, more tolerant thinking.

"Can it happen again?" asks one of the students, a young German seeking reassurance.

"I consider this democracy to be quite strong," she says. "This is not Weimar. I don't anticipate any problems. And if there are, this state can rise to them."

The students look encouraged.

A boy stands. Anger fills his face and his voice shakes as he asks: "Should our generation continue to be made responsible by the world?"

"No, but without knowledge you can't fight against these [right-wing, neo-Nazi] tendencies in the future."

"Our grandparents say they didn't know what was happening," he says.

"No one in this city can say he didn't know something was happening to the Jews," she says sharply. "Some two hundred thousand people were involved directly in the Holocaust. They knew. And all Berliners knew exactly what was going on here—so many were wearing the yellow star in those days. People knew about Dachau and the work camps. Fewer knew about the gassing at Auschwitz and the mass executions. Maybe the men at the front knew about it, but there was little exact knowledge back home. I first heard something about this in November 1942 on the BBC. I didn't believe it. No one believed it."

"What do we do about neo-Nazis now?" says one girl. "You can't even talk to them. They scare me."

"I understand there is no point in talking to them," says Inge Deutschkron. "In my day, there was also no point in talking to such people. You must simply make yourselves stronger than they are. And you are only strong in communities. You must form organizations. Band together . . ."

I couldn't help but think: What an odd way to grow up.

For these German students, this is a field trip, like my visit to the Lincoln Memorial in Washington. Our American common bond was this hero who freed the slaves and unified America. Yet Germans continue to be tied together more by this devil bent on conquering Europe and murdering *Untermenschen*.

I can still recite Lincoln's Gettysburg Address from my primary school days, but few German young even know the words to their national anthem. The original first verse, the part about *Deutschland über Alles*, has been done away with altogether.

Every child in this room has grown up with a genuine, modern-day hero: Helmut Kohl. If one looks at the facts, such a statement is hard to contest: he reunified their country peacefully and democratically. He unified Europe as well, even if it meant surrendering a good degree of national sovereignty with his support for a single currency. But in the culture of self-doubt that has followed the war, Germans don't want heroes, even of the dull, democratic type. Americans are more likely to celebrate Bill Clinton, with all his foibles and lack of historic achievement, than Germans are willing to recognize Kohl.

Like the insecure adolescent who chooses to criticize himself before anyone gets to him, Germany seems to be constantly looking for reasons to suspect itself. It isn't just the world that keeps linking the German present to the past—Germans do it themselves. The children want Inge Deutschkron to hate them. They expect it. Yet they are also relieved when she refuses to satisfy them.

Inge Deutschkron later says, when we chat over coffee at her apartment, that she is often shocked by heavy-handed performances of her play where local directors feel compelled to make the link between the Nazi past and the neo-Nazi present.

In the eastern German town of Dessau, for example, the play opened with a scene not in the script: a contemporary skinhead beat a newly arrived Russian Jew to a pulp as prologue. It was a crude attempt to give the play, set in Third Reich Berlin, a modern context. The Jew lay on stage in a hospital bed throughout the rest of the play, attended to by tall, blonde, blue-eyed nurses. Occasionally, a ballet dancer, dressed like Hitler, pranced through the scenes.

"Not very subtle," she says.

Inge Deutschkron put a stop to the performance. It wasn't her message.

"This is one of the few plays about the period where the hero is not a victim. The main character is fighting. Outwitting the enemy. The message is: we must win. This message was in me all these years, and I am trying to transmit it to them. The play shows that there were Germans who helped, who were courageous, and who survived. These young must be given hope—this is in the play. I tell them that one can't achieve anything if one doesn't have the desire to win and fight."

Germany's youth is studied, scrutinized, surveyed, and analyzed as much as any young generation on earth, perhaps because the country is so watchful of itself. Several surveys confirm a general impression: German youth are simply less scarred by the past and less preoccupied with history than their parents or grandparents. They don't feel the same need to rebel against an elder generation that itself had nothing to do with the war. The bottom line: they are more comfortable in their German skins.

The young in any country play a special role as a moral compass and motor of change, but since World War II, German youth has figured particularly large; the elder generation lost both credibility and moral authority with the Third Reich.

Richard Hilmer of the polling company Infratest Burke has made a business out of understanding the German young. "At the very latest with the sixty-eighter generation," he says, "students advanced to become important actors in politics and the main initiators of social traditions and changes in values. Never before in Germany, where the stature that comes with age and experience has always played a larger role than in America, have the youth been such decisive players."

In 1968 students vented their rage against "the parental betrayal of Nazism," says Hilmer. Many wanted to demolish everything that had been Germany and start anew. The new generation of students, however, by and large likes the Germany in which they live, and it respects the democratic society their parents helped build. Yet poll results show they are more conformist than their parents, and at the same time less characteristically German.

Polls show they are becoming more "American" in that they are more individualistic and optimistic than their parents. A ground-breaking Infratest Burke study carried out for *Die Zeit* newspaper in 1995 and reinforced by later studies suggested that, to paraphrase the popular song of the time, Germans just want to have fun. Or at least a remarkably large percentage of them do, particularly compared to students of sixteen years earlier, when Helmut Kohl had first become chancellor. Hilmer figures the next such study in the year 2000 will show the same trend, only more pronounced.

When asked to list their values, a remarkable 86 percent of young Germans polled said they simply desired to enjoy life, 97 percent wanted a profession that made them happy, 99 percent wanted good friends, and 90 percent considered a single, fixed partner to be critical to happiness. The underlying message: make the best of what is available, but don't embrace the revolutionary ideas or concepts of the past.

When asked whether they enjoyed their studies, some 85 percent of the 1998 students said yes—compared to a far smaller 68 percent back in 1979. And eastern Germans were even happier than the westerners, showing that the eastern young generation was far less sour about unification than their parents. But perhaps that isn't so surprising, since any teenager by the year 2000 will have spent more than half of his life in unified Germany.

In a society that was growing more competitive with each year, only half as many students as in 1979 (37 percent) complained of society or the university placing too high expectations or pressures on them. The message: the young broadly accept what society demands of them: few flag-burners here.

Yet even as I study these statistics and develop this image, the students themselves begin to challenge it in massive demonstrations and student strikes across the country in the autumn of 1997. I walk to Berlin's Technical University—the barricades are up. Why, I wonder, is this basically conformist group rebelling against the society with which they seem relatively at peace? Were the survey results being undone by another generational shift?

Yet when I study the protesters more closely, I see they aren't bucking the system—they are trying to preserve it by fighting against subsidy cuts. The problem is clear: over the previous two decades the number of German university students has doubled, but the personnel to teach and administer them had grown only by 10 percent. One of postwar Germany's achievements is that by 1995, some 30 percent of all youth between nineteen and twenty-six years of age were enrolled in higher education. That compared to less than 5 percent in 1960. But this growth strained university capacity. The state couldn't finance or absorb the numbers, and private schools hadn't developed to take up much of the burden.

The country had only some thirty-eight thousand professors for its 1.9 million students. And they didn't serve their constituency well, spending large amounts of time away from classrooms on one research project or the other. The most motivated and talented of young German professors often landed at American or British universities, for the most brilliant found advancement and recognition were too slow in Germany. (Rudi Dornbusch, an immigrant from Germany who had become one of America's leading economists at the Massachusetts Institute of Technology, told me that if he hadn't left his country, "I still would have been some professor's assistant, waiting for my superior to die so that I could advance.")

By the time of the strikes, seminars so bulged with students that many had to bring their own chairs if they wanted somewhere to sit. Cost cuts had prompted libraries to reduce hours to two or three per day, and many were short of books. Students also didn't have their American colleagues' entrepreneurial instincts to compensate themselves in areas where the system failed.

In today's Germany, the state remains responsible for all costs of education—90 percent of education is funded by the state, 10 percent by the federal government, and nothing by the students. Student volunteer work is still a foreign concept. Students and their parents mostly stand by as quality drops, except to make demands that can't be met by budget-strained governments.

I disagree with the diagnosis of the striking students—that one simply needed more state funding. What one needed was a more competitive system that produced better teachers and graduates. One doesn't strike for that. As it turned out, my attitude was shared by enough students to make the strikes a flop. They hadn't the fire of the sixty-eighters, partly because they couldn't agree on the cause.

The alternative newspaper *Die Tageszeitung* reported that no more than 10 percent of Germany's 1.9 million students participated in the strike—a "silent majority" had better things to do. While her Bauhaus-University Weimar is closed, twenty-three-year-old architecture student Ulrike Bahr is working at building sites in Berlin to gather work experience that might get her a job that no seminar could give her, and certainly no strike. "That's the reality," she says.

Berlin psychology student Carola Rother complained that the protests could cost her a semester at the Free University of Berlin, and she wanted to get out of school and fight for work as soon as possible. She looked at the barricades at her own school with a sense of impatient disdain: "We're cutting off our noses to spite our face."

Ulrike Bahr, the eastern German architectural student, agrees. Such protests, she says, are passé. She has career plans, and a strike doesn't help them. She has already studied in France, and she is off soon to Zurich to gain architectural office experience there. She can only smile when reminded of the sixty-eighter generation and their desire to change society through such protests. She calls the fall of the Wall in 1989 "the last great happening" shared by all of society. "It's about individualism now. There are no more ideals that tie together our generation."

The strike, which began before Christmas in 1997, dissolved at the beginning of the new year. The student activists of the preceding weeks are eager to catch up on their missed course work. "It seems as if we Germans just can't get rid of our thoroughness and discipline," says Anette Moos, a student whose purple hair matches her purple backpack, but who otherwise is an unconvincing revolutionary. "Ché Guevara could never have been a German. We are not made to be rebels. That is the real German character."

She says many of her fellow students' parents look down their noses at their children as too conformist. And it is true that the polls showed that they now view the university less as a laboratory for social change and more as a place to prepare themselves for a career.

In fact, Hilmer's poll showed that two-thirds of the students either were "convinced" or "fairly convinced" by the system. And though students, like the rest of society, said they were fed up with politics, in fact only 12 percent felt no established political party represented their views. That was only half the number of 1979, when students felt much more alienated from the establishment. And the notorious German opposition to technological progress was fast eroding: by 1995, only some 40 percent of students thought technological progress threatens people, compared to 60 percent in 1979.

Perhaps most telling, the huge German generation gap is closing. While students in 1979 felt overwhelmingly misunderstood by their parents' generation, only a minority of the 1995 students felt that way. "There has been a clear normalization of the relationship among society, parents and students," says Hilmer. "Students' own self-image has shifted more to the status of 'normal citizen.' " At least three-fourths of the students polled used establishment-friendly terms to describe themselves: self-assured, success-oriented, and career-conscious. "They are more positive, more optimistic, and seem to take more joy in life."

A week after Inge Deutschkron's performance at the Wannsee Villa, I arrive to visit the students to whom she spoke at their school, Rheingau Gymnasium, a red-brick building in a well-off section of West Berlin. Rainer Gladdis, a popular history teacher in the school, calls the pupils who study there "the Kohl generation." Or, playing with the English translation for the German chancellor's name, he smiles that they are "the cabbage kids."

But what does that mean?

For one matter, he says, it means they had never known any other chancellor. Helmut Kohl, who became chancellor in 1982, was the only national leader in their conscious experience before his loss in the 1998 elections. What they had experienced of democracy had been through him: slow, steady, ponderous, predictable and unchanging. For the Kohl generation, democracy wasn't any more a matter of debate than the overwhelming political and physical size of their country's long-time leader.

"What I see, I call post-materialism," says Gladdis. "They are also post-yuppie. They are future-oriented and have material values. They want success in their studies to help them in their careers, but they have conscience enough to care a great deal about the environment. They don't dress as well as the yuppies that came before them—more jeans and T-shirts, and the hair isn't so important. Their relationships and friendships with foreigners are much more normal than the generations before them."

"Twenty years ago, there were no Turks in the *Gymnasien,*" the better schools that are the breeding ground for college. "Now I have quite a few in the class and most are fully integrated. I'm optimistic about them, this Kohl generation, because they are more tolerant, more civilized. But at the same time they are more individualistic." That he finds troubling.

On my day in class, the students are still abuzz about their time at the Wannsee Villa. It is the first subject on our agenda as I take over the class for an hour. "What surprised me most," says Tobias, a lean and gaunt seventeen-year-old, "was that Frau Deutschkron didn't feel more bitterness toward us."

"How can she be so happy in Germany after what happened to her here?" Natalia Yanez-Exner wonders. Her hyphenated family name describes her mixed breeding—Turkish and German. She can feel only 50 percent of the responsibility—like so many children of mixed marriages. "I still can't believe it ever happened."

"It only really hits you when you travel abroad what sort of burden you must carry as a German," says Tobias. "People act aggressively to you the moment they find out you are German, and you just don't get it at first."

The class is weary of having to bear this historical burden but resigned to the fact that it will only change slowly.

Lenz, an intense young man in the front row, leans forward and speaks: "We have a feeling of responsibility, but we can't feel responsible." The class nodes in unison at this curious formulation. "I see the pictures and I'm just as shaken as you are. But this is all played up too much in today's politics. Every country has its problems. And anyone who sees the photographs can't think it would happen again here."

"We are a new generation," said Muria, a pretty girl at the back. "The world shouldn't blame us."

I ask them to explain to me why their generation buys Goldhagen's book so enthusiastically, why young people like them drive up ratings for Third Reich documentaries.

Said Andreas, a thoughtful young man: "When you go out in the world, you need to know what it is for which you are being held responsible. You need to know why you are so disliked for the misfortune of being German. We don't get this knowledge from our grandparents. So we have to learn it somewhere."

Their grandparents won't talk about it?

Muria says she has tried to talk about such matters with Opa and Oma, "But they always change the subject. Or my grandfather talks about his time in a Soviet prison camp after the war or about being forced from their homes in the East." The students all agree that the older Germans are more comfortable teaching the younger generation how they suffered rather than talking about how they made others suffer. "Then you see the films, you hear the facts. You give up at some point asking them because you don't get anywhere."

And then you read Goldhagen instead. And listen to Deutschkron.

A studious blonde girl at the back of the class stands so that I can hear her protest against the course of the conversation. She has had enough of German self-flagellation.

"The world also didn't do much to save or help Jews, and plenty of people knew what was going on. We don't deserve all the blame. You have to ask yourself a few things about Americans as well. The Americans did some things with the Indians that weren't so nice."

It seems a bit of a leap to me, but she's hit a chord with the class.

"And look at right-wing groups elsewhere in Europe and the world," says Michael, who stands as well. "Neo-Nazis are stronger elsewhere than here. The most virulent ones here are monitored and forbidden. But what we outlaw here is allowed and considered normal elsewhere."

Yet Fabian fears that Germans aren't yet fully healed from whatever sickness it was that caused the Third Reich. He says the country's rising unemployment is already pushing many youth in the country to the right. When the British are jobless, they go fishing, says one member of the class, but when Germans are unemployed, they go fascist.

They all laugh.

"It is not impossible that it could happen again," he says.

I'm watching emotional Ping-Pong. If the students hear too much bad about Germans, they defend themselves. But too much defense results in immediate rebuff. They seek some safe middle ground of accepting responsibility while at the same unearthing flaws in other nationalities, so they don't feel quite as singularly evil.

A young man stands and says he was recently on an exchange program in America. He likes the fact that Americans stand to pledge allegiance to the flag each morning. "But if someone does that here, you would call him a neo-Nazi," he says. He wishes Germans could be proud of what they are—of what they have become.

"Other countries hang their national flags out of the windows on important national holidays. I don't think it's a bad thing. But if you hang out the German colors here, it carries so much more baggage."

An Algerian-born student, who has spent most of his life in Germany, says Germans should be prouder of themselves. He is more comfortable as an Algerian in Germany than he ever would be in France, he says. Turks have more religious freedom in Berlin than they have in Istanbul, he adds. "Except for Bratwurst and beer, the question of what is in the German soul is dead. There is no German soul. The country means nothing."

"You are wrong about there being no German soul," says Michael. "There is one. But the new German soul is more modest. It is more assimilated into the world all round it."

A short moment of silence.

"I have a national pride," says Fabian. "Great pride in what we've become. I want the right to express it." I feel the class's immediate disapproval of this "pride." Fabian senses it as well. He adds: "But part of my pride in being German is knowing I'm not allowed to say it. National modesty is built into our thinking. It must be."

Lenz says they should all learn from the Algerian student. It was curious, he thought, that a foreign student would be prouder of being German than native Germans. "I'm happy to be German. I wouldn't want to be French. I wouldn't want to be any other nationality. Any other mentality. Others aren't as tolerant as we are. The way we live here is a little more orderly, too, and I like that. We talk about things reasonably before there is a popular uprising."

He criticizes the French truck drivers who just that week were striking by blocking roads and burning their tires on them. It is all so disorderly, not the way a society should come to terms with change. And that's the problem with a single currency—other Europeans simply aren't as disciplined as the Germans.

From a class of some thirty, only two raise their hands when I ask who wants this Euro, the single European currency that is soon to become reality.

"Europe is beautiful," says Andreas, "but we don't want to give up our identity to it."

Lenz can't see the potential good to warrant the risk. Most of the class nods in agreement. "We have enough uncertainties in our lives and don't need to be saddled with another one."

The Algerian-born German doesn't understand why Germans, who consider themselves so democratic, had so obediently accepted the currency without having been given a chance to vote on it, as had been the case in France, Denmark, and elsewhere.

He has a point, yet it has long been the concept of German elites that some matters are too important to be democratically decided, a leftover distrust of the grassroots from Germany's less democratic days. This new generation will be less willing to accept a leadership that decides matters dear to them without their consent. With them at the heart of German's body politic, Helmut Kohl might never have achieved the Euro.

"It is just typically German that nobody here has been asked," says the Algerian. "Other countries had referendums, but not Germany. Finally we have something to be proud of in German history, the German mark, and it is typically German that they just want to fit in with everyone else and not hang on to it."

The room reaches consensus.

They are for Europe, but are against the single currency.

They want to be Europeans, but they want the Deutsche Mark. Unlike their parents, they are less interested in trading Germany for a federal Europe. They feel less need to disappear.

"All you have to do is look at the countries who are going to be in," says the Algerian, "and you have an idea about how it is going to turn out." They all nod—as Germans they feel superior to the Italians, the Spaniards, and most of the rest in how they run their country.

After my day in class, Rainer Gladdis tells me that he still worries about the pessimism of the young, no matter what polls might show. Youth, he says, is supposed to be driven by hope, motivated by all the possibilities that lie before them. He simply doesn't get a buoyant feeling from this generation. Whatever the sixty-eighters' faults might have been, they felt they owned the world and thus could change it, he says. But the new young instead are ready to accept their own powerlessness.

Surveys show most want to work as civil servants, or in safe positions or large companies. Perhaps the greatest difference from Americans, and even many Europeans, is how few want to be entrepreneurs.

"This sniveling, these lamentations, this future pessimism. I can hardly stand it sometimes," he says. "They simply don't believe in the future, they don't have the feeling of optimism that youth should have, the feeling that you can conquer the world. That is gone."

A colleague of mine, Michael Meier, the editor of the *Berliner Zeitung*, is certain that part of the problem is the exaggerated educational emphasis on Germany's worst dozen years, the Third Reich. Meier, an Austrian, finds the most aggressive and entrepreneurial of his young reporters come from East Germany, where they weren't brought up as much in a culture of self-blame. The East Germans, being the Communists, had been as much the victims as the Jews, according to that part of Germany's teaching of the Holocaust. The approach to history might be dishonest, says Meier—like that of Austria—but it created a generation that wasn't constantly second-guessing itself.

The problem is no longer that Germans don't learn enough about the Holocaust. Instead, they learn about it often to the exclusion of all other

German experience. German schools spend precious little time on Martin Luther, Beethoven, Frederick the Great, or the great German musicians and writers of the Romantic period. Rainer Gladdis concedes that 50 percent or more of his twentieth-century history class focuses on the Nazis' twelve years, whereas World War I, the Weimar Republic, the Cold War, and German unification are squeezed into the other 50 percent.

"Other teachers spend no less time on the Nazi period than I," he says. "Perhaps it's understandable. The Nazi story is so overwhelming that it covers up all other positive history. When you try to teach more about the postwar history, how Germans created a stable state, where there is order and no enemies, the young have less interest."

The most heroic European period of the second half of the century—the pro-democracy uprisings in Eastern Europe, the fall of the Soviet empire, and the critical role of the Western alliance in ending Communism—gets less than five percent of Gladdis's attention in the course.

I tell Gladdis that the German youth don't grasp the extent to which Germany is a postwar miracle, a creation of Western values, freedoms, and resolve. Instead, they—like their parents—carp about the cost of unification and problems of Russians flooding Berlin.

"They view such statements with skepticism and distance," Gaddis says, seeming to view my statement with his own skepticism and distance.

Yet if all this is true, how can Gladdis be so sure this generation will be more tolerant than previous generations?

"When I was younger, people made jokes about Jews," he says. "I heard this one, for instance: 'How many Jews can you get in a Volkswagen? Answer: Six million, all in the ash tray.' These jokes you don't have anymore. You might hear them still, but those telling them would be marginalized in the school yard."

Yet I had heard enough anti-Semitism among the young, often cloaked in the guise of anti-Israeli attitudes. I had heard racist comments about Turks as well. Plenty of them. How could Gladdis be so sure?

"I know because I am gay," he says flatly. "And I no longer have to hide it." He says an earlier generation of students spray-painted the wall of the school with anti-gay epithets when his sexual preferences became public.

"*Faggot pig—we'll get you*—that's what they wrote," he says. "That was painted in giant red letters."

Gladdis feared for his well-being then. But now the threats and graffiti are gone. He now brings his partner to school events. "The young have become much more tolerant. They are raised by their parents to be that way. They are freer inside of themselves."

...llay of horse and hoofe and
...rare, and mangles, and scatters...
...en beneath and the blue above,
...gth and danger, and life, and
...reca, — Lacca used to ride
...mouse-gray mustang close to my
...line escape and bright-bellied...
...hed with joy as I looked at...

SIX

YOUNG DIPLOMATS

There is no German identity without historical guilt. My Germanness is defined by it. But I don't have a complex about it. Perhaps it has given me a heightened sense of responsibility . . . I have decided to turn it into something positive. In the important global problems, such as saving the environment, we must play more of a positive role because of who we are.

MARCUS BLEINROTH, AGE 30,
GERMAN DIPLOMAT

My cousin Marcus Bleinroth serves up thick, doughy, homemade pizza, assembled from ingredients bought mostly in one or another of those plentiful German shops that sell only organically grown or chemically untainted foods. The cost is greater, but he and his wife, Lingky, the daughter of Indonesian Chinese parents, try to avoid polluting their systems with the chemically tainted fare that sustain Americans and their Americanized fellow Germans.

At age thirty, Marcus is in his third year as a diplomat in Germany's foreign office, having just landed a future-paving job in the planning office, where he looks after global economics, environmental and European Union issues. He lives with his wife, a doctor, their Indonesian nanny, a student boarder, and their two children in a leafy neighborhood of Bonn, where they have settled into an upper middle-class life beyond their years. As we begin to eat, we make small talk about cuisine.

Marcus, the born German, prefers sushi, sashimi and Chinese wok cooking. When he prepares dinner, don't expect Teutonic meat and potatoes. Lingky, on the other hand, leans toward schnitzel, sauerbraten, dumplings, red cabbage. I offer the view that perhaps Marcus, the born German, has been taught to be less proud of his country's traditions. Lingky, who carries none of that historical baggage as a first-generation German citizen, embraces German ways without any of the unconscious reluctance of her husband.

Whatever their tastes in cuisine, however, they both represent for me to some extent what has become of their country—deeply conservative about some basic values yet at the same time less married to the status quo, partly because change has been so much a part of the new generation's upbringing.

Marcus has chosen one of the oldest and most conventional professions a country has on offer, that of diplomacy. The foreign office ranks are filled with offspring of nobility and sons and daughters (but mostly sons) of the country's elite.

Yet Green leader Joschka Fischer didn't appear to want to change this bureaucracy after he became foreign minister in October 1998: he didn't bring in a transition team but instead decided to leave well enough alone, reinforcing a comforting impression of continuity.

Though the country has changed demographically in a way that might enrich the diplomatic service, few Turks, Yugoslavs, Poles, Italians, or others have made their way to the foreign office. The place is still run by ethnically homogeneous, dark-suited, pin-striped conservatism.

Yet it is hard to look at Marcus and not transplant him to another era. He is blond, high-cheekboned, and slender. His posture reflects confidence and pride. The overall effect resembles that of the uniformed youth in the film *Cabaret,* who rose from his seat and stood ramrod erect while singing "The Future Belongs to Me."

But the resemblance stops there. Marcus envisions not a world that serves Germany, but a Germany that serves the world. He sees himself as an agent of change. As a trained economist, he is convinced the twenty-first century will bring some of the most difficult negotiations ever on ecological matters with developing countries, particularly China, and he has made himself fluent not only in Chinese but also in environmental issues.

"If China continues to grow and develop, global CO_2 emissions will double by the year 2020 because of China alone. That would be a catastrophe for the world climate. Ecological problems, however, are finally a question of economic policy. Without an international redistribution of wealth and a greater transfer of resources to developing countries, we have no future. That will require complicated negotiations whose importance and strategic weight might compare with disarmament talks during the Cold War."

Lingky listens and nods. She, like Marcus, is also a curious mixture of conventional and New Age. Just before she leaves the room to put their two young children to bed for Sunday afternoon naps, she speaks of her medical degree from one of Germany's first private universities, Witten/Herdecke, where she met Marcus. She studied at the respected Case Western Reserve University in Cleveland and is now an internist on the staff of the University Clinic in Wuppertal, where she practices conventional medicine. Yet her doctoral work was on unconventional remedies such as acupuncture, and she'll happily accompany Marcus to China (though she doesn't speak the language as well as he) to expand her specialty in alternative medicine. "The treatment must meet the need," she says. She explains how alternative medicines can do little for infectious diseases, but then she demonstrates where one must insert the pins (around the ears) to cure incontinence.

As Lingky takes the children away, Marcus serves us up a second helping of pizza and speaks of his first trip to America, when we had initially met. Like many of the elite of his generation, he is fascinated by the country that has the greatest impact on Germany's thinking, while at the same time he is deeply critical of America. "I was shocked by the differences between rich and poor in your country," he says. He drove through the South Bronx, and felt it looked more like a war zone scarred by rocket attacks than part of the most developed nation in the world. "In this respect, our country is far superior. Our generation doesn't want American conditions. What we want is the freedom, the mobility, the dynamism of America. I miss that in our society. The average here is better than the average in America, whether it be in our education system or our living standards, but what's outstanding in America is the top element of your society. That is what we miss here."

Marcus and Lingky are of a new German elite—well-educated, multilingual, often multicultural. They are more willing to take pride in the country than the German youth of the '50s, the '60s, and the '70s and are quicker to criticize what's failing in other countries, no longer applying the postwar censor. Their *Weltanschauung* builds in the recognition that Germany's Nazi history still shapes their world in many ways, yet they accept no responsibility for the past. They consider themselves first to be global citizens and second to be Germans. They are more pragmatic and less ideological than their parents, neither seduced by socialism nor outraged by capitalism.

For Marcus, dealing with his country's Holocaust history had been as much a part of adolescence as fighting acne. He remembers his first close contact with someone Jewish, a passage of youth most Germans can recount as precisely as their first romance. She had been an American student also studying at Keio University, the leading private university in Japan where Marcus earned a degree in economics. (He chose to study in Japan rather than America, where many of his friends had landed, because he was convinced of Asia's future importance to Germany and felt that few Germans understood the region, while coming to terms with the United States was comparatively easy.) He was surprised how quickly a "latent feeling of guilt" can come to the surface during such a chat.

But while his parents' generation transformed the Holocaust into a form of political rage against their parents, Marcus merely accepts it as a fact that shapes German foreign policy. "It is a fact that the Holocaust happened," shrugs Marcus. "I can't deny it. We have a special mission because of this. The German has a greater consciousness of his history. He more consciously defines himself according to it. Our past is the source of an ongoing moral obligation."

What strikes me as we chat, having moved on from the natural cheese on the pizza to the organically grown lettuce and tomatoes of the salad, is how comfortable Marcus is in his German skin. He doesn't wring his hands about his country's sins, nor beat his breast about postwar accomplishments. He has been responsible for neither. Yet he would factor both into his country's future. "There is no German identity without historical guilt," says Marcus. "One is always confronted by that history when one travels the world and says one is German. My Germanness is defined by it. But I don't have a complex about it. Perhaps it has given me a heightened sense of responsibility . . . In the important global problems, such as saving the environment, we must play more of a positive role because of who we are."

Marcus's maturity and intellectual confidence remind me of the impression he made on my German-born aunts in America when he visited them as a teenager. My aunts judge the young primarily by their manners. And they assess manners according to their own private formulae that factor in humility, the number of dishes washed, beds made, and such.

By those measures, Marcus had failed.

"He is impolite," clucked one.

"Arrogant," added another.

"Spoiled and lazy," said a third.

"He might as well be an American teenager," said one of them, the most severe condemnation imaginable for them.

Yet now, I view the New Germany's future to some extent through him. Postwar Germany is still a society shaped more by its elites than its masses, and in Marcus I see little reason for concern. He is self-confident, yet he is also clever and worldly. At age fifteen, he discovered that learning Italian on vacation gave him the ability to mediate between two cultures. In school, he was already learning French and English, but from that point forward he decided to expand his repertoire to become a diplomat. He spent every night of his youth perfecting one language or the other. By age thirty, he was fluent in nine of them, including Portuguese, Russian, Japanese, and Chinese. He figured Korean would be next.

As we move from politically correct pizza to cakes made with free-range eggs smothered with organically grown fruit—golf-ball-sized, succulent strawberries—Marcus explains that he, as a teenager, had as much disdain for East German socialism as he did for the American inequalities. I'd found the lack of any strong ideological motor was characteristic of many young

Germans, setting them apart from parents who, if intellectual, were often left-ist and more willing to overlook the flaws of Soviet Communism than U.S. capitalism.

When Marcus's father, a life-long Social Democrat, took his boy to East Germany as a teenager, Marcus found the girls to be homely, the food to be bad, and the people to be unhappy. After such early comparative studies of both America and the Soviet bloc, he grew prouder of his Germany, which avoided both extremes.

In Marcus, I also saw a generational phenomenon that was common. Lines between generations were more pronounced than in America, partly be-cause each generation has had such a different historical experience. His grandfather Kurt Bartzsch had been a Luftwaffe officer who, after the war, marched to the tune of the *Wirtschaftswunder*, as a dentist in Estenfeld near Würzburg. He was a conservative man who earned well enough to buy a rid-ing stable and build two swimming pools. The war and postwar reconstruc-tion were his formative experiences. Marcus knew little about his war past, and he didn't ask much.

Marcus's mother, also a dentist, belonged to a generation whose forma-tive experiences were Germany's continued division, West Germany's grow-ing affluence, and America's Vietnam War. Her politics was that of the establishment left, though she and her husband hadn't any sympathy for the radical leftists or their terrorism of the nineteen-seventies.

Marcus's formative experiences have been German unification, the Cold War's end, globalization, and the technological revolution. He sees his own politics as a mixture of certain Green values and liberalism, in the pro-business German sense. "My parents' world was one of parties, socializing, jawboning over politics, and knowing that there was a good position avail-able for everyone who had some brains," Marcus says. "It wasn't hard to achieve what you wanted in your job and get ahead. It was the generation that, without having to try all that hard, could climb up the ladder. But just look around and you see how much harder matters have become. Universities are overcrowded. Good jobs are hard to come by. I've accomplished a lot al-ready, but I needed to apply myself enormously to do it. Thirty years ago, my talents alone would have been sufficient. Our generation will get less money for more work, and those who don't apply themselves will fall by the wayside."

Marcus says his generation is returning to basic values—his free-loving parents' generation provides no role model for his old-fashioned vision of family. "I don't know anyone among my collection of friends who is having an affair," he says. "There is a move back to more traditional relationships."

Perhaps this Germany will also be more pushy. As we eat our strawberry tortes, Marcus recounts with pride how he prepared the German negotiating side to stand up to the Americans in talks about military "burden-sharing."

Something just didn't seem right to Marcus about the old argument that Bonn wasn't carrying its European defense weight, leaving Washington to pick up too much of the bill. Marcus did some investigating and found that only 5 percent of all military equipment based in NATO countries was American, contrary to the general assumption that it was some 20 percent. There was only one problem with his findings: the military equipment that really counted in the modern world—high-tech weaponry and airlift capability—was overwhelmingly American.

Yet Marcus found yet another calculation that showed Germans were paying their fair share of the "security" burden, as opposed to a purely "military" burden. Humanitarian assistance made up 0.3 percent of Germany's gross national product while America paid only a third of that level, some 0.1 percent. "One then could make the argument that this humanitarian assistance was conflict-prevention investment—as important as military equipment to keeping peace or perhaps more so." As the American Congress had itself begun to talk about "responsibility sharing" instead of "burden sharing," Marcus recalls that this was a "timely argument."

Marcus is proud to provide Germany the intellectual ammunition to stand up to America. He is also unwilling to kowtow to France within European councils. One senior foreign diplomat at the foreign office says he is surrounding himself with young diplomats like Marcus because they are less caught up in the German habit of ceding leadership to others. Says the official: "When I tell diplomats they must fight for our national interests, the older ones don't know what I'm talking about; they don't even know how to define them. The very idea of 'national interests' was discouraged before. But this younger generation is less shy about defining and then attaining national interests."

What is changing most, the senior diplomat says, is Germany's attitude toward France. In the past, the European Community—and then the European Union—was a place where France was able to exert greater global influence beyond its weight and where history-tainted Germany chose to disappear as a national force. For many years, the arrangement suited both countries.

Yet the nineties have been a decade of growing German influence, due only partly to unification. Beyond that, the European Union added members who are natural allies more to Germany than France, Austria, Sweden, and Finland. The next expansion, taking in as many as five Central European states, will only serve Germany further. The pre-eminence of American global influence also serves Germany, for Washington has a far easier and more natural relationship with Germany than it does with France. France's continued arm's length relationship to NATO—it participates politically but hasn't integrated itself militarily—keeps it out of some of the West's closest councils.

The relative French decline and growth of German influence seems as natural to this generation of German diplomats as bending to American and French will was to the previous generation. Marcus's parents embraced Europe as a place to wash away their unwanted German identity, but Marcus views it more as a place to fulfill national goals, the way France and other nations have done for years.

Marcus is one of four spokespersons for an elite circle of Germans called the *Tönissteiner Kreis,* a network and think tank that brings together Germans with international experience. Every meeting has three sessions, each of which is carried out in one of the group's required languages (French, German, and English). He once invited me to speak before one of the meetings, and it wasn't long before I noticed the generation gap between older and younger members on questions of Europe.

At the event, one of the members, an economist in his late forties, spoke of the gradual erosion of the nation-state that in the end will lead to a situation where all problems of any importance will be addressed and solved at the European level. Marcus disagreed.

"He's so out of step with the times," my cousin whispered to me. "The nation-state will grow ever stronger." Marcus views his job as defining German national interests and pushing more resolutely than his elders to achieve them. "But our neighbors need not worry about us. We are less selfish in our interests than the Americans or the French. We think more about interdependence, an approach that grows out of our history." Interdependence and multilateralism has, in his view, become part of the national interest because Germany can never again go it alone.

As we finish our dessert, I tease Marcus that for all his modern ideas, he hasn't departed from the German tradition of Sunday afternoon coffee and cakes, topped with hearty doses of whipped cream. He shrugs again that it is far more Lingky who preserves German traditions. She has learned the German recipes from Marcus's mother.

After coffee, Marcus and I set off on another German custom—the Sunday walk in the woods. As Germany's familiar gray drizzle gives way to the year's first warm and sunny days, pathways across the country swarm with walkers. During our stroll, Marcus reviews how Germany should deal with the Americans and the French.

"The older generation's policies were motivated in large part by a feeling of obligation regarding America. Understandable in the past. Not helpful now. We will more coolly assess and defend our interests."

The French?

"The French are always trying to use the European Union as an instrument to pursue their own aims. You must look very closely at French actions."

Marcus knows the world may never be able to stomach a Germany that wags the moral finger at Israel, but even here he would welcome a more straightforward German policy. Marcus doesn't think his country should stand silently by while Benjamin Netanyahu pursues policies that punish the Palestinians and set back peace efforts. Marcus isn't anti-American, anti-French, or anti-Israeli. He merely views all these relationships more dispassionately than his parents' generation. They either idealized America and idolized figures such as Bob Dylan or Joan Baez, or they burned American flags and the effigies of U.S. presidents. They worked in Israel in kibbutzes to help pay off an historical debt, or they damned Israel above all nations. If God would have allowed, Marcus's parents might have reinvented themselves as French.

Marcus has a more balanced view. He is neither of the generation that lost the war to the Americans nor did he directly profit from the Marshall Plan and Washington's postwar largesse. Yet at the same time he doesn't share his parent generation's Vietnam-bred resentments. He regards America coolly, picking à la carte what he likes and dislikes about it.

"We have another consciousness than Americans," he says. "We have a deeper consciousness. I've participated in international programs with many different peoples. I always noticed that Europeans were able to talk longer and in more depth about any given subject. Americans don't have this spiritual depth."

And in international negotiations, it isn't the French or the Americans who impress him most but rather the British. He hopes Germany will some-day breed such a class of well-prepared, professional, and goal-oriented diplomats. In this respect, they are more his model than the French, always ready to sensibly argue a position but pragmatic enough to know that compromise is an ingredient to success.

Marcus speaks French so fluently that he can be mistaken for a native, but that makes him all the more aware of how the French outmaneuver other Europeans. For years, Francophiles at the German foreign ministry were so enamored of the French that they rarely stood up to Paris on a given course on European policy. They often ceded important positions in European bureaucracies.

It was when Marcus first worked as an intern in Brussels that it struck him just how ingrained this German habit had become. The French ability to place civil servants in senior positions was all out of proportion to their contribution to the budget. Marcus followed a list of names for Germans and French who had been approved for jobs in Brussels. Though the numbers approved for Germans and French were more balanced than in the past, the French had mastered the system to get their people in influential positions more quickly—the process for German nominees often stalled.

"They fight for every job as a matter of national interest," says Marcus. "We haven't been in that habit."

Perhaps it is a matter of language, he observes, that Germans give so much regard to French interests while the French often ignore their larger partner's needs. "We all speak French in the foreign office," he says. "Because of that, there is a better chance that we will understand their interests. Few of them speak our language. They haven't had to think about our interests so much over the years. It is important for them to learn to know us better now."

When Marcus makes such observations, the tone is neutral. He's simply making a statement of fact: the world has changed and people need to adjust. As we explore the changes more, Marcus points out a bench where we sit above a gentle meadow. Rabbits scurry back and forth in front of us; the occasional squirrel stops as if to listen in.

I wonder whether Germany's lack of elite universities—the fact that it has no Harvard, no Oxford—impairs its ability to produce the elites for its growing global role. I note that many of its best professors have taken up positions at leading universities in America, France, the United Kingdom. Marcus sees unintended positive consequences in this. His entering class of foreign diplomats was made up of individuals who had received their degrees all over the world: Cambridge in the U.K., his own Keio, Georgetown in the United States, and the Sorbonne in France. "It brings a wealth of experience in foreign countries and instincts for their culture," he says.

At the same time, the French diplomats train almost exclusively at the École Nationale d'Administration (ENA). "There is inbreeding of the leadership classes in France," says Marcus. "They are all influenced by the same forces. That doesn't exist here. Our elite is much more international."

At a dinner of his friends, the entering class of diplomats at the foreign office, the consensus is that the French are arrogant and unprepared for future global challenges, while the German young diplomats better understand a diverse world. "Yet we aren't as sure of ourselves because we aren't trained as a national elite—elite is still a bad word in our vocabulary. We are more modest. We aren't prompted or pushed in the direction of the foreign office as they are. We must push ourselves."

It begins to drizzle. We rise from our bench and begin the walk back to Marcus's home. As we stroll, I tell him that the whole world knows what the American dream is, but what is the German dream? It is a question I ask my German friends often, for I am sure it goes to the core of how bad historical experience has changed them. They aren't revolutionaries who want to turn the world upside down, but instead they seek a quiet spot on the globe where no one demands too much of them.

"The German dream is far more modest than the American dream," says my cousin. "It is build your own house with its own garden and a tree. It is to settle your existence." The operative German saying is: "Raise a son, plant a tree, live in peace."

Their longer-term dreams are a version of that basic model. He would someday want to live with Lingky on an island, Greek or in the Azores, in a comfortable villa with a view of the sea. He would sit and write books and muse about the world. Lingky would found a clinic for alternative medicine where she would treat their aging friends and colleagues who would come to visit.

"America was built by those who want to fulfill dreams," he says. "A German, however, was born into traditions. You don't ask Germans what their dreams are. Those who had great dreams emigrated."

As we arrive back at his home, Marcus warns me the last great historical dreamer in Germany had a brush mustache and a stiff-armed salute. And look how that turned out! Perhaps we Americans, he says, ought not push Germany too hard to dream again. "Hitler is perhaps the reason that we are particularly shy of national dreams."

As I drive off, I want to call my aunts and tell them what has become of the boy they had considered so spoiled and ill-behaved. It is hard to fear the Germany represented by him. He and Germany will make a more difficult partner for American diplomats, more ready to stand up for German interests, but also a more useful one—more willing to use their nation's potential to influence world events.

But how would a new German generation run the world, if given the chance?

The *Bundeswehr*, the federal German army, provides me the opportunity to find out. I am allowed to observe one of the regular war-and-diplomacy games they stage for high-school students. The *Bundeswehr*'s aim: to teach young Germans how to handle international responsibility, something new to Germans and their newly restored nation-state after nearly a half-century of division and restricted influence. To thicken the plot, the students involved in the three-day exercise are eastern German, from a part of the country untamed by half a century of membership in Western institutions such as NATO and the European Community. I would have an unvarnished chance to see how Germans handle power, after a half century of being kept well clear of it. The students and a handful of junior officers, who join them in this game, assume identities and roles that put them in the world's driver's seats.

Fast forward to the third and final day of the game—which by the fast pace of the game is the sixth year of events—when the students have brought the world to the brink of World War III. The citizens of politically unified Europe have voted Hannelore Kohl out of power (her husband, Germany's longest reigning chancellor, had stepped down in her favor some years earlier). In a lurch to the left, they elect the charismatic Green party leader Joschka Fischer to replace her.

Fischer, played by one of the young officers, faces continental crisis. Balloting in Eastern Europe, which to simplify the game is a unified if democratic bloc, has brought radical populists to power. The officer complains to me that the West has sorely disappointed the East with its protectionism, keeping out East European goods, and its low level of economic support for new democracies. So he's backing out of treaties under which his region had agreed to join NATO and the European Union.

So, in one of his first acts as leader, EU President Joschka Fischer announces that this threat to the EU cannot be tolerated. His warning is clear and unmistakable: unless Eastern Europe returns to its promised course of integration with the West, he will call out the troops to enforce compliance. He moves a couple of West European divisions to Germany's borders with Poland to show he means business.

A student playing a reporter from CNN corners Fischer and angrily accuses him of bringing Europe to the brink of war. One would have thought the Germans had learned one can't take Eastern Europe by force. Behind the reporter stands newly elected U.S. President Newt Gingrich, who fumes his displeasure with Europe. The politically weak and eternally ailing Boris Yeltsin threatens to throw his military might behind the East Europeans to support their continued independent course. NATO's decision to shun him is now backfiring.

But Fischer stubbornly stays his course. "We have a lot at stake economically and politically in the integration of Eastern Europe," Fischer tells CNN. "The recent elections in Eastern Europe are taking the region in the wrong direction, an anti-democratic direction, and it is in our national interests to stop that."

And the Russians? The danger of war?

"We have concluded a secret non-aggression treaty with them that they dare not violate," says Fischer. "It will cost them a large percentage of their oil earnings to do so. Those are the rules. They would have to give up twenty energy points to the World Bank . . ."

Twenty energy points?

So goes the game of world domination played by young Germans in their formative years.

The setting is a training center in Straussberg, near eastern Berlin, in a large conference hall that is Soviet bloc in style—being, as it is, the former headquarters of the East German army. The hall still has a socialist ambiance—overhead neon tubes cast an unnatural glare; wall paneling is of cheap, fake wood; floor tiling is a drab, uniform gray.

The complex game, designed by political scientists at the University of Nuremberg, employs books full of treaties and understandings reached among regions whose political status and challenges roughly reflect those of the current world. For simplicity's sake, though, Europe is already politically unified, Eastern Europe is a defined bloc as well, and to keep matters interesting, elections are held every two years (which is roughly once a day in the three-day game).

The players in this particular simulation are students from the Sartre Gymnasium in Hellersdorf, a district of East Berlin where the successor party to East German's Communists, the Party of Democratic Socialism, draws 40 percent support. *Bundeswehr* "youth officers" have joined them as fellow players. They are members of a group created in 1956, just three years after West Germans began to re-arm themselves, whose job then as now was PR: winning over skeptical young Germans to the idea that a peace-seeking democracy needed an army.

Pulling the strings of the game is Major Mario Sellmer, a personable, compact man who for the purposes of the game is the UN Secretary General. He's a combination of bomb-thrower and peace-maker, the one who introduces economic crises, guerrilla wars, electoral surprises, and peace talks into the game, according to personal whimsy and throws of the dice.

For many years, the game was much more theoretical. Germany's troops stayed at home, and its allies handled most world affairs. But with unification and Germany's military deployment to Bosnia, the game takes on a greater feeling of urgency and reality.

"Germans have more responsibility now," says Major Sellmer. "We've been living on a fantasy island. Now we have to learn how to swim in the currents." With eastern German youth voting in large numbers either for the right-wing Deutsche Volksunion or the radical left Party of Democratic Socialism, the game's pedagogical purpose has also grown in importance.

Arranged before his long head table sits a circle of eleven smaller tables, each representing a region or country. And at each of those tables sit four individuals: the government leader, the defense minister, the economics and trade minister, and the chief of the opposition (and, where democracy doesn't play a role, rebel groups or underground opposition). The game manuals set out each of the eleven's energy import needs, export potential, and level of consumption and investment. The military strengths roughly match the actual world situation, as do the number of treaties, alliances, and political strains. A war map rests at the center of the room should diplomacy fail.

Students choose the names they wish to play under. The World Bank president, who controls the coffers, calls himself Bill Gates. Explains the studious young man, who has a slight resemblance to the multi-billionaire: "I wanted to be the richest man in the world for a few days."

The leader of Western Europe, a woman, opts to call herself Hannelore Kohl.

Why not Frau Santer, after the wife of the EU Commission President? I ask her.

Comfortable in the national skin of a unified Germany, she shrugs, "But I am a German. How can I be Santer?"

After a series of tentative first moves the first day, the plot thickens on Day Two with Russians opposing NATO expansion and East Europeans solidly set on a pro-Western course. Latin America has a guerrilla war on its hands, a Saudi oil sheikh faces political scandal over his spending of oil dollars on orgies, and Asians complain to Europe about the sex trade.

Everyone is either wooing or damning America's overwhelming resources, military might, and general influence. A flurry of activity surrounds the U.S. table—treaties, trade agreements, loan arrangements, all to the benefit of American power. This realization of America's overwhelming strength bothers all the young German students except for those who had the luck to represent Uncle Sam.

The U.S. economics minister, nineteen-year-old Kai Bonitz, concedes that he's never had such power or such fun. He begins the game as the shy but thoughtful student his teachers knew well, but he soon is baring sparkling braces as he bites into his considerable portion of international might.

"We are the chiefs of the world," he declares to me. "Getting this job was like winning the lottery. I am the economic representative of the greatest power on earth. It has improved my feelings of self-worth enormously." He puffs his chest under his Hawaiian shirt and pulls up his faded blue jeans. Young Kai Bonitz has chosen a curious name for an economic bureaucrat: General Dwight D. Eisenhower. "I have been reading a great deal about him, and his life story impresses me. . . ."

I ask the General how he plans to use his power. "You can't make a wrong step. My friends from Asia and the Arab world can get away with irresponsibility more easily. But with true power comes great responsibility."

This latter-day Eisenhower has stayed up all night studying his manuals, and his greater preparation is paying off as he strikes deals left and right. He knows by heart what resources he controls, what treaties he is party to, and what energy he must import. "The question is how I can bring big profits to the man," he says, nodding toward Bill Clinton, as played by a young officer. But at this point, he cuts off our interview. "I really must go." Trade talks begin in three minutes in the next room.

With that, he strides purposefully out of the room.

Clinton, who soon faces re-election, and the U.S. secretary of defense, who calls himself "Duke" (after John Wayne), frown at Eisenhower's cocky demeanor. "I'm afraid it's going a little bit to his head," says Duke, another young officer in his early twenties. "It's probably a little too much power to give to such a young German."

Boris Yeltsin sadly watches all the action around the Americans. As played by nineteen-year-old Matthias Hüber, the Russian leader is slight, sober, and

soft-spoken. His bent frame strains under the burden of his economic problems and the erosion of his superpower status.

"I have a significant military, but without a powerful economy I can't afford it." He nods toward Eisenhower, Duke, and Clinton. "They are in the
driver's seat. It is amazing how unbelievably strong America is, particularly
when it has Western Europe as a willing partner. You see how the world
changes when they work together."

Yeltsin is scheming up ways to get the world's attention, to cause a little
trouble. He's learned no one will finance him if things are quiet. To head off
a crisis however, they will pay. Yeltsin's needs are urgent: his military leader
and the chief of his political opposition have been sighted at other tables
around the room, including that of the Chinese, seeking financial support for
a possible coup attempt against their leader.

"It isn't much fun to be Boris Yeltsin," he says, loping off to stand in the
bread line at the American table.

A few minutes later, Bill Clinton offers to save Russia with large loans.
But there is a price—Russia must accept the expansion of NATO. Yeltsin is
outraged. He storms off angrily. The young eastern German playing the
Russian leader isn't ready for the cold calculus of international politics.
"Why won't people help me simply because I need help?" he says. "Before I
go under, we'd sell our atomic weapons to the highest bidder."

During a break in the action to cool tempers, Secretary General Sellmer
explains: "I've seen friendships die, and relationships break up over this. The
boys particularly can't understand it when the girls challenge them."

Has it ever come to war?

"A few times," he says. "But it's only come to nuclear war once, and that
was when I played the game with teachers who couldn't stand their principal,
who was the Chinese leader. It got very personal. They blew him away."

With students, he said, he would never have allowed it to come to that.
"I have an educational responsibility," he says. Even in this sort of gaming,
Germans put constraints on themselves.

When a student gets it into his head that he wants to start a war, the
youth officers declare a cease-fire, call for a United Nations security council
session, and then collect the offending students in a separate room to show
them videos. When nuclear holocaust is the danger, they show them a film

from Hiroshima. Major Sellmer also has videos that show the worst sides of chemical, conventional, and guerrilla warfare. They all have a common intention: to convince the players to negotiate peace.

Says Major Sellmer: "You don't want Maria to go home and, when her father asks what she did that day, have her answer: 'I nuked China off the map.' That would be the end of it for us." One also has to worry about the press. In a year when the German media uncovered videos of young soldiers play-acting rape and pillage—and joining in Hitler salutes—any German officer knows that he has to play carefully. "But this game always gets a little dangerous at the end."

With a roll of Sellmer's dice, the means of determining elections in this otherwise scientific game, a populist, post-communist leadership replaces Eastern Europe's pro-Western leaders, and a campaign begins against EU or NATO membership. Clinton loses America to Newt Gingrich. Western European elections bring Joschka Fischer to power. Only Yeltsin hangs on, and he's not well.

It is the Eastern European shift that prompts crisis. The new leader calls himself Vaclav Josephs for reasons he won't reveal. (Another student suggests that he's Communist, and Communists were often Jews, so. . . . Ugly stereotypes sometimes die hard in Germany.) He blames his region's inability to pay its bills on the West's greediness and protectionism—he wants no part of the European Union on such terms.

Joschka Fischer issues an ultimatum. "We would like you to be part of our expanded structures," he says, "but if you don't want to come voluntarily, we have the means to make it happen otherwise."

Vaclav Josephs begins furious discussions with his military around the war board at the middle of the room. "No need to count up your troops," says Fischer. "We've done the math. Military superiority is decisively on our side."

The man playing Josephs, Sergeant Major Jürgen Eise, thirty-three, is enraged. "We won't discuss anything at this level," he says.

The Americans won't commit; they won't risk war with Western Europe to save anti-Western leaders. The Russians are too dependent on Western financing to help. Tempers are rising; nerves are fraying. The bus is waiting in the lot to take the students home—something has to give.

U.S. President Gingrich explodes at Joschka Fischer, babbling incoherently. "You must turn back your forces . . . the danger of war . . . the need for world peace . . . the future of Europe. I can't approve of what is happening."

"You don't need to approve of it," says Fischer coolly, relishing his position of power. "You merely need to tolerate it. Don't get in our way." For the first time in three days, Europe controls events—not America.

"It's crazy what you are doing," says Gingrich, his face red and his body shaking with anger.

"Ah, c'mon," says Fischer, who is actually Dieter Scherl, a twenty-six-year-old first lieutenant. He had been growing bored with the overly peaceful nature of the game before he initiated the escalation. "Don't you think you are taking this all too seriously? If we had had more time, perhaps I would have tried more diplomatic means. I'm just testing what the game can do."

The UN Secretary General blows the whistle before Fischer's troops march into Poland. A German leader had last done such a thing in 1939, and it probably wouldn't be the best ending in front of this American reporter. The security council convenes as the third and final day of the exercise comes to a close. War is averted, the players leave the room grumbling at each other.

"That was so irresponsible . . ."

"It was peaceful for too long . . ."

"You're an officer—you should have been a role model to the young students, but instead you attack Poland . . ."

"It's only a game. . . ."

"But the game only has meaning if you take it seriously."

The players gather for a quick post-mortem and final lunch in the battleground cafeteria before heading home. In general, they all agree that they resented America's decisive power and they wished their country had more influence. Says the day's Eisenhower: "You really saw here what difference it would make if Europe could get itself together with Germany in leadership. Then it would be a counterpoint to America. It would have a larger voice on world events. You can see what fun it can be to have influence."

Kay Jäckel, eighteen, who led the Arab military, was a large, barrel-chested young man and the only one among the students who plans a military career. "We pay a lot [in the EU and to the Third World in development funds]," he says, "but we don't do much to ensure that our economic power is matched by our political power. We should become more active in foreign policy. We should do more to shape world history. We can't always stand behind the Americans."

Their second general conclusion is that Germany is too much of a mess at home to take on this role of "great power," and to fix this, the eastern German students had a simple solution: fewer foreigners, fewer asylum seekers, and more jobs.

With unemployment at nearly 20 percent in their district of Berlin, they are against the liberal asylum policy that had grown out of Germany's role in World War II. The relative tolerance that I had found toward foreigners at the Rheingau Gymnasium in West Berlin was replaced at the Sartre Gymnasium in East Berlin by a suspicion of foreigners.

Says Silvia Antowiak, who played Hannelore Kohl, "I'm not against foreigners, but other countries ban immigration over a certain number, and so should we." She complains that whenever one tries to introduce a reasonable policy restricting the inflow, history is thrown in Germany's face. "We are trying to keep everyone happy all the time. That must stop. The war is three generations away from us. This generation is spiritually much different."

"Let's call things what they are," says Andre Riehl, who had been running Asia's economy up until just a few minutes earlier. "People coming now aren't really refugees. They are economic asylum seekers. They'll cheat, they'll do anything to make Germany poorer."

They feel the invasion of foreigners is more threatening to Germany's future than anything occurring in Bosnia. In fact, the real Bosnian threat to Germany is mostly that renewed war would mean even more refugees heading their way. "The problem of foreigners isn't just one of jobs," says Jäckel, the future official. "It is also one of cultural decline. German people and culture will be fully torn from their roots."

Silvia: "The point is that we aren't an immigration country. We must set the bar for immigration higher."

The longer one talks with these eastern Germans, the more one feels their resentment. They overwhelmingly wanted unification. But since then they have suffered two shocks: they first discovered how much different they were from western Germans. And they were most different, they have concluded, in that they are far less American.

"We are still less individualistic, less egotistical than Wessis," says Hannelore Kohl. "We aren't as accustomed to marketing ourselves." Yet she is sure they will all morph into quasi-Americans in time. "Everyone is more out for himself now."

Jan Pollei looks to be the class hippie, with his long, stringy blonde hair and worn, torn jeans. Yet he is also the most determined to resist this Americanization. "They all go to Pizza Hut, wear American jeans, and want the American dream." He frowns, ignoring his own jeans. "They've forgotten they are Germans." They are shocked when I argue that they have a simplistic notion of America as fast food. I suggest that America also represents their country's democratization, its freedom.

These young are disappointed in democracy; they had expected so much more. "The distance between the government and the people is so great," says Pollei. "This democracy might be the best thing possible, so why not accept it? But it isn't as lively as I'd hoped." The others nod their agreement.

Eastern German youth have also been surprised by the extent to which the Holocaust history influences unified Germany. After all, their own country for years considered itself the representative of the victims and not the perpetrators.

Eisenhower frowns: "We are all troubled by our history, but you have to think about it in relative terms. The Vietnam War also wasn't a great thing. You might not have killed six million Jews, but nevertheless . . ."

Boris Yeltsin is sure "Germany is not a special phenomenon. This also could have happened in the United States, and it still might happen elsewhere. Cruelty is a human instinct. It's less likely to happen here now because we have a consciousness of that."

Yeltsin is still steaming about how America treated him during the game. Though I point out to him that the American representative was a fellow German, he believes the game rules created a situation where he acted pretty true to American form. Americans, he says, were willing "to exploit my economic weakness. I quickly saw that you don't get something for nothing. The United States has power, and that makes it egocentric."

The young man playing Bill Gates from the World Bank is alone in defending Washington. "Through talent and some luck, the Americans have gained something that is remarkable: a position of world leadership that is unchallenged. The country, in a way, achieved the American dream itself." He chides his classmates for being so anti-capitalist. "Workplaces are created by capitalists."

They all groan.

Shrugs Kai Bonitz, a.k.a. Eisenhower: "I saw right from the start that if there are no surprises in the world, America can't lose with all its economic strengths and political will. I noticed that the world couldn't get by without American participation—everyone was coming to me."

His attitude: you can't fight the Americans, so join them.

In time, he hopes, Germany can enjoy some of this sort of American-style influence on the smaller stage of Europe. He wants to be a diplomat, not against America but for a democratic Germany and a Europe that is close to America.

No one quibbles with this.

"Maybe we can have some fun being Germans for a change," he says.

I could almost hear the pop tune: *Germans just want to have fun.*

And one element of that, for this generation, is a desire for greater influence in the game of world politics.

ullay of horse and hoofe and
rave, and mangles, and scatters to
en beneath and the blue above,
ack and danger, and life, and
acca, — Lacca used to ride
mouse-gray mustang close to my
tue escape and bright-belled [?]
ghed with joy as I looked at [?]

SEVEN

CRIME IN THE FAMILY: PART ONE

A German will denounce anyone to serve himself . . . this is a curious people.
They are small-minded and small-spirited. Don't forget how much Hitler wanted
to promote large, blond people. And he was dark and small. Don't you consider
that a little strange?

—FRANZ KRAMER, MY COUSIN
AND AN EX-CONVICT

My cousin Franz Kramer leans on his cane on the landing in front of his third-story apartment, which lies at the top of a narrow, winding stairway. "So this is my cousin Fred," he says, lifting the cane and pulling me in for an embrace with his two powerful arms. As he pulls back, I take in his broad features, those of a prize fighter—oversized ears, a large nose, deepset eyes.

I don't see much of the sharp-boned Schumann facial architecture about him, though he has as much of the famous composer's blood washing through his veins as do I. I decide that the Kramer genes, those of his Nazi father, are dominant.

"Welcome, come in," he says in a fine English, which I would later learn was a product of studies among fellow convicts during his prison years, as was his nearly fluent French. His voice is deep, like a foghorn. My imagination hears it demanding my money. But for the moment his hearty reception makes me forget whatever misgivings had delayed my visit for so many months. I hadn't ever quite decided what I would say to the criminal son of the allegedly war criminal father—two of my less distinguished relatives.

Yet Franz greets me like the long-lost family that I am. "I've heard you on German television—that show with the foreign journalists, *Presseclub*—so I know you speak German," he says, switching to his own language. He suggests we should use the familiar "du" form as relatives: he wants to take down all artificial barriers between us. His partner, Uschi, stands behind him with a kind of cautious smile. I hand her flowers I'd brought along. She views me more suspiciously than my cousin as she invites me to sit at a narrow table that she has laid with china and a cheesecake she has made especially for my visit, a special recipe with bits of chocolate crust floating in a rich batter. The gobs of whipped cream are freshly prepared. The coffee is hot and thick.

Uschi is the homemaker, and she appears to be a decade younger than my sixty-one-year-old cousin. She has a determined way about her, organized and purposeful in her movements. Franz is more emotional as he makes family small talk. His restless energy fills the room, one of two in which they live, which is perhaps thirty feet long but only about as wide as my six-foot body stretched out fully.

It is sufficiently large to house a green corduroy-upholstered sofa, pushed against one wall, and a narrow shelf opposite it against the other wall that is efficiently enough configured to contain a small television and video machine, stereo equipment and a radio, and various knickknacks. Any free spot on the sofa holds tiny puppets, dolls, stuffed teddy bears. Franz brags about how cozy Uschi has made the place.

I can't help but think that Franz must have grown accustomed to living in small quarters. He spent nearly fourteen years and five months of his life behind bars. But he's been clean since his last release in the mid-1970s. He

still has the physique and look
of the town tough, but his
manner is soft and thoughtful.
His eyes take me in and size
me up.

We make small talk. It
seems prudent not to start
with the question I must at
some point get to: *So tell me
about your father and the Holocaust.*

Or, regarding his own
background: *So what was the worst
crime that you ever committed?* I wonder for a moment whether I am standing before a killer or a common hood, but instead I ask about the blue-and-yellow
parakeets, who I learn are called Hans and Lisa. In a cage above and to the
right of the sofa, they squawk at irregular intervals as we converse. Franz tells
me he tacked the board behind them, between the cage and the wall, because
they chip into the wallpaper with their beaks. Aside from that they are good
company, he says. He provides a description of the recent, untimely death of
one of the partners, followed by a funeral in a nearby garden, some mourning, and a new purchase, Hans, to help the widow, Lisa, get through life.

*Erich Kramer, 1940, with Alma Schumann Kramer,
Manfred and Franz.*

Franz says that he had heard "some time ago" from his brother Manfred
in San Diego that I was coming. He had expected me earlier. I didn't say that
if I had known that my ex-convict cousin would be this civilized and welcoming, perhaps I would have visited sooner.

Franz saves me the trouble of asking uncomfortable questions about the
past by volunteering the information. He tells me that he spent the better part
of his earlier life in jail. The crimes were never major: no violence, no guns,
no deaths. He was a garden-variety criminal, pure and simple: video-shop
heists, breaking and entering, common burglary. . . .

Franz figures his life began to turn bad shortly after his father returned
home from the Soviet gulag in Alma Ata in early December 1949, more
than four years after the end of the war. Franz was thirteen years old then,
born in the third year of the Third Reich. He was an unplanned child whose
own arrival followed his parents' marriage by just twenty days. His father's ab-

sence throughout most of his young life—the six years of the war and his four years in a prison camp thereafter—had made Franz the man of the family. His brother Manfred was three years younger, which in wartime days was a particularly significant gap between brothers. Both were happy enough living on their own with their mother, Alma Schumann Kramer, my grandfather's sister. As a singer at the State Opera, she was a celebrity of sorts, and Franz remembers many evenings spent on stage with his brother, where they worked as extras.

The family reunion started poorly on that wintry 1949 day. The boys and their mother hadn't met their returning soldier at the train station, Schlesischer Bahnhof, as was the practice at that time. The mistake had been innocent enough. Each night, a radio announcer read off the names of those who were coming home from Soviet camps. But when Erich's name had been read, his wife and his two sons were performing in Leo Janaczek's *Jenufe*.

Alma falsely reckoned her husband would be among the last to be released, considering the rank he had had in the military police and the weight of his twenty-five-year sentence. The Soviets had mostly released only simple soldiers by 1949, and she knew there was nothing simple about her husband's background. So when Kramer pulled into the station with a load of newly released prisoners, he was almost the only one without family to greet him.

Franz recalls standing at the apartment door with his mother, looking at this stranger whom he vaguely recognized as his father. Erich Kramer wore a blue cotton jacket and a Russian army cap. He toted a bag that he opened to release a small, mangy cat that he had brought with him from Russia and proudly presented as a gift for the children. His boys were unimpressed. "We already had a cat, but he didn't know that," says Franz. "And our cat was a fatter and more beautiful one than the one he brought. That upset him."

Franz only learned much later what most unnerved Erich Kramer in those first days home. Alma Schumann Kramer wasn't in the mood for what her husband wanted upon his return, following six years of war and four years of forced labor in the gulag. "A man needs a woman," shrugs Franz. Angry fights erupted almost immediately between husband and wife, and they were often violent. Franz was also none too happy to have his father back, for Erich was set on violently reimposing his authority over the household with his "extreme view of discipline and order," as Franz puts it.

Franz reaches into a cabinet drawer and retrieves some *Feldpost*—a stack of correspondence that his father sent to his young son from the front. The postcards are tied together with a red ribbon, which Franz's mother strung through a punchhole in the cards to preserve them for her son. He shows me one that was dated October 5, 1944—Franz's eighth birthday. The postmark is from Litzmannstadt—Poland's Lodz—where he is serving as a staff sergeant.

It reads:

My dear Lads:
   I don't want to let Franz's birthday pass without sending you greetings. Behave yourselves always and obey your grandparents, your mother, and your teachers. Don't forget your father. With heartfelt greetings. Daddy.

And then at the bottom of the page in capital letters: *LONG LIVE THE FÜHRER. LONG LIVE GREATER GERMANY.*

"You see how loyal he was until the very end," says Franz. "It was clear to everyone the war was going bad, but he was true to the cause to the very end."

We search through the cards further. The postmarks follow the course of the war, and Erich Kramer seems to have landed wherever the action was. He was part of the original invasion in Poland, and he joined the invasion of France and Yugoslavia as well. The postmarks move east to Melitipol in the Ukraine from January to March of 1943.

Most troubling to Franz, however, are the cards in 1944 from Lodz. The Jewish ghetto had been disbanded that year, its residents shipped off to extermination camps, primarily Auschwitz and Theresienstadt. The military police, Franz figures, certainly would have played a role.

"I'd rather not know what he did there," says Franz. "That was a terrible address. It troubles me a great deal what he might have done there."

I look at the front of the card from Litzmannstadt. It bears a naive paint-ing of two sweet girls with red headscarves playing wooden flutes. The date is November 2, 1944, Litzmannstadt—Lodz, Gr. Kaserne, Gneisenaustrasse.

Franz frowns: "One only chose the most trusted of the Nazis to break up the ghettoes."

I remind myself that my bloodline is different from Franz's. I find odd comfort in remembering that his father, the good Nazi, doesn't have any Schumann blood coursing through him.

My own grandfather—his mother's brother—had avoided the draft in the first world war by making believe that he was crazy. He convinced re-cruiters, an oft-told family story goes, and he thus wasn't required to go to war. He was far too soft to survive the battlefield, and knew it. I repeat this story to Franz, making some awkward joke about how ours seems to have been a typical German family: mad poets and brutal soldiers.

"In every old established German family there are such stories." Franz smiles as Uschi pours more coffee.

I read through more of the cards held together by the red ribbon. None of them speaks of the war, though all are sent from the front. Erich Kramer instead uses the small space available on the back of each card to scribble in-structions to his two boys about how they should behave themselves in his absence. This paternal approach continues through to his time in a Soviet gulag. One letter sent from "Lager 7099-3" in Alma Ata responds to a note from Franz's mother about problems the boy was having at home and in school. "Hopefully your next school marks will improve," he writes. But at the same time he reminds Franz that learning his Sunday school lessons at the Mormon church could be much more important for his later life than anything else.

The irony of the imprisoned Nazi preaching religion to his son is lost on Franz. "He felt very strongly about the church," he says. Indeed, says Franz, Mormonism and National Socialism were his father's two great pas-sions. Both worlds, Franz suggests, offer a man discipline and a doctrine of absolutes by which to lead his life. One requires absolute faith in some su-perior being, and the other demands absolute loyalty to a Führer.

What did he tell you about the war when he came home? I ask.

"He never talked about it. No, that's not right. Some nights he would wake up screaming with bad dreams. I don't know whether it was because of what he'd done to others or what had happened to him. Oh yes, and there was one story he told time and again—about standing in a stream, up to his neck in cold water, for five or six hours, holding his rifle over his head, not making a move, while Russian troops marched past on the bridge overhead. He always used that as an example of what the human being can bear."

Did he ever talk about Soviet prison? I ask.

"Not much," he says.

Erich had been captured in Silesia as he was trying to make his way West at the end of the war so that he could surrender to the Americans instead of to the Soviets. It was a common quest after German surrender, as word spread among soldiers about how much more harshly the Red Army treated its captives.

"He did say one thing after he came home. He talked about how the best prisoners to have as friends in the camp were the Japanese. They had a stricter code of honor, he told me. They never betrayed each other." Erich Kramer told his son that Germans, however, couldn't be trusted. They'd inform on each other "over as little as a piece of bread."

Franz says he's not surprised that German POWs couldn't be trusted: he often found German thieves to be a disloyal bunch. They were often willing to trade information on friends for the promise of shorter sentences. In prison, he preferred East Europeans or Africans for friends.

"That's the reason the Russian Mafia is so dangerous," he says. "The East bloc people have a sense of individual honor, something many Germans left behind many years ago. A Pole would never betray you to serve a sentence of six months less. The East European is more dependable. Most Germans are okay. But a great part you can just forget. They always blame others for their own misfortune. They never accept the consequences for themselves."

"Germans will denounce anyone to serve themselves. This is a curious people," he says. "They are small-minded and small-spirited. Don't forget how much Hitler wanted to promote large, blond people. And he was dark and small. Don't you consider that a little strange?"

The conversation flows easily from one matter to another. For a while we talk about my work and my family, then about Uschi's family and her life in Lübeck. We chat about German politics and about Bill Clinton. They are intrigued by Americans' fixation on his sexual affairs. Uschi brings out a casserole. She offers a choice of beverages; and they are both relieved that our family's Mormon roots aren't sunk so deep that I would refuse a good German beer.

But the conversation always circles back to Franz's father. That said, Franz told me that his own father had been hand-picked by the Soviets as a man they could trust among other prisoners—he belonged to the camp police. He served them, just as he had served the Nazis, loyal to whatever master. This all led up to his early release, for he was recruited by the KGB.

Franz recalls his father arriving by streetcar to pick him up from the Mormon church's mid-week evening meetings for the young. It was October 1950, less than a year after his father's return from Soviet prison and the week that East Germany was to hold its first elections. His father said he had complained to another passenger on the train about the state of the tracks: they were so bent and loose in their cobblestone bed that the train had to crawl forward at a snail's pace.

"The Communists shouldn't be wasting their money on these fraudulent elections," his father said to the other man. "They should buy new tracks instead."

Two men who had overheard his complaint stepped down from the train with Franz's father and demanded his papers. Franz's father was so nervous that he took his sons home immediately, then packed a bag for flight to the West. He'd later tell his son that the Soviets only released him early from the gulag because he'd agreed to work for them as a spy in East Germany. Yet he was so anti-Communist that he hadn't served them well in his job in the Soviet military administration of an electrical cable plant. He feared the incident on the streetcar was all the evidence the Soviets needed to realize their spy couldn't be trusted.

Erich Kramer hurried to the opera house with his son to tell Alma that he'd stay at a friend's house that night, then flee to West Berlin the next morning. The Wall wouldn't be built for another decade, so such a flight was still a relatively simple matter. Franz still recalls his father telling Alma that this would be her last performance, for she must bring her family to the West as well the next day. Otherwise they could punish her and the children and use them as bait to get him back.

Something about Erich Kramer's story doesn't ring true to me. One doesn't flee Berlin because of one complaint about elections and train tracks. The fact that Kramer was serving the Soviets as a spy would more likely have protected him. "There's more to this story than your father told you," I say to Franz.

"I've often thought so myself," says Franz.

Erich Kramer crossed successfully to the West the next morning. He requested and received political asylum, relating the story about his confrontation in the streetcar. Franz's father had foreseen the danger correctly. The East Berlin security police woke up the family in search for Erich Kramer. They then remained, waiting for him to return home. While they sat in one room, Alma and the boys hunkered in the living room, where they burned books and papers in the fireplace. They destroyed every document that could be used against her husband, such as a personally autographed copy of Hitler's *Mein Kampf.* Alma could only leave the house with a Stasi escort.

After three days of waiting, the Stasi gave up. As soon as they did, Alma bundled up her boys and took them West to join their father.

At that point, the story grows more confusing.

After a few weeks in the West, police came again to the Kramer home in December 1950—this time in the West. They arrested Erich on charges of "crimes against humanity." The Soviets, his father would later tell Franz, were getting their revenge. He had broken his agreement with them, so they would turn on him.

Alma knew that as long as she was married to a suspected war criminal, she would not be permitted a work permit in West Berlin, nor would the boys be allowed to attend school. So she agreed with Erich that they would obtain a divorce.

A year later, says Franz, police released his father due to "lack of evidence." Still, his father continued reporting to the local police station every morning and every evening for several years, hardly the actions of a man who has been cleared of all charges.

After Erich Kramer was released, he rebuffed Alma's efforts to remarry. He was happy to be rid of her, sour woman that he had helped make her, and he soon would move on to marry again. She would take her younger son Manfred and move to America. But they left behind Franz, whose troubles with the law had already begun. How often, I thought, had a move to America changed the fate of a German family? I'd often wondered how my life might have been different had my father stayed in Germany instead of coming to America in 1927, if my father had survived the war at all. But the matter wasn't a theoretical one for Franz.

His mother and brother became Americans. His brother took an American wife, served as a G.I., worked his way through the ranks at a furniture company, bought a house in San Diego with a swimming pool, and raised two children, who both married and made successful lives for themselves.

Franz has never entirely forgiven his mother for leaving him behind. He moved from one "job" to another, from one prison to another until he abandoned his life of crime at nearly age forty. Since his release, he has stayed clean, working a string of odd jobs: as a printer, a waiter in a restaurant, an aide in a senior citizens' home, a bartender . . .

"Did your father ever talk to you about what he had done?" I ask.

"Never."

"What kind of a man was he?" I ask.

"What do you mean?"

"Was he an evil man, a bad man?"

"He was strict, reserved, a closed man. He wasn't an evil man. But he viewed very harshly anything that broke the law."

"But crimes against humanity are just that," I protest.

"They didn't break the law during his time." In fact, he was upholding Nazi laws, Nazi order, I thought to myself. When one serves a criminal regime, one can quite legally be a criminal.

"His strictness went back to his own time as a policeman," Franz says. "He saw things in a way that I could never understand."

"How so?

Franz frowns. Uschi is taking away our plates to the kitchen. She casts Franz a look that seems to say *"He may be a relative, but he's also a reporter."*

He disregards her and begins to tell me about his own first arrest when he was only seventeen years old. He and a friend had made a small business out of stealing small sums of money left in the empty milk bottles that neighbors put in front of their doors each week to pay off dairy deliveries.

They supplemented this by stealing crates of beer, usually consuming the contents but earning on the returned bottles. His father got wind of his son's crime, and he didn't hesitate to exact the proper punishment. "Instead of taking me aside to talk to me, he fetched the police," says Franz, his face toward the ground like the child caught in a misdemeanor. Then silence.

"Your own father denounced you?" I asked, with evident horror. "For stealing a few pfennigs in milk bottles!"

"To my father, the crime itself was the point, not the magnitude of it. It was the *Prinzip*."

Again, I frowned, I was hearing about the German devotion to "principle." But what sort of *Prinzip* was it that would put the pilferage of milk money by one's own son higher on the prosecutable offense scale than the brutal beating of Hitler's opponents? Franz had taken some small change and broken a small law. His father had committed a grave moral offense that at the time apparently had violated no law. Both son and father were criminals, but the felon was calling the police on the misdemeanors of his wayward son.

"I will never be able to forgive him [for turning me in]," says Franz. "Never! I told him that before he died. I don't think my father ever truly understood that he was there at the beginning. It was a bitter, bitter experience."

It was the beginning of a life of crime for Franz. At such a young age, he says, one then meets other young toughs in juvenile detention centers. They become one's crowd, one's friends. During Franz's periods of freedom, he found working with these new pals was the easiest and fastest way to earn money.

Franz's expression softens as he explains that he doesn't want to blame his father. He takes credit for his misbegotten life. He considers it a German peculiarity to blame others—whether it be the Jews, the Turks, the Americans, assorted "foreigners," the government, neighbors . . . He reckons a great number of Germans are in this habit due to their many years of living in an authoritarian culture and because of their late start at democracy. Germans simply don't accept enough individual responsibility, he says. It's a part of the country's economic reform problem—so many Germans still want the state to regulate their lives.

I speak to Franz of the *Dolchstosslegende*, a particularly German concept that translates as "the back-stabbing legend." Its origins were in World War I, when the German army claimed to be winning in the field, but public opposition from Communists and Socialists was applying a dagger in its back at home. Since then, the *Dolchstosslegende* has come to represent a general German proclivity to blame others for one's own misfortunes.

Still, Franz wonders if things might have been different if his father had handled this first crime differently. "But that wasn't the way Father was. He was a man who understood the world in terms of absolutes."

From that time forward, Franz spent his life in and out of jails and prisons for fights, for break-ins, for burglary, for larceny. "I squandered a large part of my life," he says. "It took a long time before I pulled myself out of the swamp by my head."

He's certain part of him was rebelling against his parents. "I wanted to show them, if you think you have a criminal son, I'll give you a criminal son." Curiously, he thought he was rebelling against his father and breaking society's rules while his father kept them. But to my mind he was growing ever more like his father; he merely lived in a society where criminal instincts no longer served the state. While Franz spent much of his life behind bars, his father remained a free man.

After his short year in investigative custody in Berlin, the dedicated Nazi led the rest of his life as a dedicated Mormon. He was most fanatic about genealogy, says Franz. That didn't surprise me much, since Hitler himself had been such a champion of the science, known in German as *Ahnenforschung*, ancestral research. But Hitler had had a different purpose. The church's goal was, among other things, to collect names for a ritual of baptizing the dead, giving non-Mormons a post-mortem chance to gain eternal glory. Hitler's purpose was more demonic—to sift those of pure race from the *Untermenschen*.

Franz says that his father, my great-uncle Erich Kramer, became a member of the Mormon high council in Berlin, and he was responsible as well for the whole mission's genealogy work.

"What a complex personality he must have had," I say.

"He was a hard man," says Franz. "The funny thing is that I miss him more than I miss my mother. We understood each other well in the end." Franz's father conceded to his son shortly before his death that it had been a mistake to turn in his son to the police for the theft of milk-bottle money. If he'd known the consequences, he told Franz, he never would have done it.

Alma, who had left Franz behind in Germany when she emigrated to America, had never expressed similar remorse. This difference in their behavior later in his life, after he gave up crime, made a great deal of difference to him.

I want to know why Franz, after so many years as a criminal, had opted to go straight. Unlike so many others who try but fail to make a clean break, he had successfully parted ways from his old crowd and stayed out of trouble for more than twenty years. As he talks, he sounds a little like the alcoholic who can't fully say why, overnight, he stopped drinking. He gave up partly because he got too old for the game—crime is a young man's sport. He also feared he was getting in too deep—on his last job he carried a gun for the first time, and for each repeat offense the punishment grew larger. He'd always known how he'd led his life was wrong, but with age his conscience also began to weigh heavier.

Having decided to reform himself, he articulately appealed to the judge for leniency at his last sentencing with a several-page explanation. He still recalls verbatim the judge's response: "What speaks in favor of a mild sentencing is that he seems truly to be sorry this time and is committed to restart his life. What speaks against him is that with his ability to express himself both verbally and in writing, he never would have had to land in a world of crime." The judge's message: if anyone this smart is a criminal, it is because he wants to be. Yet when Franz wanted to stop, he did so as well.

"It's all about will power," he says.

Franz's big breakthrough came when he interviewed the provincial governor, Bjorn Engholm, for the prison newspaper. The politician was running for re-election, and in Germany even inmates vote. Always keen to spot an opportunity, Franz asked the campaigning Engholm whether he'd ever intervene to help a convict who was genuinely trying to turn over a new leaf. He said yes, and Franz gained his backing to become a *"Freigänger,"* the sort of prisoner who can work during the day outside the prison and come back only at night to sleep. His job was as a printer in the Social Democratic publishing shop. Early release followed.

We end our chat for the day. Franz and Uschi insist on walking me home to my hotel. We stroll by the Lübeck office of the author Günter Grass, who lives outside town. Someone has applied a fresh green coat to the door to cover the recent-vintage swastika that neo-Nazis had painted on it as some crude threat to the leftist intellectual. Franz tells me that we aren't far from the church neo-Nazis recently set ablaze because the pastor had granted asylum there to a homeless Algerian family that had nowhere to live.

Oh yes, said Franz, the local synagogue had also been torched twice in the previous year. Growing unemployment is making some young Germans turn ugly. The favorite targets for neo-Nazi graffiti artists are the author Grass, the local pastor Harig and, most curiously, Boris Becker's black wife. Their names are attached to hateful graffiti and swastikas sprayed on the sides of buildings, walls, doors.

I tell my cousin that it all looks so frightening but relatively harmless, compared to what Germany has experienced before. The country's neo-Nazi arsonists and spray painters are a tiny fraction of the two million Brownshirts, including my great uncle Erich, who at one point served Hitler. They enjoy no political sanction, I say, so they seem more to me to be a reminder of an ugly past rather than a bellwether of the German future.

"Don't be so sure," says Franz. "I fear the situation could change overnight. The mood among the young is so ugly. And no one is doing anything about it. Overnight, and without warning, the far right gained 12 percent of the vote in Sachsen-Anhalt just a few weeks ago. The police tolerate the far right, just as they did in Hitler's time. What one should do is hit them over the head hard with their night sticks and lock them up."

Fortune places Franz's favorite watering hole on our path home, and I suggest we drop in for a nightcap. The bartender, a saucy woman named Martha, barks Franz and Uschi a greeting as they walk in the door. "Where the hell have you two been?"

Money has been short, and she hasn't seen them for some time. Lots of Martha's clients are in the same precarious financial situation. The best days are around the first of the month—pay day. We order up beer and shots of a reddish, fiery home-made liquor in a bottle marked "Dracula."

It seems a good moment to talk politics. Franz surprises me with news that he and Uschi are on the local board of the Social Democrats, a party they had joined five years earlier. His father, he agrees, would roll in his grave if he knew that his son had joined the left. The fact is that he and Uschi consider themselves working class, and the SPD, in their view, is the worker's party.

We talk some about music. Franz had a hearty dose of it as a child—his mother always made a big deal about their relationship to the great German composer Schumann. I tell him that my father always figured that it was the Schumann blood that made my mother's side of the family unbalanced and emotional. We laugh a bit over this. "It may sound funny to you," he says, "but there's always been something about his music that speaks to me more than other classical music that I hear."

As fate would have it, I tell him, a cellist I knew would be performing at the local concert house soon: he'd play one of Schumann's greatest works, the Cello Concerto. I volunteer to buy tickets and return for the concert, if they will come with me.

"We'd love to," says Uschi. "How long has it been since we've gone out to such a thing?"

"A long time," says Franz. "With my bad hip, and with the cost of the tickets, it's been a while."

We agree that I'll return to talk more about the family, to explore Lübeck a little bit more, and to see the concert. Something about the idea of going to this concert of music composed by our great, common ancestor amused me enormously. Two Schumanns had come together—a professional journalist and a professional criminal (retired)—and now we would sit beside each other at a performance of our most brilliant ancestor's music.

Before we part, I ask whether Franz would sign a power of attorney for me to go through archives that might give me wider insight into his father's alleged crimes. He doesn't hesitate to agree. It's no big deal to him: he figures he knows everything I'll find anyway, and he seems to be humoring me, this American journalist in search of the German soul. After all, the court ultimately cleared his father of "crimes against humanity," so how bad could the archives be?

We embrace like brothers at the door, and I walk up the stairs to my hotel room. As I turn out the light, Dracula's bloody shots running heavy through my veins, I am sure there is some moral to the story of Franz and Erich Kramer. I take out my notebook and begin to think, but then I set it down again.

Some instinct tells me that the story of my cousin and his father isn't yet ripe for the writing. With Franz's power of attorney in hand, I first would dig a little deeper into our family history.

...llay of horse and hope and
...and mangles, and scatters...
...beneath and the blue above,
...and danger, and life, and
...acca, — Lacca used to ride
mouse-gray mustang close to my
...escape and bright-belled...
...ed with joy as I looked at...

EIGHT

GERMANS AND JEWS

Many Germans say we should forgive, forget, reach some reconciliation . . .
but in Judaism reconciliation can only come from God.
    —IGNATZ BUBIS, CHAIRMAN OF THE
        CENTRAL COUNCIL OF JEWS IN GERMANY

I could say I came here because I didn't want to let Hitler win after fifty years in his
efforts to make Germany Judenfrei. It is the right point of view, but it isn't the reason
I am here . . . Why not live here? It is easier here for a Jew than in many other places.
    —VLADIMIR STOUPEL,
        RUSSIAN-JEWISH CONCERT PIANIST

Ignatz Bubis slowly scans the room from his podium. His gaze rests for a moment on several of the young men who sit quietly before him, wearing black
caps, and white shirts with conservative ties under gold-red-and-black sashes.
There is something playful, sparkling in Bubis's eyes, as if he relishes the irony

of the moment. As president of the *Zentralrat der Juden in Deutschland,* the Central Council of Jews in Germany, he prepares to speak to a student fraternity whose history reeks of anti-Semitism and German nationalism.

The fact that the *Burschenschaft Allemania* at the University of Göttingen has invited Bubis, a survivor of the Deblin ghetto, to speak to its members and their invited guests tells a story of change in the new Germany. That Bubis has accepted, however, is perhaps more telling. After all, the *Burschenschaften*—an alliance of university student fraternities across the country—were born as part of the outburst of German nationalism following the Franco-Prussian war. They embraced Hitler, for they believed he could bring the all-powerful German Reich they sought. They founded their patriotism on anti-Semitism. To be German was to be Christian, and no member was accepted who had more than one Jewish relative in the previous eight generations.

Due to their unquestioning adherence to National Socialism, the Deutsche *Burschenschaften* dissolved themselves in 1935 as part of Hitler's *Gleichschaltung* program, bringing all such independent organizations under central control. And they joined the National Socialist German Student Organization. At the time, many *Burschenschaftler* had already joined the SA and the SS.

Someone has etched the names of the fraternity's fallen on a wooden plaque that hangs over Bubis's head. Small photographs of the group's members, some in Third Reich uniform, are arranged in neat rows on the wall behind him. Yet Bubis takes no notice of them. As he opens his jaw to speak, his white dentures appear to bite at ghosts of past enemies floating before him. He is a small man, but the restless power of his personality fills the room. Wild wisps of gray and black hair rest on a partially bald head, and bushy eyebrows rise to punctuate his history lesson. He tells the fraternity brothers how the first Jewish community settled on what would become German soil in the year 321 near Cologne on the Rhine. He tells them of pogroms that then drove the Jews eastward to Poland nine centuries later. Kazimierz the Great, the Polish monarch of the time, took them in. They lived well and developed a language which came to be called Yiddish. They called themselves Ashkenazi, a term that still describes most European Jews in Israel.

"Literally translated," Bubis tells them, "Ashkenazi" means "the

Germans." For even before there was a country called *Deutschland*, the Jews of Prague, Danzig, Budapest, Vienna, Trieste, and Frankfurt all defined themselves, spoke among themselves, and wrote to each other in *Deutsch*. Most of them considered the East European cultures in which they lived to be inferior, but they aspired to be more German.

Bubis talks about how some of this might be credited to the Great Elector, a German who, in 1812, was the first European leader to grant Jews full citizenship rights, an act of remarkable tolerance given the times. The young men sit forward. Bubis has captured their interest. I imagine they expected harsher lessons from Bubis, the man who had emerged as a voice of national conscience, quoted by the German media whenever neo-Nazis or any other evil German spirits are on the warpath. But instead, he is teaching them the history that has bound Germans and Jews for centuries.

He speaks of Germany's nineteenth century as something of a golden age for Jews. Their numbers swelled, he says, as emigrants came from Eastern Europe to prosper in the German world of relative tolerance. Jews produced great art, fine novels, world-changing scientific breakthroughs. Jews accounted for a third of all German Nobel Prize winners up until World War II; half of the recipients in the area of medicine were Jews. The historian Fritz Stern says Germans and Jews in those years "complemented each other and collaborated in a singular crucible of genius."

It all ended in 1933 with Hitler's election, Bubis says. And that's where he concludes his speech and opens to questions. He chooses not to lecture them on Auschwitz, Treblinka, and Majdanek. I later ask Bubis, who has consented to let me follow him around Germany for several days, why he didn't preach to the members of this most guilty of organizations about accepting responsibility. "Why tell them what they already know?" he says. "They need more context to understand the extent to which this crime was also against themselves."

I wonder why he talks to such historically tainted groups. He shrugs. "If I never went anywhere in Germany that had bad history, then I would never go anywhere in Germany."

After his speech, Bubis takes questions. A tall, rail-thin student rises and shyly wonders whether Bubis could ever truly reconcile himself with those in the room. I immediately hear this as my own question as well.

Would you act differently toward me, less friendly toward me, Herr Bubis, if you knew that my great uncle may have been among the worst of the Nazis? Would you even have invited me to come along with you to this event—allowed me to spend this week with you?

"Why should I reconcile myself with you?" Bubis asks the student in response. "We have done nothing to each other, have we? Now if I met the murderer of my father, who died at Treblinka, I couldn't reach any reconciliation with him, and I wouldn't try."

Bubis leans forward on the rostrum. His eyes connect with those of his questioner, who remains standing. I look to the names etched on the board above his head—the fraternity's war heroes. "Guilt, you see, is individual. What we must talk about is individual responsibility, then and now. Each of you has a responsibility that grows out of your history as a whole. You are not guilty because of what was done, but you also can't deny it. A people can't live without its history. *We* can't live without *our* history."

Bubis chooses the language carefully.

We can't live . . . without *our* history.

He picks the words and subjects that connect him, the Holocaust survivor, with the sons and daughters of the perpetrators.

Another *Burschenschaft* member stands. This one is more confident, straight-backed and proud. His gold-black-red sash stretches neatly across his white dress shirt and tie. The sash's colors have a symbolic meaning. When the members of the earliest *Burschenschaft* joined together to fight against Napoleon, they wanted to create a uniform that made a unified impression. They thus dyed some of their clothes black, the gold derived from the buttons of army officers, and the red signified the fringes on their uniforms.

"Didn't the Jews in the ghetto ever wonder why it was that God had abandoned them so?" he asks. "How could they still believe in this God?"

He sits down.

I had heard this question in various forms from Germans and others over the years, often not so politely phrased. The usual subtext: *if the Jews hadn't killed Christ, surely God wouldn't have abandoned them so . . .*

I brace for a surly Bubis response, partly because of an experience several days earlier in Berlin at a breakfast for the famous American lawyer Alan Dershowitz. A German reporter had indirectly questioned Dershowitz's moral credentials. The context was the American lawyer's work defending

O. J. Simpson. Dershowitz had responded harshly that Germans were the one people in the world who hadn't any right to ask him questions about morality, no matter which generation they might represent.

Bubis, however, is more generous. "It's a question of belief," he says. The student sits as Bubis tells the room a story. "Ten Jewish rabbis in the ghetto in Vilnius created a court and held a session to rule on charges against God. They wanted to convict Him because of the sorts of crimes against humanity that He was allowing to occur. After sitting the whole night, the jury of rabbis pronounced God guilty of what was happening to the Jews. God is, after all, all-powerful. And when they were finished, one of the rabbis opened the curtain and said, 'The sun is coming up. It is time for prayer.'"

When we meet again the next morning outside Bubis's home in Frankfurt, about to set off for the day's list of appointments, I tell Bubis that I am surprised by his response to the student. I tell him that I had been troubled by the question, which I had interpreted as anti-Semitic.

Bubis shrugs. "Sometimes we can read far too much into everything. There's enough anti-Semitism in the world so that I don't need to create it where it isn't. I'd give him the benefit of the doubt. And it's not such a bad question: How can one believe in God after such a thing?" He's sure a lot of Jews have asked themselves the same question over the years. "It's a question of faith."

I smile: the leader of Germany's Jews, a survivor of the Deblin ghetto whose parents and many other relatives were lost to the Holocaust, was telling me, the great-nephew of a possible Nazi criminal, to be more tolerant toward the Germans. He believes the young particularly deserve a better shake from a suspicious world.

"The youth in Germany is more enlightened than perhaps any other European young people," he tells me as we begin the drive to Bonn. "There is more and better political education in the schools than elsewhere, and not just about the Holocaust, but generally."

I ask the question that was at the center of my search for the New Germany. Has bad history somehow made the Germans a better people?

"It isn't that they are a better people, but they try harder than most.

They are more politically educated. And a politically interested youth is much harder to seduce than their parents proved to be. Germany will take a dominant role in Europe. There's no question about that. And the youth are ready for that, though I'm not so sure about their parents."

Ignatz Bubis's election in the fall of 1992 as President of the *Zentralrat,* which looks after the political aspects of the various Jewish communities in Germany, symbolized an important shift in relations between Germans and the Jews who lived within their borders.

His predecessor, Heinz Galinski, was a tattoo-branded Auschwitz survivor, and he created a Jewish community that defined itself apart from German society and suspicious of it. He served as *Zentralrat* president for forty-three years until his death in 1992, during which time he defined his role primarily as a Jewish watchdog who barked loudly and angrily whenever Germans misbehaved. He also presided over a Jewish community of just twenty thousand that many figured would simply die out after its aging population left the stage. Germany had hardly been a magnet for young Jews.

In contrast to Galinski, Bubis had spent his life after World War II in the private sector, starting with the black market, as did so many others, and finishing in business and real estate development. He ran for Frankfurt city council in 1996, on the ticket of the Free Democratic Party, Germany's liberals, and was elected by the biggest vote that party had ever received for that office. He once described the difference with his predecessor: "Galinski is a professional Jew, and I am a Jew with a profession." The comment, made to a friend during a flight to America, was overheard by a reporter. But Bubis is honest enough to confirm it.

Galinski, whom I had interviewed on several occasions, wore the stern manner of a soldier manning the ramparts of a post-Holocaust fortress, protecting the small number of Jews who remained inside of it. The 20,000 that remained were a fraction of the 565,000 Jews who had been registered in Germany in 1925, before the population started to gradually shrink. The number lowered to 499,682 in 1933 as fear of the Nazis grew, and to 167,000 by 1941, when transports began to concentration and extermination camps, taking care of most of the rest.

Galinski defined his realm narrowly: the defense and promotion of his community's interests. Bubis applied a broader understanding from the beginning. He rushed to the site of an arson attack on a refugee home during his first days in office, a matter that technically had nothing to do with Judaism. I tell him that although Germans seem to like him just fine, I find members of his own community to be his harshest critics. They charge that he doesn't give their narrow problems enough attention, that he worries too much about his own image and ego and not enough about the dirty work of running the *Gemeinde*—their community.

"I didn't survive the ghetto to live in another one now," he bristles as we speed up the Autobahn. He speaks passionately. "If I don't get mixed up in non-Jewish issues, I don't speak with the same authority for the Jewish community on its issues. I simply wouldn't be taken as seriously. They would say: 'There goes that Jew again asking for Jewish things.' When right-wing fanatics burn down the home of Bosnian refugees or Turkish families, I can't turn my head. I don't live on this earth just as a Jew. Survivors have a responsibility for the present and the future. We can't say that we care only about Jews."

Although both Bubis and Galinski are of the Holocaust survivor generation of Jews, Bubis seems more to represent the future. A new generation of Jews with German passports has grown to be a much more integral part of German society than had been their parents, who had frequently talked in the years after the war of living "atop packed bags," ready to leave at the first sign of German misbehavior. Not only had Jews in Germany unpacked their bags and decided to stay, a whole new influx of Russian Jews was arriving with bulging suitcases, viewing Germany (however overoptimistically) as a "promised land." Their numbers had more than doubled the size of the German Jewish community to well over 60,000 registered members by the turn of the century from just 28,000 a decade earlier. The true count, as many of the newcomers haven't registered themselves, is likely to be much larger.

But beyond the numbers, the newcomers are radically altering the nature of the Jewish community and putting huge pressures on it for educational and social welfare services. In the decade since they started arriving, the community has already brought in dozens of rabbis, some temporarily and some for a longer stay. And it has invested vastly more in expanding Jewish schools, community programs, and religious teaching.

Most of the Russian arrivals are Jewish primarily in name—they came knowing little about their faith's teachings, having been raised in an officially atheistic society. A survey in a 1996 book by Julius Schoeps, called *Russische Juden in Deutschland,* shows that of the newcomers, only 8.5 percent attended religious services even occasionally in their home countries and only half that number did so regularly. Yet the Jewish community's efforts to integrate them is showing results. As of 1996, some 25.4 percent were attending services occasionally—a tripling of the previous numbers—and about half of that number again were doing so regularly. Julius Schoeps credits the Jewish communities' efforts, the influx of new rabbis and the fact that Jewishness is the only link for newcomers who had flowed in from all over the former Soviet Union: from Russia and Ukraine to Latvia and Moldova.

A sleepy and, to some extent, bitter world of German Jewry was quickly becoming a lively, active one that was accepting a whole new population of Jews, most of whom came from areas that the Holocaust never reached. Ed Serotta, my Jewish-American photographer friend, who chronicled their arrival, says, "They have given the aging and insular Jewish communities of Germany something they had not had until now, a real future."

This Jewish revival, which began two years before Bubis's election, was one of the more curious side effects of German unification. And it was started by a very short-lived democratic East German government that served in the period of time between the fall of the Berlin Wall in November 1989 and unification in October 1990. In July 1990, the East German Council of Ministers passed a resolution that "all Jews who have faced anti-Semitic repression in their homeland are to be given a speedy and unbureaucratic acceptance."

The East Germans had made the bold gesture to Jews for several reasons. They realized that while West Germany had done much for the Jews in paying reparations, East Germany had done very little. The country lived by the myth that it was a country that also was made up of victims, the Communists, and West Germany was the successor regime to the Nazis that owed the debts. At the same time, the chief Soviet rabbi was delivering reports of new violence against Jews in his country, accounts that were faithfully reported in a newly free East German press.

After unification, German authorities opted not to reverse the eastern German resolution. After all, how could one of the first acts of a unified Germany be to undo liberal legislation toward Jews? But they predictably bureaucratized the process a bit. Jews could still come to Germany as *Kontingentflüchtlinge*, quota refugees under the Geneva Convention on refugees, but they would have to go through a more orderly processing at German consulates. One of the ironies of this process is that the Jews had now to prove that they somehow belonged to the German *Kulturkreis*—cultural crisis— meaning that under Article 116 of the German Basic Law, or constitution, they had to prove by their "behavior and consciousness" the will to belong to German *Volkstum* and no other *Volkstum*.

In the rush of Soviet and then Russian Jews to take advantage of the possibility, no one focused much on the irony that Jews, in order to gain the permanent residence in the country of the Holocaust, had to prove that they were culturally German.

That was merely a technicality. What was important was to give the powerful message that these Jews *wanted* to come to Germany, and that Helmut Kohl backed the open-door policy despite Israeli opposition. These Jews, Israel reckoned, ought to be coming to Zion. Kohl, however, understood that he had an opportunity of historic dimensions. Says Wolfgang Gibowski, a government press spokesman, "What could be a more convincing bill of health for the New Germany than the fact that so many thousands of Jews wanted to live there?"

It was as if an unbelievably forgiving God was giving the Germans another chance.

The spotlight illuminates Mark Aizikowitsch's charcoal beard, the wisps of his unruly black hair, the bear's body wrapped in black—shoes, shirt and pants. His expression is neutral; he doesn't move. He stands against a black background, elbow on a black piano, candles providing the only light except for the spot. The sell-out audience in the darkness of the small Hackesches Hof Theater holds its breath.

Aizikowitsch's face explodes in a smile, so infectious that the audience smiles with him, not really knowing why. He breaks out in a cheerful Yiddish song about a tailor and his everyday problems. The language has enough familiar words that the German audience gets the meaning.

The audience sways, smiles, laughs, applauds. They're holding one of the hotter tickets in Berlin these days, to Aizikowitsch's "Russian-Yiddish Night." It is all part of a curious revival of Jewish culture in a city that just a few decades earlier had done everything possible to wipe out Jews altogether.

Concerts of Klezmer music, Yiddish folk tunes, play to full houses, often performed by German groups who don't include a single Jew. Germans flock to theater productions of Yiddish plays they can only partly understand: Aizikowitsch's own production of *Tevye*, the original play that later became *Fiddler on the Roof*, is a favorite and now even tours Holland from its German base. Local Berlin listings include scores of exhibitions over the year on Jewish history and culture and a highly popular annual Jewish Cultural Festival put on by the Berlin community.

No one forces all this on the Germans—the market demands it.

The setting of Aizikowitsch's performance is also appropriate.

The theater rests at the back of one of several courtyards in a turn-of-the-century complex on Rosenthaler Street known as the *Hackeschen Höfe*. It was owned and run by a Jewish investor, and many Jewish families lived there. In 1916, the Jewish Girl's Club and the Jewish Women's Associate of Berlin rented some rooms. Christmas and the Feast of Tabernacles were both celebrated there.

The Jewish owner, Jacob Michael, was one of Germany's richest men and most important money lenders. He was forced to emigrate to America in 1939, a year after the Nazis confiscated most of his property. The story of what happened thereafter underlines just how intense Jewish connections were to Berlin. The *Hackeschen Höfe* were sold in a compulsory auction to Emil Köster AG, apparently an Aryan enterprise. But Jacob Michael continued to manage and own it through front men. After the war, the *Höfe* turned as gray and desolate as the rest of East Berlin. But after the complicated legal situation was sorted out, property rights went back to the Michael family in 1993, and their heirs in turn sold the complex to a property syndicate that developed it into one of the most glittering attractions of Germany's new capital.

The rebirth of the complex has coincided with the renaissance of the entire neighborhood, a part of eastern Berlin that was once home to many of the one hundred thousand East European Jews who flocked there at the end of the nineteenth century, pushed West by hate campaigns. (This was the second such migration of Jews to Germany, the first coming in the seventeenth century as a result of Ukrainian pogroms beginning in 1648 and the Russian-Swedish War of 1655.)

The neighborhood came to be known as the *Scheunenviertel*, the barn-house quarter, a name that originated at the end of the seventeenth century. Jews settled there two centuries later because the city's first synagogue was established there. It was the only public synagogue until the huge, golden-domed New Synagogue was built in 1866 on the nearby Oranienburg Street—a monument to the supreme confidence with which Jews then lived in the city.

Other buildings nearby have links to Jewish history that aren't recorded on historic plaques: a house where the Gestapo had gathered elderly Jews before shipping them off to Auschwitz, a hospital where doctors hid some Jews, the site of the first Jewish graveyard to be destroyed (which now holds only a tombstone for the philosopher Moses Mendelssohn). And against one building's high outside wall, an artist has placed, in large letters, the names of the Jews on the floors where they had lived before their emigration or deportation. The ghosts co-mingle with the living. The neighborhood is one of the hippest and most haunted in Berlin, with bars and restaurants, many of which suggest and even promote the Jewish past.

Mark Aizikowitsch is part of the new wave of Jewish immigration, having arrived in Berlin in 1993, exactly sixty years after Hitler pushed through the first laws restricting Jews' civil liberties. Aizikowitsch learned quickly that Germany had little market appetite for a portly and aging Russian pop singer and actor; he would later invite me over to his apartment to show me a film from the days when his pop group filled stadiums in places like Estonia.

First he tried to stage a cabaret act, seizing upon another bit of Berlin's history. But it apparently wasn't what the market wanted from him. He discovered his future in the Jewish past when he attended a Yiddish song concert at the Gethsemane church in the eastern Berlin neighborhood of Prenzlauerberg. "It was mediocre, but the Germans loved it," he tells me over cappuccino at a café across the courtyard from the theater. "I didn't know that many Yiddish songs at the time, but I knew a few. And I knew I could do better."

Yiddish, after all, had been his mother tongue in the small village of Poltova, where he grew up in Eastern Ukraine. He had at last found a market value in this unusual upbringing. In Germany, of all places.

Aizikowitsch keeps the show moving, quickly shifting moods from one number to another. And with each song, he cuts a little closer to the German bone, until he ends the show with a signature tune about a rabbi and his conversation with God about the misfortune that He has heaped upon the Jewish people.

After the performance, Aizikowitsch talks about his new home and the philosemitism that keeps his family afloat. "I think there must be anti-Semitism in Germany, but I haven't noticed it. They are against Turks, Vietnamese, Africans. But as a Jew I notice nothing special aimed at me."

On the contrary, I say, people seem entranced by him, seduced by him. It seems to me they almost love him too much.

We ponder the reasons. Perhaps it is because young Germans are relieved to discover in Aizikowitsch some of the culture their parents or grandparents were unable to rub out. Perhaps they want to learn something of this culture, to try to understand what it was the Nazis wanted to exterminate. (Here Aizikowitsch's show will only mislead them, for German Jews had assimilated to such a large degree that by the '30s only a minority of the oldest Jews from Russia still spoke Yiddish. Ironically, Aizikowitsch is reviving a culture that had hardly existed here before.)

There was also the possibility that Germans instinctively bonded with a culture that had been so much a part of their society.

"And guilt?" I ask. "Does it play a role?"

"There certainly is an element of guilt in any German's relationship to a Jew," he says. "We are like pet animals who you have at home. We are loved, but we have our place." German society, for example, indirectly required

Aizikowitsch to become more rather than less Jewish to make it in the German market. Certainly in the 1920s, more Jews worked in cabarets than at Klezmer music.

"I will have to watch for many, many years to really know what is inside these Germans. I look at them in my audience and sometimes wonder how they live with themselves—when you do something that bad, it has to go into your head. Into the head of your country. You never really get rid of it. How have they been able to sleep all these years? They have to dream. We all dream. So what are their dreams? Their nightmares? The dead people must come back to them again and again."

Yet the singer has no doubt that Russia poses a far greater danger to Jews today than Germany. "There are too many Jews in government," he says. He names them. "When the Russians start looking for scapegoats, they won't have to look very far. We are much safer here in Germany."

I speed with Ignatz Bubis from Frankfurt to Bonn at nearly a hundred twenty miles per hour in an armored Mercedes being led by another armored Mercedes (three bodyguards in all, all specially trained federal police officers assigned to Bubis). The Jewish leader speaks with bemusement about the protection he enjoys.

He figures the police are there more to protect Germany than him. What could be worse for Germany's image in world opinion than some lunatic killing the country's most prominent Jew? They have probably never worked such long hours: Bubis fills each day, from dawn to night, with speeches, meetings, openings of exhibits, political negotiations. One has the impression of an aging man rushing to achieve something before his days are up.

But what exactly? I ask Bubis as he fields calls on the two telephones in his car: booking flights, providing press interviews, arranging appointments, playing politics.

He isn't sure what makes him lead such a peripatetic life. "If you figure it out, tell me."

I muse that perhaps he sees that he must use every minute in his day to help reform a people that had gone so astray, to shape the young generation of a country that now is again one of great influence in the world. It's a nice bit of reasoning, he agrees, and I may use it if I like. But Bubis in this respect is more a man of action than reflection.

Just a few months earlier, Bubis had been elected to the Frankfurt city council. It had been his personal popularity that had won him the seat—his Free Democratic Party hadn't been so successful in the district for years. Bubis is most encouraged that it was the young vote that had pushed him over the top: the elders still weren't ready to throw their votes behind a Jew.

Bubis pulls a calendar from his pocket as we pull up to the museum and tells me what's ahead for our day: a photo exhibit in Bonn on Jews in Germany (put on, coincidentally, by my friend Ed Serotta); a private meeting to solve a Jewish community problem; a speech at a high school in Essen; introductory remarks for an exhibit of Chinese woodcuts done by a Holocaust refugee in Shanghai; and finally a sermon at a Protestant church in the evening. That amuses him the most.

Television cameras follow Bubis as he walks through the exhibit at the Museum of German History with Serotta, who is showing Bubis photographs from his book *Jews, Germany, Memory.*

Bubis stands for some time before photos of the older generation of Jews in Germany. Most of them, like Bubis, had come from Eastern Europe in the first days after the war to the displaced persons camps. Genuinely German Jews had all but disappeared, save the couple of thousand who had survived in hiding. It wasn't easy to be a newly arrived Jew in the land of the perpetrators. Jews around the world viewed them with such disdain that international Jewish organizations wouldn't even recognize the Jewish community in West Germany. What self-respecting Jew would live in such a place?

To understand the mixed emotions with which Jews lived in Germany one only has to look at the name of Bubis's ruling body for the Jewish community. Established after the war, it decided to call itself the "Central Council of Jews in Germany," rather than the "Central Council of German Jews," as it had been known when it was established in 1914. With world Jewry frowning on them, Germany's Jews found financial support mostly from German state and local governments.

Bubis stops by some photos of German Jews who had moved elsewhere during the Third Reich. They had become so German that they remained more German than Jewish in their adopted homes of the Diaspora. The subhead in Serotta's book rightly says: "Jewish was our religion. German is what we were." They were so German, in fact, that they had looked down their noses at the *Ostjuden*, the recently arrived Jews of Eastern Europe, and for a time couldn't fathom that Hitler was identifying them with these Jews in a way they never would have identified themselves.

As Fritz Stern had written: "It has become a common view to hold that German Jewry somehow represents the epitome of craven assimilation and submission; implicit in this view is that the fate of German Jewry and character were somehow linked, and that character was therefore historically culpable."

The reasons Jews remained in Germany after the war—or even returned there—were seldom noble. "And I wasn't an exception," says Bubis. Some hadn't the energy to move on, a few hadn't any other language except German, still others had property or businesses to inherit. Some, like Bubis, tried Israel for a time but felt more comfortable in Germany than in that foreign country of deserts, dry winds, and threatening new wars.

Bubis recalls his short stay at the Displaced Persons camp at Schlachtensee in Berlin. He says it was so odd to see soldiers in uniform posted outside the camp and its barbed wire to protect the Jews rather than to force them to remain inside. "The daily rations of white bread, milk, butter, marmalade, and meat were more than anyone could eat," he says.

Yet Bubis couldn't sleep behind barbed wire again. He moved to Berlin with the help of one hundred dollars given to him by a well-off uncle in the same camp. He turned that money into thirty thousand Reichsmark on the black market and then moved into the National Hotel, paying three months advance rent on a new life.

"I can't tell you the exact time I decided to stay in Germany," he says. Few Jews of his generation ever *decided*, they just *stayed*, he says. "Over time, I continually pushed off my plans to move abroad and start anew. In the first years after the war, I said to myself time and again: first you have to earn some money, then attend university and only after that can you emigrate. I can't tell you I felt comfortable in my first years in Germany. It was more that I didn't want to admit my feelings to myself. I didn't allow myself to feel anything."

Bubis's daughter, Naomi, had just published a book entitled *Shtika*, about the curious flight from the past that Jews of her father's generation undertook. The victims, like the perpetrators, had much they didn't want to remember. As he has grown older, Bubis thinks more and more about how he watched his father being taken away from the ghetto to his death. Should he have gone with his father? Why did he survive but his father did not?

So many questions had so long been repressed. It wasn't just the Germans who didn't think about the past. It was also the Jews.

"And by the time my daughter had written this book," he says, "I still hadn't told her my story."

For a moment, I consider telling Bubis about my great uncle Erich. Perhaps this was the right time for it, yet I was more comfortable as an American reporter than as a person of German blood. Why complicate matters?

We reboarded the Mercedes and drove on to our next appointment.

I'd known Rabbi Andrew Baker for some time, a gentle but determined man who ran the American Jewish Committee's European programs.

I ask Andy to take me to a spot in Berlin where he, as a Jew, feels most comfortable. He chooses Weissensee Cemetery. It's the city's largest Jewish burial ground. Its 115,000 graves over more than forty square hectares make it the largest Jewish cemetery in Europe.

After we stroll through its red stone gates, an attendant provides us with black yarmulkes that we perch on our heads. We walk down the plush, tree-lined paths of a place that is more a densely wooded forest than a graveyard—old trees reach so high and grow so close that their branches and leaves block out the sun. The lane leads to a wide, forged iron gate behind which rests the *Trauerhalle*—the mourning hall—for the six million Jewish dead of the Holocaust.

We don't stop at this memorial, for that wasn't Rabbi Baker's purpose in bringing me here. What moves him are the more "normal" aspects of the cemetery, the way it represents a society of Jews who had "made it." They felt secure enough to build grand family mausoleums of pink, gray, and white marble and granite. Many sites were more monuments than graves. This was not a population trying to hide, not a group fearing a pogrom. The names and titles showed the extent to which they had become part of the country's firmament: Hermann Tietz, who created Hertie department stores; Adolf Jandor, who owned the competition, Kaufhaus des Westens; publishing barons, factory owners, leading bankers, politicians, and lawyers.

And the more modest gravestones of the back plots, many now crooked, worn, overgrown with ivy, contained evidence of a society of depth and reach: doctors, shopkeepers, tailors, craftsmen, simple workers. We quietly walk through this labyrinth of geometrically ordered rows of graves, criss-crossed by main and secondary paths, a magical forest steeped in the sadness and joy of memory. As Ed Serotta writes in his book: "They saved, they planned, they dreamed."

But they did much more than that. They also changed the way Jews looked at themselves in the modern age.

"For me," says Andy Baker as we walk, "there were always two Germanys. The Germany of the Holocaust and the Germany of modern Jewish philosophy: Moses Mendelssohn, Franz Rosenzweig, Hermann Cohen, Martin Buber. They posed the critical and philosophical question: how does Judaism adopt itself to modernity, how do you reconcile being Jewish with being part of the Enlightenment? It all started at the end of the eighteenth century with Mendelssohn in Germany."

As we look for some of the graves of the more prominent Jews, Andy Baker talks about the lasting changes that German Jews introduced in religious worship during this time of reform. They built synagogues that looked more like churches. They placed the reader's desk at the front instead of in its traditional place at the center, with worshippers circling around. They added organ music and choirs—anathema to more orthodox Jews. They moved worship in many places to Sunday.

The rabbi looks about the cemetery and shakes his head. "This is so normal, as if it never happened. If there had been no Holocaust, this place where we are standing would look no different. There's no other place in Jewish Berlin where you can say that."

And that was the reason, he says, he wanted to bring me there.

No one really knows why the Nazis didn't destroy this graveyard as they did so many others. Perhaps it was simply because it wasn't dead Jews that concerned them. Nazis even brought members of the Red Cross here as well as foreign dignitaries to show their intentions toward Jews weren't so bad. And, after all, one needed a place to bury Jews. The only time the gravestones were damaged is said to have been during World War II when the Gestapo discovered Jews hiding in the tombs.

Andy Baker came to know the ways of German Jews intimately when he landed a job at a synagogue in Chicago after being ordained a rabbi. It had been founded in the last half of the nineteenth century by German Jews. "Even in Chicago, a couple of generations later, they still had certain German characteristics. Punctuality, for instance. If the service started at eleven, it damn well started at eleven, and not at eleven-oh-two. People were up in arms if you were late. It had a lot of high church stuff. Very Protestant. No guitar-playing rabbi there. No yarmulkes. The major service, with the full choir, was on Sunday morning. No children running around and screaming the way it is at so many other Jewish services. Fewer people jabbering. Here they listened. It was a cerebral congregation."

Baker's knowledge that the German-Jewish past consists of more than the Holocaust gives him a more nuanced view of the country than that of most American Jews. He wants to believe in the New Germany, but he fears signs that a more assertive, post-unification Germany is forgetting the debts it still owes for its Holocaust crimes.

What occupies him as we walk through the graveyard is how fiercely the German government of Helmut Kohl is resisting his appeal that it give East European Jews the same deal that it had given other Holocaust victims. These Jews had a double misfortune: by landing on the Soviet side of the continent, they lost both political freedom and access to postwar German reparations to individual victims.

After the collapse of the Soviet bloc, Bonn began to settle with each former Soviet bloc country through a series of state-to-state treaties, which included one-time, lump-sum payments to the government involved that would then be spread over a number of uses, from medical care to monuments. When Baker and the AJC protested, on the long-accepted principle of individual reparations, the Germans argued that they had already paid the princely sum of 100 billion dollars in payments over the years to one Jewish source or another. They were unwilling in the newly tough budget situation to commit themselves to more recurring charges.

When the AJC protested, German officials produced copies of the individual agreements signed with the governments involved. "I felt a little like I do when my kids come to me with a coloring book. They scribble a little bit on each page and then bring it back and proudly say, 'See, I'm finished.' Yet they haven't paid any attention to whether they've done it properly."

Baker wanted a more comprehensive coloring. And he wanted it in a hurry since survivors were dying off. But chancellery officials refused again, repeating the government position and the amount of money they had paid over the years. Baker was of the opinion that someone at a very high level had decided to draw the line, had decided it was time for Germany to stop its guilt payments. A quite senior government official later conceded to me that this was precisely the case. The new Germany was willing to take in a new wave of Jewish emigration from Russia, but at the same time it was trying to say no to what one of Helmut Kohl's people called "that eternal blackmail" of international Jewish groups.

"At some point, they have to treat us like a normal country," the senior official said.

Baker and the AJC launched an offensive against the chancellor, which was all the more dramatic considering their close relations of the past. The AJC's willingness to work with Bonn and to promote closer German-Jewish relations had won the organization the monicker of being "Kohl's favorite Jews" among Bonn officials. That was changing fast.

The AJC printed full page advertisements in the *New York Times* and the *International Herald Tribune* that showed a survivor of the Riga Ghetto beside a veteran of the Latvian Legionnaires and Waffen-SS saluting Hitler. The ad then posed the question: "Guess who gets a war victim's pension from the German government?" (A German documentary program *Panorama* had reported in January 1997 that the German government had paid more than DM 600 million in "victim pensions" to some 50,000 former members of military units described as criminals by the Nuremberg Tribunals, while Jewish victims at that point hadn't received any individual compensation.)

Baker was surprised by the German resistance to the East European reparations partly because the country had built up such a solid reputation for du-
tifully paying the price of its history. "People were dumbfounded partly
because of the perceived reality that Germany has dealt responsibly with its
past. We aren't surprised by disappointing responses from the Austrians, the
Swiss, and the French. But from the Germans it's more unusual. What
Germans were telling us is that it was time to draw a line. It was arbitrary, but
they felt they had to draw it and did so."

A second AJC advertisement followed on August 16, a reaction to the
fact that the first campaign evoked little more than promises to "reconsider
the matter," according to President Roman Herzog. This time a letter drafted
by the AJC and signed by eighty-two American senators appealed for German
pensions to be paid to East European Holocaust survivors.

Baker was trying to tell his German friends that one shouldn't draw a line
between the past and the present but instead build a bridge between the two.
For a unified Germany, he felt it was essential to show the same sensitivity
toward Holocaust issues that West Germany had done. "I told them: is this
really a matter of closing the book, ending the chapter of one period, or can
you make this a bridge to the new Germany? I think this is a real choice you
have." In the end, the government relented—but more due to pressure than
any conviction or agreement with Rabbi Baker's reasoning.

Rabbi Baker directs me to the back of the cemetery, where we find what
he considers the most telling section: the military burial ground. If anything
shows just how much Jews belonged to Germany, this was it. On each of the
opposite sides of a narrow aisle rest four long rows of uniform, gray stones.
Etched into them were the names, ranks, and the date of death of Jewish soldiers and officers: Musketeer Alfred Lewin, May 1917; Cannonier Arthur
Blumenheim, 1918; staff veterinarian Dr. Berthold Jacobi, December 1917;
Private Julius Lichtenstein. . . . Only one of the gravestones is lettered in
Hebrew. "I wonder how hard that was to pull off," says Baker. The fact is that
Jews in those days were more interested in proving their Germanness than
fighting over gravestone lettering.

At the end of the row of graves rests a memorial for "our fallen sons."
When Jews had been asked to aid their "Fatherland" during the First World

War, some one hundred thousand Jewish men enlisted and twelve thousand died fighting—a surprisingly high number of soldiers, considering the total number of registered Jews in Germany was under six hundred thousand. A surprising 87 percent of the enlisted served on the front. Some two thousand were officers, some thirty thousand were decorated.

Germany's Jews didn't just go along with the First World War, they embraced it as an opportunity to finally show Germany and Germans how loyal they were to their country and culture. And they could fight against the Russians who were infamous at the time for their brutal anti-Semitism. The Kaiser's proclamation of *Ich kenne nur noch Deutsche*—I know only Germans— became their banner and with it they proudly marched to the front.

Letters, poems, and songs written by German Jews about their role in World War I show they saw in their participation in the war liberation from centuries of brutal discrimination. They had hoped that they would be treated as equals in a future Germany, whose culture so many of them had embraced. One letter from a soldier is particularly memorable: "The German Jews were and are German to the bone. They have become an inseparable part of the German *Volk*. It goes without saying that they would do everything for their Fatherland . . ."

The irony was a tragic one—that many had been so willing to sacrifice their lives for a Fatherland which a few years later would disown and sacrifice them.

On our way out, we pass a part of Weissensee that doesn't fit in. It is an expanse of fresh lawn that breaks up the landscape of old stone burial sites down dirt trails that are overgrown with trees and brush. In the lawn rest a set of newly closed graves. We look more closely and see that many of the names are etched into the stone in the Cyrillic letters of the Russian language. These are the graves for natural deaths of a new population, following years during which Weissensee had virtually no new burials. Each has a small gravestone at the head of a site adorned with flowers, a more Christian than Jewish practice, where the placing of stones, representing eternal memory, is the tradition. But most Russian Jews in Germany are only just beginning to learn their Jewish traditions.

Rabbi Baker smiles. "I didn't know they were still burying here. In an odd way, it's a nice feeling to see this. It's funny to think of a gravestone as a sign of new life. But that's what it is."

An increasingly typical night out in the New Berlin:

A Russian-Jewish concert pianist, Vladimir Stoupel, is already waiting for me when I arrive at a Lebanese restaurant in a fashionable part of Berlin's Wilmersdorf district. It is early summer, and black-cloaked Hasidic Jews with their *payess* stroll past. Vladimir explains that they are leaving services at the nearby Joachimsthaler Street synagogue.

They look strangely normal—or normally strange—among the Berlin summer night traffic of chattering teens, entwined couples in light summer dress, and men in business suits, jackets hung over their shoulders. In Berlin, the curious has become everyday. No one in the restaurant pays any particularly attention to the Orthodox Jews as we order our mixed Middle Eastern plate of mixed appetizers.

Vladimir Stoupel didn't come to Berlin in the way of most recent Russian immigrants. He had been living in Paris when the Wall fell, married to a French woman. He then changed wives and cities, unwittingly becoming part of German demographic change. As he tells the abridged version of his life story, he tilts his head toward the nearby sound of a familiar music, the sound of the Hebrew language.

At the table beside ours, an Israeli artist who was born in Germany is jabbering with his Algerian Jewish wife about his new exhibit down the street. He shows the program of another show in Leipzig the following week that will include works from his family's three generations of German Jewish artists. It is part of a retrospective on the city's Jewish heritage.

After a time, the restaurant's co-owner, a Lebanese Christian, joins us as well. He speaks Arabic to the Israeli artist's wife, who he says reminds him of his aunt back in Beirut. After all, we are all Semitic, right? he laughs. Perhaps even related back some centuries. They all laugh. They make an appointment to meet and talk on another evening.

I take in the scene: the Orthodox Jews strolling by, the Israeli artist flogging his work, the Arab restaurant owner refilling our glasses with thick

Lebanese red wine, the concert pianist shifting from French and German to English and bits of Hebrew. The conversation is animated, full of laughter and self-deprecating humor, on a cool summer night with an open window on a vibrant city.

"Are you sure we aren't in Tel Aviv?" I whisper to Vladimir.

"Quite," he says.

He'll get to that later.

Vladimir reckons that he first recognized he was Jewish—and that it wasn't necessarily a good thing to be—when he was a child and his family was on vacation in Ukraine. A fat peasant woman walked up from behind them and spat at him: "So little, and already a Jew."

"I asked my mother afterward what that meant, to be a Jew. She didn't answer then, and no one has truly been able to answer me since. My mother always tried hard not to be Jewish. She dyed her hair blonde. I never liked it. If you have an identity, you keep it. I knew that instinctively even then. And Father was completely assimilated. There was nothing Jewish about them. It was better not to be Jewish."

"Why?" I ask.

Vladimir shot me the look of someone who can't believe I can be so naive as to ask such a question. "Children beat me up at school because I was Jewish."

"How did it happen?"

"They just said, 'Let's go beat up the Jew,' and then they did it. After a while, I learned jujitsu. I learned two maneuvers quite well." He stands and shows me one, how to twist a larger man's arm so that it is pulled out of its socket. "The other is a quick kick to the groin." I draw back as he begins to demonstrate.

"You must be two times as good at whatever you do as a Jew in Russia to get anywhere. If they need to choose between two people for something, whether it's a job or a concert, they will always pick the non-Jew. That's a big burden to carry on your shoulders. I always knew I had to be better. That pushed me to develop my talents. But it was also neurotic. I became better because I had to. It was overcompensation. The historic overcompensation of our people."

Yet in Germany, he concedes, the opposite is often true. One experiences a bonus for being Jewish in Germany, a reverse prejudice that often allows Jews to get ahead.

The Israeli artist chimes in, arguing that he's never experienced such a bonus, but in the same breath he brags that his work sells better in Germany than anywhere else—his agent stages from fifteen to twenty exhibits in Germany annually. He insists it is because his style speaks to Germans, but that it has nothing to do with his distributor's quite conscious effort to market him as an Israeli artist. "I'm sure that plays no role at all," Vladimir winks.

Vladimir says the unrequited love that Jews had for Germans for so many years, before the Holocaust, has now been perversely reversed. "When they exterminated the Jews," he says, "they exterminated a big part of themselves. At that time they saw in Jews all their worst characteristics: greed, miserliness, and so on. They were also envious and jealous of the Jews, who were so successful. They wanted their success. In one way, they profited by getting rid of the Jews. By seizing all their property, they took much more than they ever repaid through reparations. But now they have noticed that they also lost something that has been hard to replace: humor, art, science. Before, the Germans saw only the bad Jewish characteristics. Now they only see the good: Jews are lively. Jews are witty. Jews are musical. Jews are artistic. All the German complexes about what they are not have been turned on their head and projected onto Jews. Above all, many Germans say to me that Jews are lively and Germans are dead. And I'm afraid that it's true. There are so few lively Germans."

He says great German lovers, for example, are few.

"Jews are better lovers than Germans?"

"Why do you think there are so many blonde Aryan girls hanging out at the Cafe Oren?" It was the restaurant, owned by the Jewish community, that sat beside the New Synagogue on the Oranienburgerstrasse in the *Scheunenviertel*. A large number of Nordic-looking women—no doubt they are gentiles—always seem to populate the place.

"They want to meet a Jewish man," says Vladimir. "They say we are better lovers. That we last longer. Perhaps it is because we are circumcised. But I also think that there is something psychological to it."

"What better way," I wink, "to confirm to themselves that Jews are still alive."

Vladimir smiles at the black humor, "Are you sure you aren't Jewish?"

I ask Vladimir why he has settled in Germany; he sees so much in the German character that disturbs him. In France, for example, he says he is merely a pianist. In Germany, however, he has become a Russian-*Jewish* pianist. He is proud of his French passport, because he considers the country more of a melting pot. Yet on the other hand he is happy enough to take advantage of his Jewishness—each year he organizes much of the classical portion of the annual Jewish Cultural Days in Berlin.

"I could say I came here because I didn't want to let Hitler win after fifty years in his efforts to make Germany *Judenfrei*. It is the right point of view, but it isn't the reason I am here. Lots of Jews who live here do very well. They are successful. They make children. They do business. Why not live here? It is easier here for a Jew than in many other places. And was France that much better in history? Was the government of Vichy more enlightened than the government of Berlin?"

Vladimir, like Rabbi Baker, also has his "other" Germany. For Andy Baker, it was the one of Jewish philosophy. For Vladimir, it is the one of music. "For me, there will always be another Berlin. If countries were hotels that were judged according to their music, Germany would get four stars. I had to make my name in Germany to be taken seriously in France as a musician. Now that I live here I also get better concert dates when I travel abroad in Europe. The history was more than Hitler. For me there was also Brahms, Bach, Clara Wieck Schumann, Felix Mendelssohn. . . ." Stoupel notes that of the seven orchestras in Berlin, four of them are directed by Jews.

As we leave the restaurant, Vladimir is laughing. I ask why.

"The Israeli artist, he asked if you were Jewish."

"Me?"

"Yes, he didn't think you were uptight enough to be German."

As an American with thick German blood coursing through my veins, I find myself disturbingly complimented by this artist's comment. All things considered, I would prefer to bear the burden of the Jew to that of the German. One is liberating, that of moral outrage and survival, while the other is confining, that of inherited guilt.

I envied Vladimir his Jewishness, but I was sure he didn't envy any of my Germanness. I wondered if that wasn't what was really driving the philosemitism of the Germans: they weren't only envious of the victim's culture, they also somehow wanted to discard some piece of themselves as they embraced it. Is that what drove so many German youth to kibbutz work in Israel or to Klezmer concerts in Berlin?

Yet the overcompensation for the past didn't trouble me. All things considered, wasn't it better for Germans to celebrate the arrival in their city of a pianist like Vladimir Stoupel or a Yiddish singer like Mark Aizikowitsch than to throw bricks through Jewish shop windows?

Ignatz Bubis heard the bad news the way that he gets so much of his information—by mobile phone in his car while racing from a political meeting to a public speech. It was hard for him to fathom: a town council in Gollwitz, a village of five hundred in the eastern German state of Brandenburg, had voted unanimously to reject district plans to house sixty Russian-Jewish immigrants in a local building that had lain empty for three years and would have been fully renovated for their use.

Worse yet, the governor of the state, Manfred Stolpe, had publicly expressed understanding for the good people of Gollwitz; he called them "completely normal citizens."

"So I called him up and said that in 1933 it was also completely normal citizens." Bubis rages at the memory of the conversation.

So did the Gollwitz experience surprise Bubis?

"No. Such things are part of everyday normality. But what surprised me was that the town council, these seven people, voted unanimously. I thought that in the old East Germany you wouldn't just have right-wingers in the town council. Certainly, there must have been PDS, SPD people. But apparently they are all independents there. That's what they said."

So what lies behind Gollwitz?

"Xenophobia, *par excellence*. They would have reacted the same way if Turks came, or anyone not like them."

So it's not a sign of rising anti-Semitism?

"It's all the same for me. I don't differentiate between xenophobia and anti-Semitism. The people would have responded the same way even if it didn't have to do with Jews, if it were other 'foreigners.' But does that make it any better?"

So is the country becoming less rather than more tolerant with a new generation? Bubis doesn't think so. He insists that young Germans tend to be considerably more tolerant than their parents. Yet he fears a parallel trend—that with unification Germans are now less shy about voicing opinions that had previously been taboo. He says that the number of anti-Semitic letters he receives at his Frankfurt office hasn't increased, but the number has increased that carry return addresses with their true names.

"Two years ago, the Gollwitz people didn't think any differently than they do now, but they wouldn't have dared to say it. Now they dare. It has become part of daily discourse to say, 'We won't any longer allow others to dictate how we should behave ourselves.' "

I organize a visit to the town to draw my own conclusions.

No one comes upon Gollwitz by accident. From the newly paved highway nearby, a small road of rough cobblestones leads a couple of hundred meters to a town that seems untouched by unification. No one outside Germany ever would have heard of Gollwitz if the district council hadn't moved to house Jewish immigrants there.

A rust-corroded sign on the outskirts of town provides an odd greeting: "Dumping of any sort of refuse is strictly forbidden across the entire area of the community of Gollwitz."

I wonder for a brief moment whether the sign has a political subtext.

It has taken some time to get the mayor, Andreas Heldt, to agree to talk, given the storm of bad publicity about his town that followed the council vote. He speaks of Gollwitz as a place that was first mentioned in history in 1375 but that had been little noticed by the outside world until now.

The idea to move Russian Jews to Gollwitz had been born because bureaucrats back at the Brandenburg state capital, in Potsdam, were running out of space for all the Russian newcomers. Brandenburg had had only three Jews left shortly before unification, compared to 8,442 (not counting neighboring Berlin), when the population was at its height in 1925. By 1999, the state was again home to some two thousand Jews and counting. Yet as far as anyone knew, Gollwitz had never had a Jewish resident.

"For weeks we were living in an emergency situation," says the mayor. "All day long, from morning at eight until late at night, the phone never stopped ringing. One journalist after another wanted to know what the town had decided and why. I had to get up at four in the morning in order to get any work done at all."

The facts were that the town council had voted against a plan to take the Jewish settlers because of "the threat to security and order." The locals had read enough about Russian mafias and growing crime rates to conclude that they didn't want anything to do with these newcomers. Worse yet, the place where Gollwitz would house the Jews was the town's most notable architectural feature, a manor on the only small rise in Gollwitz, next to the town's Protestant church. The town council had voted against taking fifty to sixty Russian Jews in an empty mansion in the middle of town that locals call "the Castle"—the closest thing Gollwitz has to a historical attraction.

District officials falsely figured the town might welcome the settlers because government investment to spruce up the manor would follow. Gollwitz needed the money. Though Westerners had invested in cities and property all around Gollwitz, the town remained one of eastern Germany's many spots that had been disregarded by investors.

Mayor Andreas Heldt doesn't look the image of the right-wing, small-town politician that had been portrayed in the press, and certainly not the bitter eastern German racist many Westerners expect.

For Heldt, unification had been a financial windfall, for it brought back to his family a large piece of farm property that the state had turned into a co-op. He sold it quickly to a developer who built a shopping center on it about two kilometers out of town, and he's been well-off ever since. He invested much of the money on a year and a half of travels around the world, seeing places that the Wall and his country's travel restrictions had put off-limits for so long. He made a point of telling me that he'd been to Israel because the country had fascinated him for so long.

The mayor, it seems, is providing his own transition for talking about the Gollwitz scandal. He wants me to know that he is a sophisticated, intelligent man, and not some neo-Nazi just waiting to burn a new lot of Jews. To this end, Heldt tells me he was in Australia shortly before the town council vote, spending considerable time with aborigines. And after his world trip in 1991, he even studied management in West Germany.

He describes himself as a student of the science of administration. He is in the process of writing a dissertation on "modern performance incentives in public administration." The underlying message: he's not only worldly, he's also progressive.

He concedes that his studies had brought a change of his values. German democracy simply isn't democratic enough—not enough power at the grassroots. If you truly wanted democracy, you had to listen to the people. And the people didn't want the Jews.

So anti-Semitism is democracy in action?

Definitely not, he says. Anti-Semitism doesn't exist in Gollwitz.

Xenophobia, then? I venture.

Mayor Heldt is sure it isn't that either.

He finally agrees that one could safely call what has happened *Fremdgruppenabwertung*, one of those German words one often invents when one doesn't want to say things quite so precisely. It translates literally as "foreigner-group-debasement," with the word "foreign," *fremd*, conveying the sense of strange or unfamiliar.

"That sort of thing does exist," he says. It is only natural that such a small community would have fears about such a large group of "unfamiliars."

Of course, he says, one must add to their instinctive rejection the fact that the manor was something of a local symbol: it had grand, spacious rooms and a large fireplace. Even in its dilapidated condition, it was still the only building in Gollwitz with that sort of soul. District officials who came up with the concept just weren't thinking.

The mayor had explored all sorts of concepts: conversion into private apartments, a senior citizens' home, or the establishment of some sort of private school. The town council would have approved any of these concepts. But the investors hadn't been there, and dreams became illusions. That's the way matters go in eastern Germany these days: dreams to illusions. So the locals were already out of sorts when this new idea came along. For them, this was the final nightmare of unification. Not only were the hopes of unification a mirage, now they were being replaced by unwanted Jews.

That said, Mayor Heldt concedes that he was surprised by the heat of the opposition. One of the council members had even suggested putting a prisonlike, concentration-camplike fence around the building should the new immigrants move in despite local opposition. Another cursed Bubis and suggested he open up his own house to these new Jews. "That I had to discover such anti-Semitism in people that I thought I knew, that shocked me."

So there is anti-Semitism in town?

He shrugs that one has to give normal people their right to speak. "This European house isn't just one of advantages," he frowns. He speaks of the failed efforts to meld Berlin and Brandenburg, a plan with logistical logic but roundly defeated in a referendum because politicians didn't understand the fears of eastern Germans that their interests would be swallowed and lost if they became part of Germany's new West German–oriented capital. "The politicians paid the bill for not taking the little people seriously."

After two hours' conversation, we end our chat. But before I leave town, I try to pay a visit to the Protestant pastor, who had remained curiously silent during the entire scandal. He was said to have supported the town council rejection of the Russian Jews. Given the church's history of looking the other way during the Holocaust, I wanted to ask him a few questions. Why hadn't the pastor spoken to his flock about the need for tolerance? Why did he still refuse to talk to any outsider about the town council's controversial decision. Why did he support it?

The mayor doubts the pastor will see me, but he lives next door so it is worth a try.

When the doorbell rings, a woman in her fifties opens up. Yes, she is the pastor's wife, she says. What do I want?

Her already suspicious face turns dark when she hears that a reporter stands before her. Her husband isn't home, she insists. And no, there isn't any reason for me to return. Her husband won't talk to me no matter when I come back.

How long had she lived in the community? I ask politely, hoping by way of conversation to get a foot in the door.

No, she won't answer that either.

Can she at least give me the copy of the statement he had given during the height of the controversy?

No, she can't do that either.

She shuts the door before I finish my next sentence.

By the time I arrive with Ignatz Bubis to his last appointment of the day at a Protestant church in Essen, the slide show from Auschwitz has already begun. Young members of the congregation had brought back a heap of black-and-white transparencies from a religious retreat they had taken to the concentration camp: simple shots of the *Arbeit Macht Frei* front gate, the remains of the barracks, the stacks of clothing, the chimneys of the crematorium.

The crowd is too absorbed in the slides to note the arrival of their star attraction for the evening, Ignatz Bubis. We sit silently at the back. The room is hushed. No words. No music. The only sounds are the clicking of the projector and the burdened breathing of the congregation as one slide after another flips viciously onto the screen.

The pastor, Dieter Schermeier, is one of those activist Christians one meets now and again in Germany, his 1968 awakening transformed into religion. He is sixty years old, but his wild wisps of white hair and hyperactive pacing and gesticulating give the impression of a much younger spirit. The meeting that night is part of a regular series of mid-week consciousness-raising events that he organizes for his congregation, and every seat is taken.

After the last slide, Pastor Schermeier announces, "We will now sing an aggressive hymn." And they all sing aggressively, letting out a communal rage for what Germans before them had done to humanity.

Behind the podium stand large, identical, life-sized black metal stick figures—thirteen of them in all. After the singing finishes, Pastor Schermeier decorates each with a green military helmet. In a matter of a minute or two, the neutral figures become soldiers. He then removes the helmets, and two teenage girls from the congregation stick yellow Stars of David on their chests. The soldiers are transformed into Nazi-era Jews.

"You see," says the pastor, "the uniformity dehumanizes the victims just as the helmets dehumanized the perpetrators. We are dealing with a simple model of a *Massenmensch*—a mass-produced human being. The *Massenmensch* goes along with everything."

The girls remove the stars and put an array of different heads atop the stick figures: black, Asian, white. Red hair, brunette, and blonde. All ages. All categories. "It all looks a lot different now, doesn't it?" the pastor says.

The audience applauds. This is the world they want: multi-cultural, not all Jews with stars, not soldiers with helmets, but a rainbow of peoples and colors and nationalities.

Bubis smiles at me. For all its naiveté, this is the Germany we both believe in, the one that teaches and takes the lessons of the past.

The pastor then launches a short sermon against German uniformity and conventionalism. He appeals for individual courage. Then he hands the floor to Bubis. "Do you mind if the happy figures remain behind you?" he asks.

"Not in the least," shrugs Bubis.

As if he has a choice.

Bubis, happy stick figures as his backdrop, comments on an earlier speech by a local official about right-wing youth. It isn't the violent young who concern him, he says. It is the attitudes of their parents and grandparents that poison them.

"The spiritual arsonists who stand behind them are the problem," he says. He tells them that anti-Semitic language—hate language, in general—is growing more acceptable again, a fact he repeats at every stop, adding, as he did to me, "Nasty letters that were once mailed anonymously are now sent to the Central Council of Jews in Germany with a return address and full name."

He fears this is a result of reunification—and of the time and distance from the Third Reich. "There is a feeling among some that they now are liberated from the old constraints. It isn't that people have changed—they were always this way. They are merely more willing to speak their minds."

At the end of Bubis's comments, the pastor poses a question that he says is on behalf of all those in the room, perhaps all those in Germany.

"When is it—" he asks, pausing theatrically for a few seconds—"when is it that I, as a German, and you, as a Jew, can have a normal relationship?"

He almost reaches out toward Bubis, as if he expects some sort of embrace. But Bubis deflects any such gesture as too cheap for so profound a history. "There are many people in Germany who love me and many who hate me," says Bubis. "And it always has to do with my Jewishness. I will welcome the day when people love or hate me simply for what I do as an individual."

At the end of the service, many in the congregation gather round the two men to shake hands and exchange views. I ask the pastor about the awkward moment of a few minutes earlier. Was he bothered by the Bubis response?

"I wish it would be possible to have this normal relationship," says the pastor. "I wish he could come here and give me permission."

He wants Jewish absolution, as do so many other Germans. They desire that the world Jewish community—any Jewish community—grant them forgiveness in recognition of the $100 billion in reparations they have paid and of the sort of people and country they have become.

A photographer pulls the pastor away from me and lines him up beside Bubis for a shot. They stand too far from each other for the frame, so the photographer coaxes them more closely together. They edge hesitantly nearer one another. Still, their elbows barely touch as the shutter snaps and the flash explodes. Awkward smiles.

I think back to a conversation I had earlier that day with Bubis. I asked him whether he could ever entertain the sort of absolution that Pastor Schermeier seemed to want. I told him a Jesuit priest had told me that such a Jewish pardon was what modern Germans needed to become healthy.

"That's Catholic theology," said Bubis, "where absolution and reconciliation play an important role. But it is different in Judaism. In Judaism, reconciliation exists only with God. No, I have a different view. I'd say to your Jesuit, did you do anything to me? No. Did I do anything to you? No. So why should we two reach reconciliation? If your brother kills my father, is it right for me to forgive your brother? No, only my father can do that. I don't have that right."

I recall this conversation as I watch the German and the Jew, the sixty-eighter pastor and the ghetto survivor, stand stiffly with their arms by their sides as the photographer asks for one more pose.

"A little closer, this time, please," he pleads.

ellay' of home and hoofe and
vare, and mangler, and scatters h
en beneath and the blue above,
eth and danger, and life, and
reca, — Ltcca used to ride
mouce-gray mustang close to my
he escaped and bright-belled ep
hed with joy as I looked at

NINE

THE TURKISH CHALLENGE

We are not a country of immigration.
—HELMUT KOHL

If we aren't a country of immigration, I am a fata morgana.
—CEM ÖZDEMIR, THE FIRST TURKISH-GERMAN
MEMBER OF THE BUNDESTAG

From the highest perch at the farthest corner of Dortmund's Westfalen Stadium, Mehmet Erbakan supervises an army of workers preparing the venue for the next day's gathering of forty thousand Muslims. They will fill the stadium for the largest meeting ever of the fastest-growing Islamic group in Germany, *Milli Görüş*, of which Erbakan is secretary general at age thirty-one.

With an organizer's pride, Erbakan looks through his wire-rimmed glasses on the busy scene: women in headscarfs and body-length cloaks swipe seats clean with damp rags, young men in white shirts and dark ties practice their roles as ushers, workmen install a ten-meter-high screen and speakers, rank-and-file members blow up balloons and stuff them in huge nets to be released over the crowd, and other volunteers drape enormous flags over entire bleacher sections at the front of the stadium. The banners are Turkish, German and, most prominently of all, the green-and-white banner of *Milli Görüş.* The official German name for the group is the Islamic Community for a New World Vision. The shorter Turkish version, *Milli Görüş,* translates roughly as "national vision."

Erbakan explains, however, that the nation to which it refers isn't Turkish and certainly not German, but is instead Islamic. "We are Germany's new Jews," he says, absent-mindedly rubbing together his dark brown prayer beads. "Watching how the Germans come to terms with their Turkish population, the world will learn what sort of people they have become. With us, they can show the world that they've changed. The Jews stand for their tragic past. We stand for their uncertain future."

The statement seems a bit too well practiced to be impromptu. Erbakan knows pushing the hot "Jewish" button is the quickest way to attention in Germany. Yet hyperbole aside, one is forced to agree with Erbakan that the country's 2.5 million Turks—far more numerous than were Jews in Germany at the height of their numbers—are a litmus test of some sort and will be a central factor in shaping the new country.

If Erbakan wants to draw on this historical comparison, I tell him that he must concede that the fact that his organization can gather so freely demonstrates how tolerant Germany has become. Turkish laws never would have allowed such an Islamic rally in Istanbul. Adolf Hitler, I argue, would only have gathered so many "non-Aryans" in a soccer stadium as a staging point for concentration camp transports.

Erbakan grins darkly. He's heard this all before. "We are not holding up this Germany to its low standards of the past," he says. "We are holding up this Germany to the high standards that it sets for itself now. And in this respect, this Germany has a very long way to go."

Erbakan cites citizenship laws that, though later liberalized by a new German government, had discriminated against German-born Turks for years. The roots of that attitude went back to laws first enacted in 1913 that established a view of nationality based on blood rather than a liberal, republican view of citizenship adopted by most other European countries. That, in the view of Erbakan, is part of the reason for a continuing German mind set that will demonize Turks long after the changed law. When unemployment rises, he frowns, many Germans still instinctively point the scapegoat-seeking finger at their so-called *foreigners,* who are often actually second or third-generation residents of Germany. He complains that ethnic German immigrants from Russia, who often speak only broken German, automatically received citizenship due to this obsession with German blood, while Turks who were born and educated in Germany were left waiting.

Just that morning, a local radio commentator sneered that the *Milli Görüş* event was "the largest meeting of Islam in Europe since the Turks stormed Vienna." And a newspaper editorial criticized the soccer club and city officials for providing the venue to "the most fundamentalist Muslim group in Germany." Erbakan speaks of how, up until a week before the event, his lawyers had been fighting legal efforts to cancel their annual "Peace and Cultural Festival" on security grounds. Stadium authorities argued at the last minute that the stadium had to be kept empty due to a track meet in a field next door for which emergency rescue teams would have to have the stadium available as a helicopter launching site.

"You learn to live with all that," says Erbakan, whose famous uncle, Necmettin Erbakan, had been Turkey's first Islamist prime minister. The links between his organization and his uncle's Islamic movement were so tight that the Federal Office for the Protection of the Constitution was monitoring Erbakan's group at the time as a potential Islamic Trojan horse, which it feared was out to disrupt democracy and help create an Islamic state, in Turkey if not in Germany.

"The authorities should learn that they are lucky to have us around," says Erbakan. "They should thank us for channeling the Turkish young in a positive direction. We take them off the street, out of gangs, away from drugs. We give them purpose."

Yet it is just that purpose that worries many Germans, for it diverges so radically from their own fiercely secular, nonconfessional, and often atheistic nature. *Milli Görüş*'s success also flies in the face of German confidence for many years that Turks, given the chance, would integrate themselves more and more in German society. For many Turks, that is certainly true, but familiarity has also bred distance among many Turks who still felt themselves rejected by Germany, even as they became a larger and more permanent part of its society.

Only twenty-five hundred Turks were living in Germany in October 1961 when Bonn invited the Turks as temporary guest workers through a state-to-state agreement. Those numbers will have grown more than a thousand-fold by the end of the century. What Germans wanted in the sixties was simple: a shot in the arm for their labor-short *Wirtschaftswunder.* What they'll end up with, more by accident than design, is Germany's first politically important ethnic minority. And that will have an impact on foreign policy as well. Germany has long had a strained relationship with Turkey over human rights and other matters. How Germany comes to terms with this country will set the tone for the European Union, which is pursuing a tricky policy aimed at preventing Turkey from turning anti-Western while at the same time not embracing it as a potential EU member.

The September 1998 election of the red-green coalition of Social Democrats and Greens accelerated the growing influence of Germany's Turkish community. One of the first policy initiatives the new government announced, against virulent conservative opposition, was a significant easing of citizenship requirements. The parties estimated that the changes would allow close to three million of some seven million "foreign" residents of Germany—or some 9 percent of the population—to become German citizens. Although some 220,000 Turks have become citizens through existing laws, those numbers could grow quickly to more than a million. The legislation grants automatic citizenship to any child of foreign parents who is born in Germany if one parent was born in Germany or has lived there since his fourteenth birthday. Foreign residents may request German citizenship after eight years of residence instead of fifteen. Most important to Turks, Germany would allow dual citizenship. In practice, many of the Turks who had become German citizens reapplied for Turkish citizenship after giving it up to get their German passports. Yet despite those loopholes, less than one percent of the foreigners in Germany obtained citizenship each year.

What the new laws recognize is one of the most important changes the country has experienced in the postwar years: Germany has become less

German. Aside from some 2.5 million Turks, the country is also home to some 800,000 Yugoslavs, more than 600,000 Italians, and about 350,000 Greeks. The number of residents whom German statisticians consider "foreigners" has grown more than tenfold in the last forty years. That trend began with agreements to import guest workers from Italy in 1955, Turkey in 1961, and Yugoslavia in 1968. Europe's most liberal policies toward accepting asylum-seekers fed these numbers. Yet Germany continued to have a far larger quotient of "foreigners" than England or France because its laws made it so difficult for the *de facto* immigrants to become citizens.

Safter Çinar, a Turkish leader in Berlin, was relieved that the change he had long wanted would finally come. "The atmosphere of this country is going to change as the notion that we are all German citizens, independent of our roots, takes hold. It will take a long time [to change attitudes], but it will happen."

The long-time visitor to Germany experiences the dramatic demographic changes in mostly pleasing ways: a huge growth of ethnic restaurants, foreign films, and intermarriages. My German friends prefer the "foreign"-run restaurants for the simple reason that the service is better and friendlier. "It's like going on vacation," says Gerhard Stockheim, the chemistry teacher, when we eat at his favorite Greek restaurant.

And Germans, who only sixty years earlier took the most brutal measures to preserve the purity of their so-called Aryan race, now were passing laws and taking personal action to dilute their German blood. Among my friends, schoolteacher Stockheim has adopted a mixed-race Peruvian son; mathematics professor Norbert Heldermann married and produced children with his Argentinean wife; psychiatrist Stephan Ehebald was doing the same with his ethnically Indian, South African partner; and writer Peter Schneider was wondering why his children, conceived by his Polish-born wife, should share in the German historical guilt.

Yet Germany is far from being an American-style melting pot. Uncle Sam's newcomers, by and large, arrive with the old "American dream" in their heads: that hard work will make them prosper in the land of opportunity. Germany's immigrants, however, arrived first either as guest workers or asylum seekers. For some, the "German dream" is gaining access to the protection of the country's rich welfare system. Germans have trouble accepting they are an immigration country because, being a people that prides itself on planning and organization, they never intended to become one.

The idea, after all, was that after the Turks finished their contribution to the *Wirtschaftswunder*, they would return "where they belonged" and invest their savings from Germany in Turkish property or a business. Yet the rotation system to ensure that no individual Turks stayed long never worked well. And when Germans stopped importing workers in 1973 after the global oil crisis, only a small percentage of them accepted company or federal programs to return "home." Germany's history of cattle cars stuffed full of unwanted humanity prevented any serious consideration of forced mass deportations. Indeed, the postwar German conscience gave rise to programs under Chancellor Willy Brandt that, by promoting family reunification, brought in even more Turks and made their stays more permanent. Berlin soon became the largest Turkish city after Istanbul and Ankara.

To Germans' great surprise—and to the surprise of many Turks themselves—the guest workers put down roots. A new generation spoke German better than Turkish and had no intention of going home. Parents had grown old and often sick in factories and coal mines. They preferred to stay with their children rather than return to Turkey's less developed social and medical care.

When I return to the stadium the next day with Erbakan, it is full of Allah's soldiers under Nike banners that fittingly announce, "Just do it." The southern stands are brimming with Islamic women in modest Islamic cloaks and an understated kaleidoscope of headscarves. Not a strand of hair is to be seen. The north wing overflows with menfolk, a sea of macho: dark hair, thick mustaches, deep voices shouting greetings to one another in brotherly tones. The strict segregation shocks the few German journalists who have taken their Saturday to cover the event. But the participants appear more than content. They laugh, sing along with folkloric groups, and wildly cheer Turkish politicians.

"For the German government," says Erbakan, waving his arm across the expanse of people filling the stadium, "we were a political accident. They simply missed their chance to send the Turks back home. It is like the woman who gets pregnant even though she is taking birth-control pills. Then the baby is born. It is in the world. You didn't plan on it, but now you have to deal with it. The Turks never should have become a minority group here, and because this was the official thinking, for a long time, authorities couldn't accept that it had happened."

So the guest workers, I say, became immigrants without the permission of the Germans?

Erbakan winks. "Anyway, I have never understood this term 'guest worker.' In what sort of society do you ask your guest to work?"

Erbakan is an odd mix of Turkish and German qualities. His cool, mid-European composure, his aides say, is a product of his German mother. His Islamic passion and occasional temper outbursts, they reckon, are from his Turkish engineer father. His mother, as a medical student, had met and fallen in love with his father, who studied machine-building in Aachen, when she was a volunteer introducing visiting Turks to Germany. The result was this unusual offspring, with his pale intellectual's pallor and intense eyes. He looks out at the world watchfully and thoughtfully. He is simultaneously rational and emotional. He is cool under pressure but turns angry when he feels crossed. His mother is a typical postwar German child, who talks to him of how a black GI saved her life when she was almost trampled to death while being evacuated from Cologne on a train. She grew up with Bill Haley and the Comets. But he and his father prefer the cry of the muezzin.

One of the *Milli Görüş* leaders asked the clever boy Mehmet, who was then age fourteen, to organize a trip to the museum for his youth group. He bought the streetcar tickets and organized the food. Erbakan enjoyed the task, and his masterful handling of it led to official positions. He joined the board of *Milli Görüş*'s young leadership at age sixteen. By age eighteen, he was on the youth board for Europe. The adults elected him to the general board at age twenty-one, and he became secretary general a couple of years later.

It is rare to find anyone in a position of power in *Milli Görüş* who is much older than thirty. The organization exudes youth and dynamism and a confidence that it can only grow in strength. Erbakan shrugs off German official monitoring of his group as a potentially criminal organization. He argues they've found nothing about which they can prosecute *Milli Görüş*, and even the interior ministry concedes that is true. No serious person can believe *Milli*

Görüş can turn Germany into an Islamic state, Erbakan says. And as for the virulently anti-Israeli statements in various mosques that so alarm Holocauststained Germany? How much different are they from what one hears in German society, he says, and he couldn't censor the mosques even if he wanted. "We live in a democracy, after all, remember?"

And the charge that *Milli Görüş* is trying to help his uncle overthrow democracy in Turkey?

"We aren't the ones threatening to ban political parties or restrict their freedom of speech," he says. Indeed, he says, it is more the military that has done so in the name of protecting the secular nature of Turkey. (It inspired the banning of his uncle's Welfare Party in 1997, after which it reorganized and renamed itself the Virtue Party.)

Erbakan scoffs at charges that his uncle's party finances his group. It is more the other way around, he insists. This event's total cost of a million marks would be funded primarily by its better-off members, he says. He reads off a long list of prominent Turkish business people. Erbakan not only has Islamic faith behind him in a country that has otherwise few deeply held religious or political beliefs, he also has funds.

Yet Germany, he insists, shouldn't fear him or the change that is coming. He places his face close to mine and asks if I can imagine him, chest bared and sabre clenched between his teeth, plotting to overturn Christian Germany. We laugh, for he looks none of these things. I can't help but think he is a new breed of individual who exists only in the new Germany, a devout and determined man who is a product of two cultures but who fits easily in neither.

As much as these Turks are products of Germany and, with every year, more permanent fixtures in it, they choose not to assimilate themselves in a manner many Germans would like. Yet none quibble anymore with the fact of their permanence. They are buying homes and investing in businesses in ever greater numbers. The consulting group KPMG carried out a study for the European Association of Turkish Business, fittingly entitled "The Unseen Power," showing that Turkish companies would employ 650,000 by the year 2010, a fourfold increase from their levels in the mid-1990s. Their turnover would grow at a similar rate to more than 110 billion dollars (190 German marks) in the year 2000 from some 30 billion dollars, including 25 billion in investments in some 42,000 companies. Though no one keeps statistics, schools and universities report a growing number of better educated Turks, rising from their working class roots to attend the more elite high schools, where Turkish faces were once rare. This increased education in many cases has bred a greater cultural awareness rather than assimilation. Just as more educated Blacks in America often defined themselves in contrast to the white society, so have Turks done so in Germany. The growth of discos and clubs that cater predominantly to Turkish teens and college students has been dramatic, though the working language is most often German.

Technology has also allowed them to remain apart from Germany more than was possible before. While only a third of Germans had satellite TV hook-ups by 1998, some 60 percent of Turks did, so that they could receive a half-dozen Turkish stations, a good portion of which relied primarily on Islamic programming. Turks in Germany also are more likely to read Turkish than German newspapers. The largest of the papers, *Hurriyet*, a mainstream paper with close ties to the military, had in 1998 a circulation of more than 110,000. Each Turk in Germany travels home an average of twice a year; a round-trip tickets costs as little as 199 German marks.

"Emigrants from England to America in the eighteenth century didn't care if they ever saw England again," says Erbakan. "Or if they did care, they didn't know how to bring it about. This new world of smaller distances has a great impact."

Erbakan should know.

When Turkey began to grow more openly Islamic in the nineteen-nineties, a mirror impact in Germany followed. In Turkish elections in March 1994, Islamists swept into a majority of local administrations, including for the first time in Ankara and Istanbul. *Milli Görüş* is by no means the representative of all Turks in Germany, but it grew fastest in response to this trend. Erbakan counts 161,000 dues-paying members (men who attend Friday prayer). With their families, he reckons his organization's numbers swell to a half million, making it by far the largest group in the fractious Turkish community, which has dozens of mosque associations.

Rivals claim that Erbakan exaggerates his strength, but they agree that by the late nineteen-nineties *Milli Görüş* had become a phenomenon, so well financed and organized with Koran schools and youth groups that it was likely to be an ever-growing force. And unlike in Turkey, where the Islamic movement has grown fastest primarily among lower classes, in Germany it has also grown quickly among the young, among university students, and even intelligentsia.

The shock of a shift within Germany's Turkish population toward Islam and Turkish chauvinism came home with a study in 1997 that became known as "the Heitmeyer report," a striking bit of research showing that the will to assimilate was declining. The most outspoken of its three authors, Wilhelm Heitmeyer of Bielefeld University, says of his general finding, "We have registered a considerable measure of Islam-centric feeling of superiority and a religious-based readiness to engage in violence."

Nearly 75 percent of those polled answered that they could never consider themselves as Germans because they didn't belong. And more than 65 percent said they considered themselves first as Muslims, before either Turks or Germans. What alarmed Germans most, as measured by the focus of press reports on the poll, was the finding that 35 percent declared themselves ready to engage in violence against non-believers if they felt their Islamic society was threatened. (Whereas the press reports suggested that Turks were ready to initiate violence, a close reading of the question posed by the survey shows they were merely willing to react violently if threatened themselves, a less surprising response.)

Critics of the study charged that Heitmeyer and his team loaded the questions to get the results. Farukh Şen, of the Institute for Turkish Studies in Essen, charges that they needed the most alarming outcome possible to justify continued and increased funding.

Yet almost everyone, including both Heitmeyer and Şen, believes that one central event in 1993 in an industrial town called Solingen had much to do with the shift reflected by the study. During the night of May 29, 1993, five Turks died in flames that destroyed the house of the family Genç. Following a closely watched judicial process that lasted eighteen months, a Düsseldorf court in October 1995 convicted four locals between ages sixteen and twenty-four with sentences ranging from ten to fifteen years. The court established that the four had poured some three liters of gasoline in the entryway and lighted it. Those burned to death were the senior Genç's five- and nine-year-old granddaughters, a twelve-year-old niece, and two daughters aged eighteen and twenty-eight.

The Solingen attack drew particular attention because it was the climax of several recent attacks against so-called "foreigners" in Germany. Turks didn't respond violently but with fear and a resolve to better protect themselves. A 1996 book, *The Solingen Files*, listed the measures Turks began to adopt. One sixty-five-year-old woman, Riza Öbzkürt, who had lived in Germany for three decades, said, "As long as I've lived in Germany, I've never had such fear. For twenty marks, I bought a thick rope. I tied it to the radiator in front of the window. If they set a fire here, we'll save ourselves by sliding down it." If the threat instead walks through the door, she had a bread knife within reach on the kitchen table, and took a pocket knife with her whenever she went outside—and was thinking of buying a gas-cartridge pistol.

Her view was typical of the Solingen aftermath. And although the panic subsided, Turkish attitudes shifted in a lasting way. The distance between Turks and Germans grew, and Turks for the first time began to compare themselves publicly to Jews. Turks began to band together more in their own groups—community and mosque organizations. *Milli Görüş* enjoyed its fastest growth ever. Fewer Turks trusted German society to take care of them, an attitude made stronger by Chancellor Helmut Kohl's own failure either to visit Solingen after the attack or convincingly to voice any moral outrage. For a generation of Turkish youth, Solingen was the proof that they couldn't trust those who were controlling their society. The Heitmeyer study made clear Solingen's critical role: more than 60 percent of the respondents said that Solingen showed Turks must bind themselves closer together. Some 75 percent responded that Solingen showed they must learn to protect themselves.

Erbakan is certain part of the Jewish mistake in the nineteen-thirties was trying too hard to assimilate in a society that wouldn't take them. "Integration shouldn't mean assimilation," he says.

He is certain that if the Jews had shown as much unity and power as *Milli Görüş* now does, Hitler might never have had the guts to start the Holocaust. "The Jews now number more than fifty thousand in Germany again. If I were [Jewish leader Ignatz] Bubis, I would fill this stadium with them. But I'm sure he'd be afraid to do that. Can you imagine what a target that would be for right-wing extremists? All the Jews in one place?"

Erbakan doesn't fear the same for his Muslims. "We can take care of ourselves," he says. He figures his most compelling argument against those who were trying to prohibit his group from using the stadium was when he told city authorities that forty thousand Muslims would be brought to Dortmund in buses, cars, and trains anyway; local authorities could either have them all in the stadium where they could be watched, or face the challenge of their large numbers throughout the city.

If Mehmet Erbakan is the Turkish-German who causes Germans to lose sleep at night, Green party parliamentarian Cem Özdemir is the Turkish-German of their dreams.

"Comparing us to the Jews is absurd," says Özdemir in his Bundestag office before Germany's 1998 elections, which made him the new governing coalition's most important voice on Turkish questions. "Such comparisons are an insult to the dead of Auschwitz and to every citizen of modern Germany. We aren't those Jews and the Germans aren't what they were then."

Özdemir was elected on October 16, 1994, as the first ethnic Turkish member of the German Bundestag and he stands against Erbakan's efforts to define Turks apart from a German society that he considers, on balance, to be enlightened and welcoming. It was that society, and not Turks, that elected him, after all.

Erbakan and Özdemir are roughly the same age, having both been born in 1967. Erbakan dresses in conservative slacks and open, short-sleeved dress shirts, the uniform of Germany's Turkish elite. His face is pale and his demeanor that of a far older man than he is. Özdemir is boyish, movie-star handsome and clean-shaven, and he wears the casual chic of his German Green generation—jeans and turtlenecks. Erbakan studied medicine and was a surgeon before he shifted his operations to German society. Özdemir followed the usual studies of the German left, social work, but his avocation from the beginning was politics.

While talking to Erbakan, one's eyes wander to the prayer beads he restlessly kneads. With Özdemir, the eyes focus instead on the tell-tale golden earring, a trendy bit of young-and-hip German branding.

At Özdemir's political rallies, populated mostly by the non-Turks who have elected him, he deploys the inclusive pronouns "we" and "us"; he wants no psychological borders between himself and his constituency. But Erbakan's constituency is Islamic and Turkish and he makes a living out of creating just the sort of separate definition that Özdemir resists. Between them they represent the two major trends of the Turkish population in the country: assimilation and alienation.

Erbakan believes the way Turks will secure their position in Germany is through the "in-your-face" approach of the Dortmund festival, where they boisterously stand up for their very different culture and religion. Özdemir cautions against demanding too much too quickly from a German society that is nervous enough about demographic changes. Gradualism, he argues, is the better policy. What gain is there in making Germans afraid?

Özdemir doesn't like the fact that I am spending so much time with *Milli Görüş* and Mehmet Erbakan. He pleads with me to get to know the Allowites instead—the largest ethnic group within the Turkish community. The Allowites are the second largest community in Turkey after the Sunni, making up some 20 percent of the electorate. They have been the heart of the secular Turkish state and, because they define themselves less according to Islam, and they worship in family homes—if at all—instead of mosques, they have better assimilated in Germany. For me to truly understand Turks in Germany, he says I must attend the Allowites' own rally, where he will be speaking, that coming weekend.

So, I ask Özdemir, does he disagree with statistics that show that Erbakan's course is the one gaining popularity against his own, more secular vision of the future?

He frowns and concedes that Erbakan truly does have the momentum, and he blames Germans partly for the fact that *Milli Görüş* wins over the young so easily.

"What we're watching is a self-fulfilling prophecy," he says. "Because Germany hasn't embraced the Turks, the Turks are becoming the types of people Germany doesn't want to embrace. Thus begins the vicious circle.

Because they aren't included, Turks go their own way. Germans and Turks distrust each other more, communicate with each other less, and live beside each other instead of with each other."

Özdemir catches me surveying his office and guesses correctly that I am searching for signs of his Turkishness. I find little except for a parking sign outside the entrance: "No Parking Except for Turks." He picked it up in some ethnic neighborhood in America. "You are much more comfortable with ethnic backgrounds in America because no one uses them against you in questions of citizenship."

Özdemir says Germans come to his office all the time to check him out. "They want to see the Turk they've read about and seen on TV. Is he kneeling on his prayer rug? Does he smoke hashish from a water pipe? I am happy to receive these groups because I know how much I will disappoint them. Frankly, what do I have in common with Erbakan and the fundamentalists?"

I argue that well-off, assimilated German Jews of the nineteen-thirties also felt they had little in common with the poorly educated, often more Orthodox Jewish working class that had newly emigrated from Eastern Europe. Their differences were great, I say, but in the end their shared race ensured a common fate.

Özdemir harrumphs. "It was Hitler who bound those Jews together. We don't have a Hitler. We don't have anyone who forces me to associate myself with them. And I don't think that will change. I know of no other people that takes such a ruthless accounting of its own history. A people that takes such an open view of the negative sides of its past is in a better position to tackle the problems of the future."

I had seen a clip of Özdemir from a show that was sent out on Turkish national television. One of the Turkish participants said that Turks would become the new Jews. He argued that Germans were as racist as ever, and that matters could turn nasty at any moment.

"If that's the way you feel," Özdemir replied, "rush to your home right after this program, pack your bags, and go. Don't lose any time and don't ever come back. Otherwise, hold your tongue."

Özdemir smiles as he remembers the TV confrontation. "Many Turks were taken aback by what I said. But I react very aggressively to this unqualified comparison. It is becoming too fashionable for Turks to cloak themselves in the garb of the victims."

So was it Özdemir's view that all the bad history had created a better, more tolerant breed of Germans?

"The Germans are more normal. And the migration of so many other types of people has helped." In fact, Özdemir is one of the co-founders of *Immi-Grünen,* a group of Green parliamentarians that wants Germany to remain open to immigrants from all countries. "The Germans today are more relaxed. Just compare them with the German society of the fifties. Look at all the street cafés. The easy-going life. All the different sorts of restaurants. This has become a multicultural society. This is a society where every citizen can enjoy all the changes that came with postwar development—the reconstruction and, with the help of the Americans, the democratic re-education. Democracy is firmly anchored here now."

Özdemir doesn't think the trend toward *Milli Görüş* is unstoppable, and he'll use his newly gained power to prove his point. "This can be fought—and prevented—but only if Germany strengthens the Turks' feeling of belonging here. Accelerating naturalizations is the best way to do that. Democratic principles tell us that people who live here should participate in political life."

And as naturalization of Turks increases, Özdemir hopes that will also lead to the creation of more Turkish "elites" like himself who serve within German society instead of those like Erbakan who build their world outside of it. "What Turks living in Germany need is more role models," he says.

Many Germans celebrated Cem Özdemir's election in 1994 as happy proof of their own tolerance and of their society's ability to integrate its foreigners, much in the way that Americans had greeted Colin Powell's potential run for the White House. Official government and foreign ministry publications make him their cover boy. Talk shows have booked him and his father, a retired factory worker who assembled fire extinguishers, as the picture-perfect immigrant success story. A German publisher even printed the thirty-one-year-old Özdemir's autobiography, entitled *Ich bin Inländer*—a play on the German word for foreigner, *Ausländer,* a title telling readers that he is more "in-lander" than "out-lander." For all this, Germans love him, but

Turks are divided. For some he is a role model, but for others he is an Uncle Tom.

"I have had to live with this charge since I entered the Bundestag," he says. "There is a danger that some might want to use me to show the world, 'You see, we're not as bad as they say we are.' But I don't have any trouble identifying myself with this society. And if all the attention I get brings more notice to the legislation I introduce, then the price is worth it."

Indeed, when he senses rejection by Germans, he has several tricks to convince his listeners that he's one of them. The first is to turn on the broad, comfortable dialect of his native Swabian village. "It confuses people," he says. "Who can call me a bloody foreigner when I'm speaking Swabian? It just doesn't fit into their clichés, and it inhibits their aggressions."

He then tells his constituents his family story: how his parents have lived and worked in Germany for more than thirty years, where his father labored throughout his life in a local factory like thousands of other Germans. The point is to show how much his life is like their own, except that his parents only became citizens shortly before his own election day, October 16, 1994.

His parents were the happiest voters in Germany that day, he tells the crowd, and everyone smiles and cheers. What he doesn't say is that his parents almost didn't gain citizenship in time to cast their ballots, and only did so, Özdemir says, because he threatened to name the offending bureaucrats on television on the day of his election if they didn't clear the way for his family's citizenship.

He tells them that his parents didn't know what to do when they were in the voting booth. "Here were two people near retirement, who have spent most of their lives in this democracy, and they didn't know what it means to vote, to be able to decide. Others had always decided for them. It is incomprehensible." He speaks here, only near the end of our talk, with the fire of an American civil rights activist.

For all of Özdemir's praise for Germany, he still won't call himself "German." To avoid awkward moments and to win a laugh, he tells voters that he's an Anatolian Swab—loyal to both the regions of his origins, Anatolia in Turkey and Swabia in Germany—but not to the countries they inhabit. "The problem," he tells me, "is that Germany didn't lay out the welcome mat to me at my birth. This country said to me, as I viewed the first light of the world, 'You are a foreigner.' "

Still, Özdemir says he didn't notice any racism against him as a child. In fact, his biggest adolescent conflicts were with his parents over the fact that he was becoming so un-Turkish. The first crisis came when Özdemir, at age fifteen, joined the Green party's youth group in his home town of Urach. At that moment, his parents would have been more comfortable if he had chosen the path of Mehmet Erbakan, who at the same time was taking on a teenage leadership position in *Milli Görüş*.

Özdemir says his parents, like many Germans, viewed the Greens "as a place where women breast-feed their children at party gatherings, where dogs run up and down the aisles, and where everyone smokes dope. They feared I was doing something illegal—they were certain that one day the police would come to our house and arrest me. They were accustomed to a Turkish political culture where such radical politics resulted in imprisonment or execution. What I was doing frightened them."

To his parents' thinking, his situation turned from bad to worse. Özdemir applied for German citizenship at age sixteen, in large part because he didn't want to serve in the Turkish army. This was a blow to his parents in a Turkish community where most families still proudly sent their boys back to Turkey to enlist when they reached military age. Özdemir won German citizenship at age eighteen after two years of battling with German bureaucracy.

That didn't end his "Germanization."

His parents' dread turned to horror when their son announced at age seventeen that he had decided to become a vegetarian. "For them, a Turkish man who voluntarily forgoes eating meat is suffering from a self-inflicted form of mental illness," he recalls. "Can you imagine what all this meant to my parents? They thought I was committing suicide in installments."

At age eighteen, he came home from a Berlin outing with a dangling earring, the last proof his parents needed that something was seriously askew. "They didn't understand the world anymore," he says. "I didn't make life easy for them."

Yet a dozen years later his mother joined the Green party. And the family's Turkish neighbors now collect at the family's home whenever Cem is in town to get help with their citizenship applications. "You see every day how times are changing," says Özdemir. "Many are coming to terms for the first time that they are going to stay here. They see that they have laid down roots. They see that the idea of returning to Turkey is a chimera. And if you are going to stay, it starts to make more sense to use all your rights and duties. That's what I tell them."

And they listen.

Whatever the final course of Germany's Turks, both Özdemir and Erbakan are certain that Turks will form a new political force for Germany in the early twenty-first century, the first politically significant minority that the country has perhaps ever had. What's less clear is which direction will dominate the community: Özdemir's secular message of integration or Erbakan's Islamic differentiation.

"That is the most suspenseful question," says Özdemir.

And he wasn't about to wager on the answer, though he's certain more liberal citizenship laws will help his cause. He knew, though, that the odds had turned against him in recent years, and he needed a German society that understood the stakes to help him turn the tide.

When I ask Erbakan to answer the same question of whose direction is more likely to win, he doesn't have the same doubts as he looks over the flood of humanity filing through the gates of Dortmund's stadium.

"So, what do you think?" he asks.

I had first met Erbakan at a seminar on Turkish identity—in Germany and in Turkey—put on by the Körber Foundation. The Hamburg-based group runs some of the most ambitious and visionary programs to promote understanding between Germans and Turks, both domestically and between the countries. A Who's Who of German and Turkish politicians and professors attended.

Mr. Erbakan wasn't impressed. "This only proves why we [at *Milli Görüş*] are having such success. What sort of identity is it that a room full of academics can't define after two days of discussion? Certainly not one that attracts most normal people."

German identity isn't inclusive, he said at the time, and Turkish identity isn't sufficient for a generation that was born in Germany. Erbakan told the collected professors, to their dissenting muttering, that the leading identity among Germany's Turks would increasingly be Islam. He had a confidence about this future that I didn't detect in Özdemir when the latter appealed to the same gathering to concentrate their efforts on building more Turkish elites at important levels of German society.

"Who wants to belong to sixty million Turks whom no one wants to accept in Europe," he said to me during one lunch break, "when you can be part of 1.5 billion Muslims around the world who can't be ignored?" When this statement, lifted from the off-the-record hearings, later raised dust in the Turkish press, he backed off it. But there is no doubt that it reflects the underlying philosophy of his organization.

When, at the Dortmund Stadium, I remind him of what he had said at the Körber Foundation event, he takes another look at the Nike banners and their fluttering "Just Do It" message. He speaks calmly, "How do you say it in English: 'Think Big.' "

And that's exactly what he does in Dortmund, acting much more like a German than a Turk as he attends to details, from the regiment of women wiping the seats to the army of clean-cut young men getting precise orders as ushers from a cluster of his top lieutenants.

We watch the ushers in their coats and ties, after receiving their instructions, stand at attention before their squad leaders.

"Are you ready to serve Allah?" the leaders ask.

They answer in joyful shouts, "We are ready to serve Allah."

In each year of its existence, *Milli Görüş*'s annual get-together has grown. The first was in 1984, when four hundred faithful gathered in a Hannover meeting room. The numbers grew gradually until Erbakan began to call the meeting the "Peace and Cultural Festival" and then moved it to a Dortmund basketball hall in 1996, where twenty-two thousand faithful assembled. His next move was the ultimate Turkish chutzpah—he rented the stadium for the 1997 festival that I was attending. It provided him plenty of room for future audience growth on the field itself and in the end zone bleachers, which for this event were covered by his giant flags.

Erbakan climbs high in the stadium and then walks around it, inspecting the view of the stage from every angle. His staff trails behind him, taking orders and passing them on through their mobile phones, which ring every few minutes with new information and updates on preparations. From the highest point in the bleachers, underneath the superstructure, he climbs a ladder to an even higher catwalk where young men are hanging nets full of balloons, which will be released at the end of the festival.

The staffers and I, paralyzed by vertigo, look on as Erbakan leans precariously off the catwalk, helping to attach one of the nets. While there, he asks one of his teenagers to tell me the boy's story, of how *Milli Görüş* found him in a train station, drunk and lost. And how *Milli Görüş* dried him out, put him to work and gave him purpose. The boy shyly tells his tale as best he can.

"We've given him a family," says Erbakan. "If he weren't blowing up balloons for us, he would have stolen at least five cars this year. I'm saving German authorities more trouble than they know, and they call me a threat. They call me a people-eater. Do I look like a people-eater?"

We sit in the empty bleachers and talk about how misunderstandings occur between Turks and Germans who have grown up alongside each other in the same country.

I think to myself how curious it is that a man who has a German mother and Turkish father, equal parts of both national bloodlines, had chosen the Turkish identity over the German one. I had experienced that so much with mixed nationality or mixed-race marriages that involved Germans. German identity, it seems, is something one decides against when given a second option. Even with two German-born parents, I opted for the adopted American identity, never for a moment feeling myself German during my upbringing.

"One thing strikes me about Germans," he says. "When the bill at a restaurant is twenty marks and three pfennigs, the German waiter always makes sure he gets the three pfennigs. The Turk wouldn't do that. It is so unnatural. Another example: if you were sitting here with a German and he pulled out a sandwich, he would fall over dead before offering you a part of it. But a Turk would die before he doesn't offer you part. I also am capable, unlike Germans, to say *Kismet*—to rely on fate. I don't need to say yes or no. I can say *Inshallah*—God willing."

Will the rain hold off for his festival the next day?

Inshallah.

He hasn't even looked at the weather prediction.

Will everything go as planned? Doesn't he fear neo-Nazi upsets outside the stadium?

Inshallah.

He hasn't heard of any reports. But anything can happen.

Will the German media call this the rise of radical fundamentalism à la Iran or Algeria, or will they praise it as a non-violent, cultural, and religious festival of a growing minority in Europe?

Kismet.

Who can say what will be their fate in the hands of Western media? He can't be troubled by what he can't control.

Seems pretty pragmatic to me, I say. But then again, I ask, isn't it true that his religion commits him to *jihad*—to holy war?

He smiles. "What you will see tomorrow, when we fill the stadium, that is also a form of *jihad. Jihad* means spending your energies toward Allah's purposes. That can be public relations, it can be recruiting more members for *Milli Görüş*, it can be organizing meetings. It can be talking to you. An actual holy war is only the exception, when one faces aggression from others, as in Afghanistan. Only in the worst case do you turn to holy war."

Any prospect of that in Germany? I ask.

"For us," he answers, "in Germany there is only a holy peace."

Yet up the road in Duisburg, a group of Germans are on the warpath over Islam's growing influence in their country. More specifically, they are trying to block the application of two local mosques to amplify the muezzin's call to prayer.

The conflict had begun with bureaucratic requests from a mosque group in Laar and another in Marxloh—two working-class districts of Duisburg—that were passed to lower-level city officials. The amplification of the call to prayer is an everyday practice in the Islamic world, but has only occasionally been practiced by Islamic groups in the West, and virtually never in Germany. The city officials knew the issue was too hot for their lowly positions, so they kicked the applications upstairs. Their bosses balked as well, and before they reached a verdict the issue leaked out to the public.

By the time I reach Duisburg, national television cameras had arrived to chronicle a town gathering at the market square in Laar. The opening scene of the program, which the channel WDR called *God and the World*, shows fearful rage: locals with jowls shaking and lips quivering stand before the camera, one after another, complaining variously about the anti-democratic, anti-feminist and anti-Western nature of Islam.

"We live in a country where church and state are separated," barks a voice like the others, a fiftyish woman whose face is distended by anger and red from the chilly weather. The camera moves in closer. "The Koran violates human rights. It is against the equality between man and woman. The Koran and Islam are against human rights."

The crowd cheers.

The camera then homes in on their leader, Pastor Dietrich Reuter, and the moderator asks him about a half-page advertisement he has taken out in the local press that throws oil onto the flames of conflict. It contends, among other matters, that "Christians and Muslims don't have the same God."

He tells the reporter he only bought the ad once he saw the press wouldn't represent his views accurately in reports about the matter. "The muezzin's call to prayer," he says, "is an affront to Christian believers ... Sura 39 of the Koran teaches that those who say Jesus is the son of God are damned. The call to prayer proclaims the jurisdiction of Allah, the God of Islam, over the territory where [the muezzin's call to prayer] can be heard. What the muezzin cries is that there is no other God than Allah. This Allah recognized by the Koran is set against the God of the Christians, and damns those who find their way to God through Christ and according to the Bible. So don't be confused by the words of seemingly Christian preachers."

The crowd lets out a cry of support. Clearly they are with him. Reuter is encouraged. He issues a smile of self-satisfaction.

The moderator is taken aback. He takes the microphone away from Reuter and tries to calm the crowd, noting that some of the strong feelings might be attributable to a high unemployment rate in the city, which had reached 20 percent, and to the uncertainty such a situation breeds.

Claudia Kleinert, an expert on Turkish affairs who works in Duisburg, watches the whole affair on television. She has been working on projects backed by government funds to bring Turks and Germans closer together. Many of these projects were born in response to the arson attack on the Turkish family at Solingen in 1993.

She is part of the positive side of the German story, a representative of the hundreds of Germans who have joined community groups, citizen initiatives, and party rallies on behalf of Turks and other "foreigners" in Germany. Foundation or government-backed programs seem to exist for every such problem in Germany. For her part, Claudia Kleinert has organized seminars that promote intercultural understanding before groups ranging from police officers to senior citizens.

In the angry faces of the crowd, she sees her work being undone. Yet these aren't the faces of those who attend her consciousness-raising events. She recognizes none of them. Pastor Reuter is awakening the politically apathetic, the "normal Germans" who have been so misused by their so-called moral leaders in the past. She is seeing for the first time how ugly her fellow citizens can turn, given the right circumstances. "I had the feeling," she says afterwards, "that if the TV people hadn't been there and someone had acted as leader and given them a torch to burn a mosque, at least some would have responded to the call."

The Turkish community wisely, and by the design of its leaders, has stayed away. The only Turks present are a few teenagers listening apprehensively from the back corners of the square and one Turkish fellow citizen who will later take the microphone for a short, calm statement. The mosques, hoping to avoid escalating the conflict, have opted to keep their spokesmen home. In their absence, Pastor Reuter regains the microphone and calls upon the Turks in Duisburg—a city that has forty-three mosques, and one where Turks and Germans had lived peacefully for more than twenty years—to reject the attempt to amplify the call to prayer and thus stand against growing religious conservatism.

The Duisburg mayor, Josef Krings, interrupts—to take on Reuter. Duisburg, he says, must remain a city open to the world. "This is a harbor city [on the Rhine] and we live from the ability of different groups to coexist." He says that an American journalist is in town to write about the situation. "If this journalist sends a message to the world that the Muslims don't have a place in Duisburg, it would be a disaster."

The crowd shouts the mayor down.

They want more of Pastor Reuter. But the moderator holds the microphone away from him. He hands it instead to Gerd Bildau, the Duisburg official responsible for education and "foreigners."

Bildau looks at the offending pastor. "Herr Reuter, you have a great responsibility in these days, and you aren't accepting it as a Christian."

Whistles pierce the air against Bildau. Shrieks of support for Reuter.

Bildau stubbornly shouts into the microphone over the clamor. "Good citizens of Laar, Herr Reuter's words take us back to the time before the Enlightenment. To the era of the eighteenth and nineteenth centuries, ladies and gentlemen. That was a time of religious wars, of misunderstandings, of intolerance. Pastor Reuter doesn't speak for the entirety of the Protestant church."

He begins to explain Reuter's membership in a group of dissidents in the synod, fundamentalists themselves. He wants them to understand that Reuter doesn't represent mainstream church thinking.

More shouts. The crowd wants Reuter's message, not that of Bildau.

But Bildau stubbornly holds onto the microphone. He reminds townspeople that the Turks, when they first came to Germany as guest workers, were invited to pray in the Cologne Cathedral as a sign of national welcome. Certainly, he says, you don't want to go backwards. Pastor Reuter "says he's talking in the name of Christianity, but he is setting people against each other. And then he says at the end of his service that they should 'go in peace.' That is anti-Christian."

One of the pastor's lay supporters, Erich Christ, takes the microphone. The newspapers had been carrying his letters of support for Pastor Reuter's campaign. He speaks calmly about the unconstitutionality of the call to prayer. He talks of an article in Germany's Constitution that protects "negative freedom of belief." No one need share in a belief they don't hold—and that the cry of the muezzin is a violation of this freedom. Some say ringing church bells are louder and represent the same invasion, but Erich Christ avers that as Germany is a Christian society, the bells don't represent the same offense.

The crowd is happy again.

Heads nod, voices agree.

The nationally televised event had been shocking enough to the Protestant church that it came down hard on Pastor Reuter; he was silent for months thereafter. Though Reuter won't discuss details of the conflict with his church, he tells me when I reach him by phone that he can't meet with me "for the time being" because of pressure against him. Perhaps in a few months.

In the meantime, he suggests I call his lay supporter who had spoken out on his behalf in the square. When I phone Erich Christ, he says that he and his brother, Peter, would be happy to meet with me. They have taken on some of the burden of the pastor's good works, answering letters, fielding phone calls, gathering signatures on petitions, and raising contributions for "the cause" against Islam. They are willing to meet with an "objective" reporter, which I declare myself to be.

The two brothers and their wives meet me in front of Peter Christ's neat home in a suburban Duisburg neighborhood of freshly painted houses and tidy gardens. They greet me at the roadside and invite me inside for cake; it is that time of afternoon. The table in the sitting room is set with fine china and filled with the aroma of fresh coffee.

Erich explains how he first woke up to the Islamic threat. It began when he received a mission newsletter in September 1996 from a place called Dillenburg, in the federal state of Hessen, where a debate was ranging over whether the local mosque should win permission to amplify its call to prayer. The article coolly reported that two German communities had already approved similar applications.

"Something felt wrong about this," says Erich. "I immediately had the feeling that this was a massive provocation from the Turkish side." He was so troubled, he says, that he educated himself more. "I wanted to understand better what was eating at me, the reasons that might lie behind it."

His wife, Elisabeth, pours me coffee. Just the right amount of cream. She has done up her hair and put on a nice dress for our meeting. The Christs are a German middle-class couple right out of central casting, well dressed, softly spoken, and gracious.

"Sugar?" she asks sweetly.

As I decline, she provides me her view about the controversy. "It's all about power. That's what they want here. It's what the call to prayer symbolizes. They are penetrating my air space with this call to prayer. And that disturbs me. It doesn't belong here—maybe in Damascus, Ankara, or Istanbul. When I go on vacation to these places with southern European flair, I expect it. But please, not here."

It was early on that Erich told his younger brother Peter what was troubling him. Says Peter: "I thought, that's the last thing we need. The Turks have tried to take Europe twice, and now they are at it again."

Eric senses my skepticism. So he provides a short history lesson. The Turks' first try to take northern Europe, he says, ended in the year 732 when Charles Martel defeated and destroyed the Arabs at Poitiers. In 1389 a Turkish army under Sultan Murad I defeated a southern Slav-Serbian force under Lazar I Hrebeljanovic, bringing Serbia under the Turkish yoke. In 1529, Suleiman the Magnificent had to withdraw from his siege of Vienna due to the Hapsburgs' bitter resistance. In 1683, the Turks' second siege of Vienna failed and was followed by the Europeans' retaking of Bulgaria, Serbia, and Transylvania, and the peace agreement of Karlowitz in 1699.

What Germany is now experiencing, he says, is a new Islamic onslaught with modern methods used for modern times. "They are at it again," says Erich Christ flatly. "We insist that this Occidental country, this country of Christianity, be defended as the last bastion against Islam." In his view, the role that Germany was playing was that of a modern-day Vienna—but lying undefended before Ottoman conquerors.

The problem, he concedes, is rallying the population to recognize the threat. The country's bad history had dulled its good sense. Some originally courageous citizens, he says, even asked that their names be removed from petitions they had already signed against the muezzin's call or in favor of Pastor Reuter. And the Christs had gathered far less money than they had hoped in their fund-raising campaign.

Erich's wife Elisabeth complains, "If you say you are against the Turks, then you are called Nazis. But it is because we are against fascism that we are against what's happening. The problem is that they, these Turks, don't want to integrate. They want to build a state within a state. Turks go into the street-car and tear up seats. They threaten people. But we don't have a right to say anything strongly against this because we are guilty of the death of the Jews."

As if to prove that their politics aren't Nazi, Eric pulls out a book that he has been reading called *The White Rose.* It is about the siblings Hans and Sophie Scholl, whose acts of resistance as Catholic students at the University of Munich resulted in their execution in 1943. Erich Christ views himself in their tradition, stopping the forward march of radical Islam and the new threat of religious fascism. "I see a danger for our Western community. You must act in an exemplary manner when democracy is endangered."

Peter shows me the advertisement that had so inspired the Christ broth-ers, placed by Pastor Reuter in November 1996. It had so impressed him that he and his wife traveled across town to attend Pastor Reuter's Christmas ser-vice. He then played the church organ at Reuter's services on New Year's Eve. "I even remember what I played: Praise be to God."

After that, the Christs began volunteering their time to Reuter, helping him answer the flood of cards and letters he received from all over the coun-try. Most of them were supportive, they say. After Reuter was attacked by church authorities, they gathered signatures to stabilize his position within the church, four thousand in all.

Peter Christ shows me another book I should read: *The Mullahs on the Rhine.* His brother later ships me my own copy. They are missionaries trying to win a convert.

"The bottom line is these Turks don't want to be Germans," Peter Christ insists.

I tell them about my time at the Dortmund Stadium. How I met many Turks who wanted German citizenship. I say the Turks there didn't strike me as all that threatening, merely wanting to practice their religion in Germany. They smile in unison as if thinking, You poor, naïve American, you really don't understand, do you?

Elisabeth speaks of an Islamic law called the Taqiya. "They're allowed to lie by their religion. The Koran says they are required to lie to us if it serves Islam."

I check this later in a book by Dr. Ursula Spuler-Stegemann, called

Muslims in Germany, which explains it a bit differently: "One can hardly translate this concept into German . . . Taqiya means that the Muslim can conceal his religious identity or his true intentions in case of threat."

"They don't have anything in common with us," says Erich. "They don't walk in the woods on Sundays. They don't ride bicycles. They don't go to the theater. Our country doesn't mean shit to them. But we swallow all of this because we can't take pride any more in being German. Our history is too burdened."

Elisabeth says she knows a couple of Turks, good Turks, who agree that 75 percent of their kind should be sent back "to where the pepper grows." She worries particularly about new Koran schools that *Milli Görüş* is establishing which "indoctrinate against the Germans. They want to introduce Islamic laws here. The girls won't participate in gym. They don't join the *Wanderwoche* [the week of hiking introduced by an earlier German president to get the natives out into their woods at least once a year]."

Her brother Peter nods. "Let's not mince words. He who wants to integrate here, who is ready to accept our ways and traditions, is welcome. He who can't adjust to our ways can take off from Düsseldorf airport, and the German government should buy his ticket for him."

I note that Germany's history of deportations might make such forced transports unlikely.

Erich doesn't agree that Germany's treatment of the Jews should make them shy of deporting uncooperative Turks. The latter had come as guest workers, he argues, and now there is no more work and thus no more need for the guests. It is time to go home. "Sending them away isn't repeating Auschwitz. We've got to get over that way of thinking. Auschwitz was an extermination camp. In Anatolia, the sun shines, there are blue skies and beautiful beaches. Flowers grow. That's no punishment. They'll be better off."

Elisabeth smiles and asks whether I want another cup of coffee. I nod and she refills my cup.

"The problem was that the Jews didn't have their own country," she says.

Peter agrees. "They had nowhere to go. No one wanted them. That is not the case with the Turks."

Adds Elisabeth, "The real problem is how they reproduce. In a generation, there will be ten million of them. And we are becoming fewer all the time because of our own low birth rates. And then there will be pressure from here to bring Turkey into the European Union. Then we're all finished." Erich notices my look of consternation. He wants to make the matter crystal clear to this uninformed American: "The problem you have with Blacks is what we'll have with the Turks. They'll be our niggers—only worse."

"Your niggers?" I say.

His wife whispers in his ear.

"Take out the word nigger and call them colored."

His wife says perhaps "Blacks" is the more appropriate English word to use in my text. I nod that it is.

"Change it for me, please. I don't want anyone calling me a racist," says Erich. "But the fact is that Europe and Islam are a contradiction in terms."

I ask whether they support the rebuilding of the synagogue in Duisburg, which was being largely funded by German federal and local financing. I won't catch them there.

For the first time, Peter's attractive young wife speaks. She has been quietly nodding and occasionally voicing agreement. "I am so proud that thousands of Jews are coming back here. The Russian-Jewish immigration is something we all welcome. I even contributed money to the synagogue."

Says Peter, "If Islam gets established here, the Jews may all have to leave again. For them especially it will be a dangerous situation."

He wants to return to the Turks' proliferation, their central concern. He talks of how Muslims aren't allowed to use condoms or pills. "They're reproducing like rabbits." He recalls a conversation where he heard a Turk say to a German woman, " 'We will fuck you *kaputt*.' Excuse my language."

"The more you read about it and learn, the more your hair stands on end," says Elisabeth.

I only discover later that the statistics don't quite back up their fears. It is true, however, that the "foreigners" share of new births (13.3 percent in 1996) far exceeded their proportion of the population (some 8 percent) and contrasted with only 1.9 percent in 1962 before the arrival of the first Turkish guest workers. In that latter year 18,803 "foreigners" were born, compared to 106,229 in 1996. In Berlin by the end of the century, Turks alone will provide more than 10 percent of live births, though they make up only 7 percent of its population.

The Christs complain that Germans no longer are allowed to express their fears lest they be called Nazis. While French courts had ruled against Islamic girls wearing head coverings in schools, German courts didn't dare take similar action. "We are beginning a liberal dictatorship," complains Peter. "What we can say is proscribed. We can't be against anything. There are no benchmarks any more."

"When you try to show the dangers, they rip you through the shredder," says Erich. Some of the advertisements proposed by their group had been rejected by newspapers, he says.

I mention that for all the action they've taken against the amplified call to prayer, the Turkish community has been unusually silent. They backed off from their demand without protest.

"Yes, they've behaved themselves just fine and have stayed quiet," says Peter. "They can wait us out. Do you have any idea what their numbers will be in a hundred years' time? At current birth rates, there will be sixty-four times more of them." His math is hard to prove, but that doesn't deter him. "At such reproduction levels, we'll go down the tubes. They are fucking us up against the wall."

In dozens of conversations with Germans about Turks, it is surprising how often the complaints revolve around the women's headscarves.

They are unclean.

They are out of the Middle Ages.

They are a demonstration of the women's refusal to assimilate.

They are a sign of oppression of women.

At Dortmund stadium, the German television cameras can't get enough of the sea of headscarves. When I try to make my way to the women's side of the stadium, the ushers block me. The closest I come is an area under the stands where a number of vendors are selling goods to the women.

There is a stand for books on Islam for adults and children, including comics teaching values of the religion. There is a stand for Islamic children's toys, and one for CDs, of which the most popular involves an Islamic freedom fighter. By far the largest stand holds rack upon rack of women's clothing—the modest cloaks and a bottomless supply of scarves in subtle tones.

The women's giggles can be heard from the back, where they are trying on the latest models and assessing each other in the mirrors. All that is un-Western about the scene is the nature of the attire that the women are trying on for size.

After the festival, I catch a group of women outside the stadium. They are happy to speak with me. They are excited about the size of the crowd. "Islam is slowly coming to life," says a twenty-year-old from Stuttgart, Semra Gulergun. She compares it to *Kirmes*, the annual church festival that many German villages hold.

Her German is fluent, unaccented, but why shouldn't it be? She was born in Germany. Her father works at a Thyssen factory and her mother is a housewife. She says many Turkish women of her generation are getting more religious. "Lots of us were wearing jeans and tight T-shirts several years ago. We like this better. But we live as Germans—go to movies, theater. We celebrate birthdays together with our German friends."

The half-dozen young women who circle around all agree that is true. "As Islamic women, we can live more easily here than in Turkey," says her twin sister Suna. "We are more likely to be harassed there. Here everyone is for himself. You wander around the way you like. Nobody sets rules about it. You are put down in Turkey if you're too Islamic."

I ask Semra why she stopped wearing her jeans and T-shirts. Did she have some moment of revelation, of clarity, of conversion?

"I came to this festival because I wanted to be together with my friends," she says, sidestepping my more direct question. "I've been wearing the headscarf for two years. I've been married for a year and a half."

So you did it for your husband?

Partly, she says. "I feel far more comfortable now. I've read, I've learned. I've found my culture. If I go to Turkey, they say, 'The German is here,' and in Germany they always call me a foreigner. I'm only at home with *Milli Görüş*."

Several men are watching me and moving closer. The women look over to them and shrug. They didn't invite me to come talk to them, but they are too polite to send me away. The men don't like my presence. One jerks his head to the left, as if to tell me to go. I ignore him.

What is the attraction of *Milli Görüş* for young people? I ask.

"Milli Görüş offers many opportunities," says Semra. "It brings together young people who think the same. For some, it is a replacement for hash, heroin."

The men regard me with increasing suspicion. Two move closer. It is time to end the interview.

Semra stops me. "You asked what my life was like before, and now I will give you the answer. I was a punk. I had green hair, close shaven. I had a ring in my nose." She points to a tiny scar. "I did everything possible. I can't tell you the half of it. Now all that is gone. I am so much happier. My life is much more regulated. Much more full. Many of my German friends respect that direction. Some of them think I've taken a step backwards, but I think I've come forward. But I remain more German than Turkish. I don't know what Turkish culture is, what people talk about in Turkey, how people have fun."

I tell them that some Germans fear the Turks will someday launch a Holy War against them, once their numbers are large enough. Suna says, "If we get our rights, there is no need for war. If not, it can end that way. But the only time there is *jihad* is when we are threatened. The new *jihad* is this"— she points to the stadium—"that is why we are here."

My last stop in Duisburg was at a youth center called *Kiebitz* in the heavily Turkish district of Marxloh, named for a bird that likes to look in other nests. I wanted to see close up one of the many projects in Germany whose aim is to promote understanding between Turks and Germans.

One of the highlights of the year at Kiebitz is its "Theater Days" when high schools from throughout the region perform plays that act out whatever may be the students' concerns. The play that was getting the teachers' unofficial vote as the most troubling of the year was entitled, *Perhaps Someday It Will All Be Somehow Different.*

When the lights go down, the spot focuses on a star-crossed couple, a German Romeo and a Turkish Juliet. The students of Comenius Hauptschule from nearby Hamborn have added an ingenious twist: Turks are playing Germans, and Germans (some with painted-on mustaches) Turks.

The plot is simple enough. A Turkish girl has started an innocent friendship with a German boy, and that is turning her friends, her family, and particularly her brother against her—and naturally, against him. The Turkish family scenes are ugly, full of violence and shouting. The overbearing brother is brutal and threatening. The scenes among the Turkish girls are touching but telling: all counsel their friend to dump the German.

The drama builds to a final scene where a Turkish and German gang confront each other over the honor of the girl and her family. "Go home to where you came from," shouts the largest and angriest of the Germans toward the Turkish gang.

"I'll show you where I'll send you," says one of the Turks (a role-playing German girl with a mustache painted on). She raises her knife and prepares to plunge it into the chest of the offending German.

Müjgan Bayur, the director of the center, shudders as she talks about the play afterward. "Is this really what our world has become?"

She says her generation of Turks in Germany was much more assimilated and less religiously influenced than the current one. "That play is their reality. It reinforces all the prejudices we might have had—the violent family, the girl without rights, the separation between German and Turkish societies. As a Turk, I took a lot of deep breaths. It was so authentic! But these conflicts are new. I grew up in German culture. What they are talking is another culture that now exists in Germany that I don't know. I thought to myself, this just can't be true. All that saved me was the ending."

Just before the gang member can sink his knife into the German's chest, the brother shouts from behind.

"*Stop!* What's happening? Have you all gone crazy?"

They freeze in place.

"You started it all," says the distraught sister. "This is your work."

"But I never wanted *this*," protests the brother. "What is happening to us? I just wanted the guy to lay off of you."

"But we like each other. We should be able to like and love who we want. Why can't we be with each other if we like each other?"

Then the bad German walks out from his gang to deliver the final message to the audience.

"Perhaps one day it will all be somehow different."

TEN

CRIME IN THE FAMILY: PART TWO

The name Kramer at the time was for me as well as for all the prisoners there the embodiment of one of the worst ruffians and sadists of General Pape Street.
— HANS-JOACHIM SCHLESINGER,
FORMER PRISONER

I regret today most deeply the events of that time and can only say in my defense that the political circumstances played a large role . . .
— ERICH KRAMER,
MY GREAT-UNCLE

I wait but briefly at the unguarded gate that stands between me and my family's darkest secrets. The compound behind it is engirded by ten-foot high, chain-link fences, wired to be electronically monitored and reinforced by a crown of concertina wire. It is as if someone is warning me not to enter.

Yet the physical security is all that remains of the building's past residents, the East German foreign intelligence operation. The time-soiled, gray complex behind it—of the prefabricated construction characteristic of postwar socialist architecture—once contained some of the country's most secret documents, collected by more than a thousand agents whom superspy Markus Wolf ran in the West. His branch of the *Stasi*, East Germany's state security apparatus, shredded most of what could incriminate it before it was disbanded.

The building now serves as the vault for other archives, collected by the Stasi on a miscellany of other subjects. What had lured me are documents East Germany collected on the Nazi pasts of thousands of Germans, East and West. This cache served the Stasi as leverage to convince reluctant citizens to serve as informants. The intended threat was clear: if they didn't cooperate, they would, at the very least, see the dirty laundry of their past hung out for general viewing, and, at worst, they could be imprisoned or executed.

I throw open the unlocked gate and enter a Communist ghost town. The hallways are still painted in the sorts of unnatural melon and green pastels available only in a country liberated of consumer tastes. The scent of socialism rises from dull linoleum floors; the odor of cheap detergent hangs in stale air unperturbed by ventilation.

I walk down a long, empty hallway toward the sound of distant typing. An apparatus involving heavy string still hangs outside many doors, a crude security device that allowed the Stasi to seal shut offices with hot wax each night. Before the days of digital locks, and in such an authoritarian country, that's all the security that was needed. Workmen are in the process of removing each of these devices as they repaint the halls. No one uses them anymore now that the building's purpose is to open previously secret files to the public.

Near the end of the long hallway, whose only sign of life is a forlorn, meagerly decorated Christmas tree, I find the office of the archivist. An emergency flashlight still hangs in a small box on the wall of her workroom, left from the days when even Markus Wolf couldn't stop the frequent power outages of an inefficient economy. She keeps the flashlight filled with batteries, though she can't remember when it was last used.

Here, with the twenty-first century just around the corner, I was nearing the end of my search for the *new* Germany—a search that had drawn me to a stadium filled with a new Islamic minority, to the homes of my Berlin basketball club, and even to Bosnia with young soldiers on postwar Germany's first combat mission abroad. Yet I was again being drawn as by a magnet to Germany's *past*.

Before he was hanged at Nuremberg, Hans Frank, the Third Reich's Governor General of Poland, said, "A thousand years will pass and the guilt of Germany will not be erased." Now, more than a half century later, the past was still returning. In 1998, it assumed the shape of victims' suits against banks and industrial concerns which had profited from the Holocaust. In one, American lawyers sought the entire ten-billion-mark worth of Degussa AG, a company that once had provided the gas that killed Jews and then exploited the gold fillings from their mouths. And one of the hottest election issues that year was whether or not to approve a monstrous Holocaust memorial in Berlin.

Each new generation of Germans would be seized by a need to understand how one of the world's more civilized countries went mad. So it isn't surprising that I, too, wanted to know more.

Months after I had launched an investigation of my family's past, I received notice that Stasi files contained information on my great-uncle Erich Kramer. And that is what had led me to this curious complex in the far outskirts of eastern Berlin, in the Hoppegarten district that is best known for its horse racing track.

The archivist wears thick-rimmed glasses and a gray pallor to match her surroundings. She hands me a small key and sends me to a room across the hall, where I find lockers for coats and belongings. "Many people who come here," she says, "remain for several days or even weeks, so we try to make them feel at home."

By the looks of what she's about to hand me, however, my stay will be a short one. The Erich Kramer file is disappointingly thin: a single folder containing only a small booklet and twenty or so other single-sheet, yellowing documents. If this is all the Stasi had on my uncle Erich, considering the German passion for record-keeping, he must have been small-fry indeed.

I turn to the booklet first, its brown cover dated May 1951. I flip quickly through its pages and see it contains the photographs and histories of a couple of dozen suspected war criminals, a rogue's gallery compiled by some group that called itself "The Association of Nazi Victims." I return to the cover page and its bold headline: *Wer kennt diesen Mann?*—Who Knows This Man? The publishers are looking for help. A smaller headline underneath makes the appeal: *Witnesses from concentration camps are being sought.*

The cover boy is my great-uncle, his large ears sticking out from a gaunt and severe face. The Association of Victims has determined that he is the worst of that month's featured perpetrators. Small type under his name provides a short biography: "born on January 6, 1905, in Berlin, was with the field police on General Pape Street and there he was one of the most brutal thugs and he is considered guilty of committing crimes against humanity on the prisoners." The pamphlet says nothing more about him, except to provide specific directions about where to deliver leads.

I look around the workroom at others toiling at their desks. Two older men hover at separate tables over thick, bound books of documents, stacked several high to form a wall in front of them. A young man sits at the only other occupied work area, absorbed by documents far more plentiful than my own. I feel a sense of file envy. They take no notice of me; they are working with the practiced concentration of men who have been at this for some time. In another setting, I would have taken the time to interview them, probing the secrets they wanted to unearth. But for the moment, it is my own family's skeletons that absorb me.

The first page I fall upon outlines the charges leveled against Uncle Erich by eastern German authorities: crimes against humanity at an *Auffanglager,* or reception camp, that had been established in February 1933 for the "incarceration, interrogation and torturing" of Hitler's political opponents, mostly among Communists and Social Democrats. The Jews would only later become Enemy Number One.

President von Hindenburg had named Adolf Hitler chancellor on January 30, 1933. Almost immediately thereafter, the then-Prussian Prime Minister Hermann Göring converted thousands of Hitler's *Sturmabteilung* (SA or storm troopers) into auxiliary police, or *Hilfspolizei.* With that action, Göring was giving official sanction to the unruly street gangs that had helped bring Hitler to power. Hitler himself explained that he was giving the

Brownshirts broader police powers "to replace that portion of the other police initially considered unreliable."

The documents offer an ugly glimpse at how the storm troopers would help Hitler consolidate and expand his power through terror.

The first witness statement is from a Karl Duft, described as a local founder of the Communist party in Erfurt. He had been arrested on June 6, 1933. By that time, in the words of William L. Shirer in *The Rise and Fall of the Third Reich*, "Judges were intimidated; they were afraid for their lives if they convicted and sentenced a storm trooper, even for cold-blooded murder. Hitler had become the law."

And Uncle Erich was his enforcer.

Duft says the storm troopers first forced him, upon his admission to the "reception camp," to stand for four hours in a corner of a dark cellar and watch them beat other prisoners. He quickly came to know Kramer "as one of the most notorious thugs." Continues Duft: "After standing there for four hours, I had to take my place on a bench in the hallway of the cellar. In the passing of the following night, a Jew who was sitting next to me explained that he had just been forced to lick clean pools of blood in the lavatory that had been left by an anti-fascist by the name of Lemke who had been shot in the courtyard of the building and been brought to the lavatory afterward (apparently to remove his clothing, before sending off the corpse) . . .

"The next morning I had to return to the cellar where I was interrogated. They demanded that I give them the names of anti-fascists and where they could find more political materials. After I refused to give the information they requested, I was so beaten by several SA thugs that I lost all my teeth and had a hemorrhage. I can't tell you anymore exactly how many SA men hit me, but I know for certain that . . . Kramer operated as one of the most terrible of the ruffians."

Duft was brought to the sick bay of Moabit prison the next day, then was sentenced to two years in prison for preparing high treason. An investigator's note on the back of Duft's account reports that the witness easily identified Kramer from photographs.

The next several affidavits include similar accounts of brutality, but the witnesses couldn't identify Kramer from photographs, nor did they know his name. Perhaps, I think, that is why Kramer got off in the end. If only this Duft could testify against him, this was hardly sufficient for conviction. How credible can testimony be from a leading Communist, questioned by East German authorities about a Nazi Brownshirt only five years after war's end?

But whatever slim hope I harbored about my great-uncle's innocence evaporates as I read further. A Karl Albert Ulrich, described only as an antifascist, confirms Kramer was part of the prison's permanent staff and "liked to show off as a particularly cold-blooded thug." He relates a story of how Kramer roughed up his own brown-shirted colleagues who had been on the wrong side of a power struggle that resulted in the purging and execution in 1934 of SA commander Ernst Röhm, a long-time friend of Adolf Hitler. In the days that followed, Hitler announced that sixty-one persons were shot, including nineteen higher SA leaders. Thirteen died "resisting arrest" while three "committed suicide." A later trial would conclude that a thousand SA men in all were slain.

Kramer cleverly cast his lot with Hitler and against his fellow storm troopers. "I specifically remember, for example, a case where Kramer, in my presence, beat one of the SA leaders over the head with the butt of a carbine," recounted Ulrich. (I later learn that he had probably been eager to prove his loyalty to Hitler; he'd lost his party card three years earlier for being on the wrong side of an SA leadership rivalry. The National Socialist Party would soon restore his membership, following the personal intercession, his wife would later tell her children, of Josef Goebbels.)

One page after another paints a similarly ugly picture of Erich Kramer. Another former prisoner, Hans Felix Lindner, says Kramer's clubbing cracked his skull and his jack boot ruptured his testicles. Kramer held a pistol to his head to get a confession which, of course, he provided.

There is a sameness to the testimonies, yet one particularly catches my eye, from a Käthe Elsa Antonie Ziburski. She is described as Erich Kramer's first wife. I had read in the Horst Wessel biography about their curious courtship. Kramer had been guarding the grave of Wessel, SA martyr and friend. She had come to visit the grave of a previous SA lover. On the spot, however, Kramer wooed and won her. The story echoed Shakespeare's Richard III. And like Richard, Kramer had a deformity by which all his victims remembered him: a cataract-fogged eye produced a one-eyed, ice-cold stare that his prisoners seldom forgot.

Kramer told his son Franz that he had divorced Käthe because he'd caught her sleeping with one of his SA comrades. Yet she tells investigators that Kramer sought the divorce on grounds that she was half-Jewish, an unsuitable partner for a man of Kramer's employment. He moved in with his second wife, my great-aunt Alma Schumann Kramer, the opera singer, even before he appears to have been divorced. He married her on October 25, 1936, twenty days after the birth of Franz, whom she would have conceived while Kramer was still married to Käthe.

Käthe Ziburski reports that she often witnessed her husband, in a drunken state, cooking up new forms of torturing the prisoners with his buddies. "For example," she says, "they talked about how they would cut open the soles of prisoners' feet and then spread pepper in the wounds." It was her husband, she testifies, "who always suggested the greatest cruelties." He even told his wife a couple of times that he'd like her to be the witness to his methods so that she would know what might await her if she should ever stand against him.

The report on his first wife's testimony is only a page long, but every line increases my pain. I let out a low, pained sigh, which goes unnoticed by the others in the room who have their own histories to digest. Käthe says that even hard-core Brownshirts pulled away from Kramer, and some even shed their uniforms and sought other work because "they couldn't witness or join in the cruelties any longer."

To be fair, the report notes Ziburski didn't personally witness her husband's inhumanities. Still, I can't imagine a more damning character witness than such a wife. I wonder how he was ever able to get off on grounds of "lack of evidence."

I close the folder and fill out the form that requests copies of all the enclosed documents. Franz and Manfred, Erich Kramer's two sons, want to see whatever I find. I wonder whether they will thank me or damn me.

I return the file and the form to the archivist.

"Did you find what you needed?" she asks.

"I'm afraid so," I say.

She smiles at me knowingly.

I seek comfort, not for the first time, in the thought that Kramer hadn't any Kempe or Schumann blood. He merely married into our untainted family, I remind myself. Yet I know my larger luck is that I was born American. Germans with far less connection to the Third Reich than our family had grown up with far more historical burden than had I.

As I fetch my coat and bag in the locker room, I chat with one of the old men who is also preparing to leave. He and his friend are former East German military officers. They had led proud lives, but unification had cast all sorts of doubts about the integrity of their National People's Army, its links to State Security, to the Communist party and to Moscow. They want to know the truth behind their lives.

The younger man, who joins our conversation, is a free-lance journalist who makes television documentaries. He'd met a woman who only discovered late in life that her father had been a notorious SS man; his job had been to infiltrate opposition groups, often leading to the arrest or execution of their members. The journalist says he might produce some television documentary about the man, or perhaps he would simply pass his findings on to the woman.

He suggests we drive to the local McDonald's, just down the road, to chat further. He stops at the sign of the golden arches after each day's research. "It makes me feel as though I've returned back to a healthy world," he smiles.

Free hot-air balloons float by the entrance; children help themselves on the way to the playground in front. The only reminder that one is still in Germany is the offer of beer on the colorful board over the cash registers.

I order one with my Big Mac. The reporter asks for a McRib sandwich. We sit and I chat with the journalist about the SS man he's studying.

I am an American correspondent again, safely back on home turf. I've escaped Adolf Hitler's Reich for the land of Ronald McDonald.

A letter from Berlin District Court authorities arrives several days later, confirming that after a considerable search they have found the records on the Erich Kramer trial.

By the time I finally stand in the entrance hall to the Moabit District

Courthouse in Berlin, six more months have passed and countless letters and telephone calls had been exchanged. The place has the imposing aura of a cathedral to justice: high brick walls from the turn of the century rise cold and dark to several floors of offices above.

It is also a place of history: the trial of former East German leader Erich Honecker took place here; he sat in Moabit prison just across the road before spending his final days in South American exile. Former East German State Security boss Erich Mielke was prosecuted and imprisoned here as well, before his release on health grounds. Like Kramer, he was tried for prewar crimes, his murder of a Third Reich policeman. (I had begun to wish the murdered policeman had been my uncle Erich.)

It's a busy morning in Moabit, and I stand at the end of a long queue behind one of the two metal detectors. I wonder whether the security isn't a little overdone until a slender, inconspicuous young man in front of me empties his pockets of a switchblade and brass knuckles. He steps to a desk to surrender and register the paraphernalia, takes a receipt, and passes through.

I wait behind him carrying a heavy, portable copy machine awkwardly under my right arm. In my left hand, I hold a special permit to bring the copier into the building. I've endured a long, bureaucratic process to gain access to the archives and to copy their contents.

At first, the court officers said I could see only part of the material due to "protection of data" laws that would require the sanitizing of documents with names other than that of Erich Kramer. After Hitler and then East Germany so abused the personal details of its citizens' lives, democratic Germany has lurched to the other extreme—protection of data far-reaching enough to frustrate census-keepers and Internet builders.

My American passport makes the matter all the trickier—for "the transfer of data abroad," I would need the formal okay of the Berlin Senate's Administration for Judicial Matters. And that could take many months.

It is only the power of attorney I have from Kramer's son, Franz, that allows me to avoid these particular spools of red tape. With it the state attorney consents to open all the Kramer files to me. But by the time he has done so, three months have passed. And more red tape lies ahead. When I ask whether I can make copies of all the files, the state attorney informs me that the office where I'll be working hasn't a copier and the archives can't be removed to any other part of the building that might have a copier. That said, I am invited to apply for permission to carry a copier into the building, which I would have to carry with me.

Only after I receive that clearance from the state attorney, several weeks later, to use a copier, do I learn that an entirely separate permission is required to bring the now approved copier into the building. This one must come from the President of the District Court himself. When I question this distinction, the state attorney's office explains that it is only logical that the state attorney rules on its bailiwick, whether one may copy documents, while the court rules on its bailiwick, whether one may bring the machine to copy the documents into the building.

And at this point I reach conclusions about German bureaucracy:

1) Germans apply the random and often illogical practices and rules of bureaucracy in a more exacting way than most of mankind. Rules don't need to make sense, for they are respected as the necessary glue that holds society together.

2) Germans in one realm of bureaucracy will seldom volunteer information about potential problems one might face from a related but different bureaucracy.

Our absurd exchange could have continued, had I let it. Something like this:

"Why didn't you tell me I would need an additional permit for my copier?"

"But you didn't ask."

"But you must have known from previous experience."

"I am only required to comment on my area of responsibility."

In this case, such an exchange doesn't transpire because I recognize bureaucrats can be petty. A small argument like this could endanger my ability to get at the truth about Uncle Erich. So I bite my lip.

Now I ask the security guards where I must go to find the archives of the public prosecutor. No one knows. And no one seems interested in finding out for me (not their area of responsibility). After additional prodding, a guard finally dispatches me to the basement.

A confusing labyrinth of hallways awaits me there, with stacks and shelves of files on all sides—a scene out of Kafka's *The Trial.* A worker appears out of one of the rooms, looks suspiciously at my copier, and informs me that I am in the wrong place. He escorts me and my apparatus up a freight elevator to the top floor, directly under the roof, a similar maze of files. The stale air is thick with dust.

The house archivist, with whom I have been corresponding, spots me and invites me to his office. He is upset I had so much trouble finding him—the people at the security desk ought to have known where he was located. He has many visitors every day. I'm lucky today that I'm his only customer, he says. He has already fished out two thick stacks of documents on Erich Kramer for me, stuffed in red file folders that I had seen by the thousands downstairs.

It is noon, however, and the archivist informs me that I only have two more hours before his day ends. After all, it is Friday, and like any other good civil servant he ends his week at two in the afternoon. I set up my copier on a desk in his office and plug it in. I must copy as much as I can in the time available, a curious rush after so many weeks of waiting.

There's no sign from the files that anyone has looked through them since the case was closed. I separate pages that are stuck together, careful not to rip them and lose their content. The brittle ends of the decrepit paper crumble in my hands. I place one sheet after another under the hot lamp of the copier. When I finish, the table is littered with paper shreds from the decaying sheets. I sweep them into a garbage can. I reckon the fragile sheets will only stand up to one or two more readings before they simply dissolve. I replace the files in their folders and bid farewell to the archivist, copier under one arm and copied documents under the other. I ask him how long his office will preserve such files before destroying or discarding them.

"Forever," he says.

The Kramer matter is considered a political case and such matters are never destroyed, he says. He rolls his eyes as he says this, because for him this is a catastrophe; he hasn't room for all the documents.

I excuse myself to return home to read my family history.

I keep the several hundred pages of files separated into the two categories under which they were organized: the first chronicles the investigation and the questioning of witnesses, and the second documents the court case itself and Kramer's acquittal.

I read through the first.

It turns out that police first got on to my great-uncle, after his return from Soviet prison camp, because he was spotted by one of his former victims while walking down the leafy Prenzlauer Allee, near Dmitroff Strasse, in eastern Berlin during October 1950. For years, Franz thought his father landed in hot water after Stasi men on a streetcar overheard his father's criticism of the coming "fraud" elections. But the Stasi already had been trailing him at the time.

The man who fingered Kramer was A. Schierz, a civil servant who had only been twenty years old when he first encountered my uncle's cataract-scarred, gray-filmed right eye and the rigid, inflexible stare of his left eye. Erich had the archetypal look of a villain, a look one witness after another recounted. Schierz recalls that Kramer hit him in the face as he entered the holding facility.

Kramer was often the acting supervisor at the General Pape Street facility. He wore the title of *Obertruppenführer*, but he had the responsibilities of the more senior *Sturmführer*, as his own superior was rarely there. The pages contain accounts of cruelties that went far beyond what I had read before. The result is that the Berlin State Court, as it was known at the time, charged him in 1952 with murder, crimes against humanity, and applying torture and violence to gain confessions.

The witness statements read like pages from a period thriller. The Reichstag was set in flames on February 27, 1933, less than a month after President von Hindenburg named Hitler chancellor on January 30, thus beginning a twelve-year and four-month Nazi rule that was to have been a thousand-year Reich. At the site of the fire, Hermann Göring shouted with excitement to the Gestapo chief Rudolf Diels: "This is the beginning of the Communist revolution! We must not wait a minute. We will show no mercy. Every Communist official must be shot, where he is found. Every Communist deputy must this very night be strung up."

On the day following the fire, February 28, Hitler prevailed on President Hindenburg to suspend individual and civil liberties, thus allowing him not only to legally gag his opponents but also arrest them at his will by making the trumped-up Communist threat "official."

Truckloads of storm troopers like my Uncle Erich roared through the streets all over Germany, breaking into homes, rounding up victims and carting them off, usually to the sites of SA barracks, which often contained the sort of makeshift prison that was found at General Pape Strasse. The first documented date of a death there, apparently as a result of torture, was March 22, which was also the day the first Nazi-controlled Reichstag was convening to vote an "Enabling Act"—the "Law for Removing the Distress of People and Reich." Hitler had enough members of parliament arrested, detained, or otherwise blocked from reaching the Reichstag building that his victory was ensured, 441 for and 84 against. This was the vote that made his dictatorship official.

Even as my uncle Erich was kicking prisoners and torturing them, fellow storm troopers outside the Reichstag and Nazi deputies inside sprang to their feet to sing the song that his fabled friend Horst Wessel, the SA neighborhood leader killed in 1930 by Communists, had written.

Raise high the flags! Stand rank on rank together.
Storm troopers march with steady, quiet tread . . .

From March 23, 1933, onward, Hitler was the dictator of Germany, and my great-uncle was one of the storm troopers who would ensure that his political opponents hadn't any recourse. In the words of the historian Allan Bullock, "The street gangs had seized control of the resources of a great modern state, the gutter had come to power."

Kramer represented that gutter.

In a statement a month after his arrest, Kramer described his job thus: "A short time after the Reichstag fire, I was taken into the newly created SA *Feldpolizei*—the military police. I enjoyed the rank of *Obertruppenführer*, carried the brown SA uniform with red collar patches and two stars with a braid. After a short time, the collar patch was replaced by a white collar patch and besides that we got a small police star put on it and on the hat. At the General Pape Street location my area of responsibility included the receiving, supervision and the handing of evidence, and the processing of all the individuals who entered the building or left it . . . I also received the assignment now and again to conduct interrogations . . . In exceptional cases during the questioning I conducted I got carried away to the point of beatings. If you ask me whether in these cases I used a whip, my fists, or whether I even gave prisoners a kick, I must explain to you that today I can no longer remember."

As I read further, I discover there's a great deal my uncle Erich can't recall. For one thing, what he did to a Jewish doctor named Fränkel—who testifies he was stripped naked, covered with a red flag, and forced through all the cells repeating, "I am the biggest rogue and swindler, I've always betrayed my people."

Ah, the innocent early days of Nazism. These were small crimes compared to what would follow at Auschwitz. And for the moment, a German's leftist politics were still considered more dangerous to him than his Judaism.

Kramer also can't remember Kurt Friedrich Otto Knobel, who says Kramer's beating broke his nose and lower jaw, knocked out fifteen of his teeth, and resulted in a hernia, not to mention long-term damage to his heart and nerves. Knobel recalls fainting from pain. When he came to, he lay in a room with several prisoners all of whom were bent over in pain and groaning.

Prisoner Hans-Joachim Schlesinger draws a gruesomely vivid picture of the sadistic world of the General Pape Street holding facility. Schlesinger neglected to hand over his watch to Kramer, who was booking him into the facility. "That was enough for Kramer to reach over the desk and hit me with the flat of his hand in the face and curse me with words like *Lausejunge*—you blighter! Then he came around the desk and smashed his fist in my face."

Schlesinger speaks of "sport" nights every second evening, when the SA men would tank themselves up on drink and then bring the prisoners out of their cells to the dark cellar. The worst of the torture and beatings took place in this dungeon, in the glare of powerful flashlights that the Brownshirts turned on victims' faces. Schlesinger was one of forty or fifty prisoners who had to run the gauntlet, being beaten down the line by one storm trooper after another with whatever weapons he happened to be holding: club, iron bar, pistol butt.

Schlesinger says he doesn't want to bore the investigators with long lists of specific inhumanities, but he feels he should provide detail about one, in July 1933, because it involved "deliberate murder." Schlesinger watched

Kramer badly beat two prisoners, one of whom was then strapped to a gymnastics vaulting horse, draped with a red flag, and wrapped in chains to be mocked.

"This prisoner had been arrested a short time before in a bar and was still drunk enough to defend himself. As a result, he was shot there and then. We other prisoners had to put our faces to the wall (so as not to watch) and were threatened that if we also decided to resist, we too would be shot immediately." Schlesinger nevertheless says he saw the murder out of the corner of his eye, though he couldn't say for sure that Kramer pulled the trigger. The next day, in early afternoon, Schlesinger says guards stopped him as he tried to make his way to the washroom. Looking through the open door, he saw two bodies lying on the floor. "I can't say for sure that one of them was the prisoner they'd strapped to the gymnastics horse, for I only got a quick look. I also can't say that Kramer fired the shots; I only know for sure that he was present."

At this point I become certain that my great uncle Erich Kramer was a killer, regardless of what the court had determined. I look at my fingers, as if expecting them to be soiled from the grime of what I was reading. I saw only fragments of paper. Then I read on.

Schlesinger concludes, "The name Kramer at the time was for me as well as for all the prisoners there the very embodiment of the worst violence and sadism of General Pape Street."

The prosecutor then asks Schlesinger about a statement he made at a previous trial of one of the SA toughs, Ulrich Gaguns, that two field police officers spit in the mouth of a Jew and then made him swallow their phlegm. Schlesinger said he had been mistaken in his statement—only Gaguns was involved. But I can't help but imagine that Uncle Erich would have joined this "sport" as well, if only he had been given the opportunity.

The 1948 trial of this Ulrich Gaguns fed my bewilderment that Uncle Erich had not been prosecuted. The court had sentenced Gaguns, a man of apparently lower rank, authority, and brutality, to ten years imprisonment. During the trial all the witnesses agreed that Kramer—in a Soviet POW camp at the time of Gaguns' trial—had been the crueler of the two.

Gaguns' statement from his prison cell for the Kramer investigation is damning: "Almost everything at Pape Strasse ran according to his command . . . Even the chief there, *Obersturmführer* Fritsch, took his direction from Kramer's suggestions. For his brutality, bordering on sadism, Kramer was the man the prisoners hated most."

Amidst this chronicle of horrors, I fall upon a letter of recommendation for Kramer from the Church of Jesus Christ of Latter-Day Saints, the Mormons. The Mormon Mission President, Walter Stover, who notes in his letter that he is a U.S.A. citizen, intervenes on Kramer's behalf. He asks that Kramer be released to his family on parole, with the church as his guarantor. He's willing to put up the two thousand Deutsche Mark bail.

"Herr K. is personally known to me as a member of our church," he writes, "and I am convinced that he will keep himself available to the court at any time and hasn't any intention to suppress evidence or to leave Berlin." He writes that the mission's appeal is also based on the fact that Kramer had spent six years for the military in battle followed by five years in Russian captivity—enough punishment for any man.

Next in the file is the most damning testimony against Kramer. It comes from Alfred Johler, whom storm troopers had arrested when he was just thirty-three years old on charges that he had destroyed documents of an aviation sport club to which he belonged. The SA wanted to break up the group and bring all private flying under the umbrella of its own club. More to the point, many of the members of Johler's club were poor; they were financed by their richer members, many of whom were Jewish. Johler figures the SA wanted the club's papers, to gain more information about these Jews.

As Johler arrived at the station, Kramer (who many knew by the nickname "der Schwarze"—the black one) cursed him "in the most offensive language." Kramer asked him why he thought he was there, a standard opening line that was an understood request for confession. Johler's answer didn't satisfy him, so Kramer smashed a fist into his face and broke Johler's cheekbone. That was day one.

Johler recalls the dreaded cellar as well, which he remembers was dark except for a lamp that burned in the farthest corner. He and others stumbled through the dark along an obstacle course laid with boxes and benches that one couldn't see, and they occasionally hit their heads on low-hanging steel bars. If anyone cried out, a guard posted in the dark by the benches would strike out at him with a rubber truncheon or other blunt weapon. After about twenty minutes of this, Johler asked Kramer to have consideration for his war injury, a crippled left arm. "He roared at me, 'For you pigs there is no consideration.' "

Kramer ordered them to walk for another twenty minutes through the dark, then he made them stand with their faces against the wall. He left the room as they did so. After holding their positions for some two hours, one of Kramer's colleagues, a man named Kell, asked: "Which of you is thirsty?"

An old man answered that he wanted a drink, but the others remained silent because they suspected a trick, says Johler. But when the guard brought the old man water, the others eagerly asked for a drink as well.

Kell nodded his head toward one of the lower-ranking guards, and he returned with a container of liquid manure collected from the toilets in the prison. He placed it at the entrance to the cellar and then called for Kramer to come downstairs to watch, according to Johler. Kell said to him, "Now you can see how pigs swill." And then he gave the order: "Suck it up!"

I recall at that point the statement from Kramer's first wife, who testifies how her husband and his friends would get drunk and dream up new forms of cruelty. Kramer, she had said, always was the most original in his bestiality. I imagine the scene of Kramer and his friends dreaming up this little number after a few beers.

Erich, the business with the beatings in the cellar is getting a little bit old.
You are right, Hans. But I have a new idea.
Tell me.
A bucket of shit. We have plenty of it, God knows. It's all those losers are good for. We can make them drink it.
(laughter)
Oh, yes, Erich, that's a good one. But before we bring it in we'll make them all so thirsty that they want to die. And we'll ask them if they want a drink.
Ah, very good, Hans. They'll hesitate, distrusting us, but the first one who asks will get a glass of water.
But the next one . . .
. . . will drink shit.
(hilarious laughter.)
Käthe, bring us all another beer.

Says Johler: "Because no one made a move to drink this sewage, Kell took the prisoner standing closest to him and forced his head into the container. The prisoner vomited in the sewage. Kell tipped over the container with his boot, and we had to wipe the cellar [floor] dry with our jackets. After we wrung our jackets out over the container, we had to put them back on. . . . During the whole affair Kramer was always present."

Johler was then brought to Cell #3, which several witnesses describe as the holding chamber for those to be handled most brutally. Some ninety to a hundred prisoners resided there at any one time; Johler lists names and backgrounds—there's no lack of potential witnesses for Kramer's prosecution, it seems. When Kramer entered Cell #3, says Johler, the prisoners had to shout "*Achtung.*" He'd beat any who didn't with a steel pipe or rubber hose filled with lead or copper.

Far larger Nazi brutalities would follow that would make such incidents a bloody footnote. Yet the witness statements make me wonder about what sort of crimes Erich Kramer might have committed as a staff sergeant for military police at the front. If he was willing to handle fellow Germans so brutally, how might he have dealt with Poles, Ukrainian Communists, or East European Jews? I recall the postcards home that put Kramer in Ukraine in 1943 and in Poland at Lodz in 1944, during the breakup of the Jewish ghetto. Franz had told me in passing that his father had never applied for his military pension for fear of the sort of attention that might draw. That fact seems a little more important with each page of testimony against my great-uncle.

The court officers finally list all the cases of "crimes against humanity" that Johler raises:

Case Number One: In July 1933, Kramer led Johler and a dozen other prisoners to the cellar. He forced one to write a goodbye letter to his loved ones because he would be, in Kramer's words, "finished off." When the prisoner finished his letter, he was strapped tightly to a stool. Before being blindfolded, he was allowed to see an assortment of dissecting knives in front of him.

The Brownshirts clattered the knives and gave the prisoner the impression that they were going kill him by cutting open the arteries at his wrists, which would leave the world the impression that he had committed suicide.

One of the men then poured a small pot of water slowly over the arteries to prepare them. He asked the prisoner whether he noticed anything and when he didn't answer, one of the guards poured sewage from the latrine over him.

This liquid manure, known in German as *Jauche*, seemed to be the all-purpose humiliation, a detestable substance in plentiful, unending supply for whatever sadistic "sport" Kramer might choose.

The storm troopers, Johler says, then sent the prisoner, blindfolded and dripping with brown goo, through the cells. They forced other prisoners to beat him. "Kramer was present through all of this," says Johler. They then escorted him upstairs to the guards' quarters, where the thrashing apparently continued. After prisoners carried him back to his cell the next day, a doctor among them named Präetorius inspected his injuries. The doctor told Johler that the prisoner had a fractured skull and on his forehead an open wound large enough to stick his hand through. Says Johler: "The man was brought into another cell where he died. Where his corpse was taken, I don't know." A lower-ranking storm trooper named Truppenführer Franke, who according to Johler treated the prisoners properly and didn't participate in any of the beatings, said later, "It was Kramer who finished off this man."

Much of Johler's evidence is hearsay. But atop everything else, the case against my great-uncle is accumulating considerable weight.

Case Number Two: A few days later, Kramer took another ten prisoners including Johler into the dreaded cellar again. He picked out one of the prisoners, whom he said is to be shot, and who, like the previous one, was made to write a farewell letter. Kramer ordered the man to spread out sheets of paper on the floor and forced him to lie down on them to be sure they'd catch his whole body after he was shot—not wanting to dirty his floor. He ordered him to rise again, then blindfolded him. Five SA men then loudly loaded their weapons near the blindfolded man's ears.

Kramer left the room at this point, says Johler, and handed over command to *Obertruppenführer* Schmidt—nicknamed "Gypsy." Schmidt ordered the SA men to shoot the prisoner, and they indeed pulled their triggers, but on blank cartridges. "The prisoner, to the delight of the SA men, almost died of fright," says Johler.

Still his terror wasn't over. The SA men then chased him out of the cel-

lar and into other cells while beating him with clubs. They forced fellow prisoners, again, to join in the beating. "I never saw the prisoner again and I heard
that he died of the consequences of that day," says Johler.

Case Number Three: A few days after the first two cases, Kramer threw a rope
in front of a prisoner, a policeman alleged to be the treasurer of a group of
Communists called the *Schräder-Verband.* Kramer charged that he had tried to
escape. "If you want to escape, then go hang yourself now," said Kramer, who
then marched him off from the cells to the lavatory.

The next day, Johler heard from two other prisoners that they had cut
down the man, who had either hanged himself or was hanged in the lavatory.
He provided the state attorneys their names. Guards prohibited the prisoners from using the lavatory that day, the only one available to prisoners, an
event Johler remembered well because most ended up having to dirty themselves. The women, who were housed in Cell #2, received a bucket for their
own use.

Case Number Four: Johler tells of the murder of a man named Michalak, a
Social Democratic Party functionary who had been one of the longest serving prisoners, having been pulled in shortly after the facility opened in March
1933.

It was July 1933 when Kramer told him to pack his things and prepare
for his release. "At 21:00 Kramer called Michalak to come upstairs . . . M.
went with his things . . . in the belief that he would receive his release papers.
After Michalak was gone from the cellar for fifteen minutes, we heard shots
from the courtyard. We then heard that a body was being dragged across the
courtyard and down the cellar steps and through the cellar hallway to the
washroom. We further heard in the cellar how Michalak screamed . . . then
more shots in the washroom.

"The next morning, other prisoners and I were called to take away the
dead Michalak, who lay in the washroom, across the hall to the hair-cutting
room. I could see that Michalak had several bullet holes in his back and also
in his face. Guards then made the prisoners clean the blood off the washroom
floor and also wipe up the bloody track along which the body had been
hauled from the courtyard."

Kramer and his men spread the story that Michalak had been shot while trying to escape. "He gathered all the prisoners to tell them the same fate awaited any others who tried to escape."

Case Number Five: Johler spoke of a Pole whom Kramer put through the usual gauntlet of beatings, but he added a new twist this time: the prisoner had to run constantly in a circle and sing Polish and Jewish songs. He was hit all the harder if judged not to be singing loudly enough. At one point, Kramer was said to have forced the Pole to run in circles in the courtyard, barefoot over gravel, while SA men chased after him on bicycles. "The SA men called this the fox hunt," says Johler. The Pole suffered similar treatment almost every day. Johler reports that his clothes hung from him by shreds. "One could see the spots on his body, suffused with blood and ruptured from the blows," says Johler

There is a sameness in the tone of the reports, yet I can't put them down. I close my eyes and try to transpose myself to a period when such cruelty was the norm of what only months earlier had been considered one of the world's most civilized societies.

Case Number Six: In the women's cellar, a female prisoner was incarcerated for having laid a wreath at the base of a lamp where a Communist had been hanged by SA men. Kramer struck her with an iron bar; her screams and curses against him, by name, could be heard by Johler and the other men in the adjoining cell. Prisoners later heard that she died of her injuries while being transported to the hospital.

Case Number Seven: In the buildings behind the garage of the Pape Strasse barracks lived a family that would often look out of the windows and curse the SA men below. The screaming of the tortured prisoners and the occasionally drunken revelry was disturbing the order of the neighborhood. The family father complained loudly, more about the noise than any crime it might suggest.

On a Sunday, says Johler, the storm troopers imprisoned the family father to shut him up and introduced him to their "sport" evenings. When his wife was caught looking into the prison's windows to see if her vanished husband was there, Kramer had her pulled in as well, says Johler. The husband stayed somewhat more than a week, and the wife a few days. I imagine they never complained publicly about the noise again.

Oh yes, adds Johler almost as an afterthought, Kramer incarcerated two storm troopers for having beat up the owners of a tavern called the Nürnberger Trichter in the Augsburger Strasse. Kramer was happy enough to lock them up, but he gave them free rein of the prison, and they returned the favor by carrying out some of the worst punishments on other prisoners.

Johler concludes his statement. "These are the important cases that I still remember and in which Kramer played a substantial role." Now Johler wants to break off the questioning and go home; he is spent. But investigators instead want him to face Kramer and identify him.

The typed statement, I am certain, doesn't capture the drama of this moment.

Johler: "I recognize the person who has just been brought into the room, without any reservations, as the former *Obertruppenführer* of the field police at General Pape Street. As I already described in my statement, I remember Herr Kramer well because of his disfigured eye and other circumstances. Against my expectations, he hasn't changed much in how he looks."

There is a German saying, *Unkraut vergeht nicht*—weeds don't die.

Kramer: After the name of the witness was made clear to me, Alfred Johler, and his nickname, "the racing driver," I declare that I can't remember this man either by name or appearance.

Once investigators confront him with Johler's evidence, Kramer turns testy. He denies all the charges and condemns the prosecutors for so clearly believing Johler. Because of this prejudice against him, he says, he won't talk to the criminal police anymore and will save any statements for the court. "I will never enter this room again, not even compulsorily," he says.

The defensiveness of the guilty, I think to myself.

I thumb through the remaining witness statements; the case against Kramer is overwhelming. And Kramer's lengthy response to the many accusations is unconvincing.

—On the Michalak murder charge: Kramer says he once "by chance heard" that a prisoner was shot while trying to escape and later died of his injuries. He had nothing to do with the case, and knows nothing about the screams and the shouts in the washroom followed by a final shooting, as related by witnesses Meissner and Johler.

—On allegations about his own vicious beating of prisoners: He doesn't deny that he hit prisoners now and then. But, he insists "it was only in cases when the prisoners were denying some accusation. He knows nothing about the witness Schlesinger speaks of, when someone was strapped to the gymnastics horse and was beaten and shot. If prisoners ever heard shots in such situations, Kramer insists they were blanks. As for charges that some prisoners were beat unconscious, he can't recall specific cases, "but I wouldn't rule out the possibility."

The half-denials come one after the other, in such number that the transcriber adopts a shortcut to record one of Erich Kramer's most repeated phrases when asked about specific events: *"m. E nach"*—short for *"meine Erinnerung nach,"* or *"to the best of my memory"*—it didn't happen.

The closest he comes to a confession: "Things happened at the Papestrasse that a morally sensitive human being can only condemn quite sharply."

But again, he is only tangentially involved, an observer sometimes who could stop little, and never a participant, except in relatively minor offenses unlikely to be prosecuted.

The doctor who attended to the prisoners at General Pape Street provides a report to the court listing names of five prisoners who died on the grounds of the holding prison and five others who died of injuries suffered at the hospital to which they were brought.

Ten names seem inconsequential when measured against the six million Holocaust victims. Yet I still feel sick as I read each name. These are some of the first victims of Nazi rule.

Kramer closes his response to his accusers with the following: "I regret today most deeply the events of that time and can only say in my defense that the political circumstances played a large role, particularly as the other side acted in a similar manner before the takeover of power."

This was the closing shot to the investigators. After all the evidence is placed before him, my great uncle Erich can only say he "regrets" the events of that time and blames the political mood and similar brutalities by the "other side."

The second stack of files, documenting the court process and the acquittal, provide an anti-climax. Eyewitnesses are lacking for the murder charges; many have died or won't testify in West Berlin because they are Communists in the East and don't recognize the court's authority. The court is able to prove lesser charges—forced confessions and assault—but Kramer's state-appointed lawyer discovers a technicality that gets his client off.

Whatever crimes Kramer committed, short of murder, are void due to a five-year statute of limitations. The date taken as the legally applicable one for Kramer's crimes was May 1945, the point at which prosecution for his crimes would have been possible because of the war's end. As Kramer was charged and arrested in December 1950, some five years and six months after that date, the court determined it hadn't any right to prosecute him.

No such statute exists for the Third Reich's war crimes or murder, but prosecutors had dropped the murder charges because the witnesses needed were dead or missing. Kramer's lawyer successfully argued that the SA Feldpolizei served the party and not the state, though it seemed to me that the lines between the two had disappeared by 1933.

By the time the ruling came down, my great-uncle had been living relatively freely anyway, working as the chief of the Mormon church's genealogical work. It is the final irony that Uncle Erich chose a form of church work that came closest to his Nazi obsessions—*Ahnenforschung*—the sort of research into ancestors and ethnic backgrounds that drove some of the worst Third Reich crimes.

In a letter to the court seeking leniency, the head of the Berlin mission, Herold Gregory, concedes that when he first met Kramer in 1949 and 1950 during an earlier stay, Kramer hadn't been an active church member. He had been imprisoned shortly before Gregory left the country. Thus he was surprised by Kramer's transformation thereafter to a pious soul who held "a very responsible position in the leadership of the mission."

"I quickly reached the conclusion that I hadn't any reason for reservations. In every respect the work and behavior of Herr Kramer is irreproachable and praiseworthy. . . . Beyond that he was hardworking, loyal, industrious, and full of enthusiasm. He was extraordinarily kind and affectionate to my small daughter, even when he thought that no one was watching. My daughter likes him almost the best of all the people in the office even to today. This is because he always talks to her reasonably and deals with her properly."

He particularly praises Uncle Erich's leadership of the mission's genealogical work. "He is very exact and doesn't rest until a project is finished. He is in this respect a very talented man . . . Between 1951 and 1953, Herr Kramer underwent a significant change in his life. His brothers in the church and I were so convinced of this that the priesthood of the Berlin district at a conference on 6 November 1954 ordained him *der Ältesten* . . . This is the highest office of the priesthood that one has in the missions of the church."

Attached to this paper is another, showing that the church had paid his 2,000 DM parole. I look in passing at the names of those three members of the mission presidency who signed it. One is Franz Schreyer, my uncle and the stepson of my uncle Arthur Schumann who had served in the mission at the time. A family member had intervened, it seemed, to help save and stand up for my criminal uncle.

Kramer's final statement at the end of the trial concedes that the mistreatment of prisoners "was the usual course" of things and "was also committed by me."

Yet on the first page of the judgment, the division for criminal matters of the Berlin District Court rules that on November 8, 1956, nearly six years after the case first came before the authorities, the accused was being "acquitted at the cost of the state treasury of Berlin" of the charges of forcing confessions—the last of the many charges that had at first been leveled against him.

The judges said "legal reasons must lead to acquittal on the charges of forcing a confession." One of the judges scribbled under the printed text, almost as an afterthought, "Which, mind you, says nothing about the reprehensibility of the deeds of the accused, which are beyond question."

After six years of war, five years of Soviet prison, a year of investigative custody in West Berlin, and a further four years of investigation and trial, Erich Kramer walked free. His crimes, though terrible, weren't prosecutable. In a world of much more heinous deeds, they weren't enough to catch much attention. His acquittal wasn't even reported in newspapers.

The six years' worth of documents reflected a change of mood in Germany. The prosecutors who had so eagerly started their work against Kramer were replaced by others who seemed to have lost heart. A court that wanted to prosecute war criminals enough to bring a series of charges against Kramer had accepted in the end an arguable interpretation of law that would set him free.

A new Germany was in the midst of a *Wirtschaftswunder* and a Cold War in which America needed it as an ally. It was time to move on. Erich Kramer would escape any punishment due to a statute of limitations, yet the stain of his era's crimes on Germany had no expiration date.

ELEVEN

AMERICA'S STEPCHILD

Bob Dylan had far more impact on my left-oriented politics than Karl Marx ever did.
—JOSCHKA FISCHER, FOREIGN MINISTER

We are in their marrow. It has been said we are part of the unwritten constitution of this place.
—JOHN KORNBLUM, U.S. AMBASSADOR

On a hot summer morning in August 1995, Joschka Fischer awakened in his Bonn apartment and walked groggily to the bathroom to wash and shave. One of the most publicized diets in German history had taken fifty pounds and a double-chin off him, but he still didn't like what he saw in the mirror. News reports had confirmed a Serb massacre of Bosnia civilians in Srebenica; European troops stood helplessly nearby. German soldiers slept through it in their bases back home.

It was only the latest bit of evidence that the continent was encountering its first genocide since Germany branded the world's conscience with words like Auschwitz and Treblinka. Yet Fischer's Green party was still more than three years away from the elections that would bring it into government and make Fischer foreign minister. It remained stubbornly pacifist.

Fischer, the party's parliamentary leader, had agonized for months over how a modern-day German should respond to Balkan "ethnic-cleansing"—parlor language for mass murder. His sixty-eighter generation had been raised on the slogan *Nie wieder Krieg*—never again war. That, they reckoned, was the simple lesson of the German past. But a new European war was already raging.

Perhaps Washington had a point, Fischer thought to himself, that one now and again had to use democratically harnessed might to crush evil and promote good. The majority of his party viewed that sort of thinking as unforgivably American, but what was the alternative? What was happening in Bosnia stretched beyond party politics to moral questions. What did it mean to be German a half century after the Holocaust? Wasn't it Germany's duty to remain on guard against new Hitlers? Fischer concluded that he had to speak out after such a long silence. He had to back allied plans to protect Bosnian safe areas with military force.

When Fischer reached his office that morning, he wrote a "Dear Colleagues" letter. The words had been buzzing in his brain for so long that it didn't take long. He sent it to party allies, fellow Bundestag members and the press. And he would read it on the floor of the Bundestag. It sent shock waves throughout the country, for with it the German left had crossed the Rubicon. Fischer's message: properly applied violence was necessary, in some cases, to achieve a just peace.

Such a conclusion was heretical for Fischer's generation, which had been raised to abhor the abusive militarism of his parents' and grandparents' generation. One senses Fischer's agonizing in every line:

"It is precisely a policy of non-violence . . . that is particularly violated when war again becomes a successful and effective European policy tool—you can then simply forget a non-violent future for European nations. What's at stake in Bosnia is also fifty years of progressive integration and peace in Europe . . .

"Can pacifists, can especially those who stand for non-violence, simply accept the triumph of brutal, naked violence in Bosnia? What is one to do, when all previously tried means—embargo, protected zones, control of heavy weapons, negotiated settlements—have simply failed or at least have proved inadequate against military force? . . . Thus arises the question for Europe, after sixty years: where does accommodation stop in the face of a policy of force?"

Three years later, Fischer sits in his Bundestag office and recalls his bombshell letter and all that came after. He knows that the Dayton accords, which at the same time brought a fragile peace to Bosnia, resulted from NATO's decision to militarily punish the Serbs and thus force them to the negotiating table. Fischer can take no credit for any of this, but he can at least look himself in the mirror again. His Greens for the first time have debated the morality of pacifism in the face of aggression.

What Fischer hadn't counted on is that Germany at the beginning of 1997 would contribute to the peace by sending combat troops to Bosnia. In fact, Fischer's letter warned that a German military return to the site of Nazi war crimes would do more to unsettle Bosnia than help it. Yet the opposite was true. All sides welcomed the German military. So much was changing so quickly for Germany in Europe that it was hard to stay visionary for very long.

Fischer never could have expected at the time I met with him that only a few months later he'd become foreign minister. Nor would he ever have wagered that his party ranks would overwhelmingly back him in the first crisis to face him in that position: the question of sending German war planes on a potential combat mission to stop a war in Kosovo.

But it all started with the Bosnia story and Fischer's speech, all a part of his effort to prepare the future: Germany in the twenty-first century needs a "value-oriented" foreign policy, he says, one that calls for "more of an American approach than a traditionally German one" of cold, calculating *Realpolitik.* "I am strongly convinced that our interests can only be interpreted on the basis of values." What he wants is to marry Germany's historic obligation to the idea of national interest.

He sees Germany as drawing a good deal of its postwar identity from a curious parentage, that of Nazi history and American influence. "What sets this Germany apart from those of the past," says Fischer, "is that we are the children of the Nazis. It has an impact on almost everything we do. That history will stay with us a long time. When you look at these twelve years with some distance, they are decisive years in German history, years in which Hitler exploited the grandest feelings of the German people for the most terrible crime of modern history. But we are also America's children. What my generation has in the way of democratic experience, what we have learned about democratic culture, we have to thank America and no one else."

The message is as simple as it is compelling: Germany must be driven by a sense of moral mission because it is yet again called upon to lead Europe. Though many Germans would prefer a Swiss-like sideline role, the country is too large and brimming with pent-up ambitions. Just as many Americans believe their country has a global calling to promote democracy and human rights, so must Germans embrace a similar vocation. Germany's role will be more geographically limited than that of America. Yet this moral mission is crucial in the European effort to expand Western institutions and democratic values eastward.

While America's mission grows out of a self-image as an historic do-gooder, Germany must be inspired by the ghosts of the past and the more encouraging spirits of the past half century.

As Fischer had said in his landmark 1995 speech regarding Bosnia, urging his colleagues to abandon their religion of pacifism: "If we don't use our means against the carnage and do everything humanly possible to prevent further victims, isn't our generation threatened with the same political-moral failure as that of our parents' and grandparents' generation in the thirties? Can we place principles higher than human life?"

Fischer put his finger on what I was coming to view as one of the least attractive German characteristics: this blind attachment to *Prinzip* that often seems to defy the most salient logic. German pacifists thought for too long that genocide wasn't enough to abandon the *Prinzip* of non-violence.

"And what will become of our principle of non-violence," Fischer added, "when it bends before violence contemptuous of humanity? . . . Bosnian Muslims are fighting at the moment for pure survival as a people and a cul-

ture, and therefore no one can deny them the right to defend themselves."
Here, he was backing many members of the American Congress who wanted
to lift the arms embargo on the Muslims. But he went further. He said that
even giving the Muslims the ability to resist their extinction wasn't enough:
"Can we fail to help them defend themselves?"

His answer was a clear "no."

His view was surprisingly close to that of many members of the
American Congress who argued that one should lift the weapons embargo on
Bosnian Muslims so that they could at least defend themselves—if America
wasn't willing to defend them. Fischer's embrace of the same thinking
brought him perilously close, in a party saturated with pacifist thinking, to
American notions of might-can-serve-right.

Two young German journalists, Michael Behrens and Robert von Rimscha,
wrote a perceptive book published in 1998 that compares the U.S.-German
relationship to that of an older and younger brother. There is merit to the
metaphor: the big brother sets an example but all too often neglects the
needs of his little brother. The younger brother imitates his elder brother and
resents him at the same time.

The image is sufficiently powerful that I offer it to a friend, the writer
Peter Schneider, for his consideration. Studying the German-American bond
is one of his life's hobbies. He reckons a more accurate picture is that of stepfather and child. Schneider argues that Germans after the war had to reject
their natural fathers because they had flopped as role models. The children
needed an ersatz father.

"Our fathers were those who fought in this unjust war. Then along came
these new fathers, the Americans, good fathers who had triumphed in this war
against fascism. It was these ersatz stepfathers we pointed to when drawing
attention to the mistakes of our blood fathers. They became the acceptable
alternative, and they took over the authority of our discredited fathers."

I ask Schneider with some skepticism whether he really believes young
people en masse turned against their fathers and embraced this intruder who
had conquered their country.

"Many of us worshipped the Americans," insists Schneider. "We gold-plated them. But as soon as they made a mistake, they were of course much worse than our own fathers. And that mistake was Vietnam."

It is only in this context, Schneider says, that one can understand the virulent protests of German young against the Vietnam War. The stepfathers' unjust war, he says, was moral betrayal. The stepchildren, who were looking for reasons to believe more in their real fathers, and hence also in themselves, were eager to condemn America.

I come equipped with this stepfather image when I meet Joschka Fischer a few weeks after our first chat, at his favorite restaurant in Frankfurt called Gargantua, owned by one of his friends from "the movement." Fischer's secretary warns me that the dinner might not be much fun. Her boss has lost more than thirty kilograms through dieting, he runs ten kilometers every day, and he's not likely to eat much more than dry bread and raw vegetables. Perhaps, I think, this Americanization of Germany has gone too far.

When I reach Gargantua, however, Fischer is hungrily viewing the menu. The worst of his diet is over; he is on a maintenance program. The owner, however, is a walrus of a man, both in his mustache and girth. As he comes to our table, Fischer says, "I was once as fat and gluttonous as he was." His friend departs, casting a disapproving glance over his shoulder.

I ask Fischer how someone as identified as he with anti-Americanism could consider himself a child of America. I remind him how he campaigned against the Vietnam War, against the deployment of medium-range American nuclear missiles on German territory, against NATO. "Bob Dylan had a far greater impact on my left-oriented politics than Karl Marx ever did," says Fischer, who was born in 1948. Forget the great Communist rallying song, the *Internationale:* Fischer says his early life's theme music was "Blowin' in the Wind," "Don't Think Twice, It's All Right," and "It's All Over Now, Baby Blue."

"That and the hobo music—the living-on-the-streets music," he says. "And that's what we did, live in the streets and reject the generation of our parents, who were too connected with the Third Reich. We didn't want any bourgeois constraints."

"Sure, we were against Vietnam. We were against McNamara, against Johnson, but who of our generation in America wasn't against them? This wasn't anti-Americanism—it was just the opposite. We felt the shots at Kent State University as shots on ourselves. We marched in solidarity with Berkeley. We experienced the riots in Chicago at the Democratic Party conference as our own riots. Woodstock was a happening for us, too. The whole culture of protest, the experience of the civil rights movement, we got all of that from America. For us, that was the shock—our great ideal suddenly on stage in Vietnam as a colonial oppressor. It was as if our own values, the morals by which we were defining ourselves, no longer applied. The Americans were violating their own values and, as Robert MacNamara says today, it was a terrible mistake that cost many young Americans their lives."

Yet Vietnam, Fischer says, also helped bring true democracy to Germany. Before then, he says, democracy was more of a formal set piece, the acting out of democratic rules and practices that had been provided by Germany's allies. But just as America helped create Germany's democratic system, so did America's Vietnam inspire the protest movement that gave that system its first serious test. "I was never anti-American, but like so many Americans, I was merely against a specific form of American policy."

He understands that the essence of Germany's Americanization has nothing to do with McDonald's or Pizza Hut. He knows that America either helped create or inspire the country's Constitutional Court, its federal system, strong anti-trust legislation, broad protection of individual and civil liberties, relatively free market economy (implemented against the wishes of the German left at the war's end), and the Bundesbank, the highly independent central bank based to some degree on the American Federal Reserve, whose model also helped inspire the independence of the European Central Bank.

Fischer calls the stable democracy of his country "one of the great success stories of American policy." Perhaps at no time in history have Americans so lived up to their perceived role as gladiators for democratic progress. The United States not only provided the decisive blow to Hitler, it then laid the basis to replace him. America has shaped German history throughout the twentieth century, from its intervention in World War I to the spread of the Internet, far more dramatically than most Germans realize or like to admit. Americanization, to German elites, is something to avoid. Yet to reject it now is to reject a considerable part of themselves. Some of the values America promoted in Germany are, in fact, universal, indeed, have been championed by Germany itself at one point or another in its history. But America's influence was especially powerful because of the vacuum into which these ideas were poured after World War II.

Some American policy makers express concern that a new generation of Germans, so many years after the Marshall Plan and Berlin air lift, will distance themselves from America. Yet the new generation's relationship with America is far less bilateral and much more internal: American thinking and habits have been built into them. They surf the Internet using American English, they've grown up in a far more multi-ethnic society than their parents knew (again, more similar to America), they've known nothing but democracy and relative affluence, they wear Levi's jeans, eat at Pizza Hut, wear Chicago Bulls T-shirts, and watch MTV—never thinking consciously that these are particularly American habits. The filmmaker Wim Wenders once called what happened to his country after the war "the American colonization of the German subconscious."

The French writer Jean Cocteau put it another way: the Americans had it easy because they just wanted to be American. Life was harder for Germans because they wanted to be American and German at the same time.

Fischer parted ways with Germany's radical leftists when their approach turned ugly, reminiscent of Nazi Germany. He was particularly disgusted, he said, when the Red Army Faction kidnapped and then executed Hans-Martin Schleyer in 1977, president of the Employers' Association and the Federation of German Industries. They garroted him with a piano wire.

"The way they held him in solitary confinement, the means by which they tried and prosecuted him, and even the way they killed him was all too reminiscent of the past," he says. "The revolutionaries had become like fascists." It was when the radical left became too German again that many German young—not just Fischer—parted ways from them. By slowly shedding its extremes, Germany was developing a strong, if duller, democratic center so characteristic of the United States.

When John Kornblum took over as America's ambassador to Germany in 1997, a storm of newspaper profiles, television interviews, and speech invitations followed. He was treated more like a pop star or powerful German cabinet official than like a foreign envoy. Some of the attention arose from Kornblum's sophisticated knowledge of German culture and language. But something larger was at work, even after unification and its accompanying release of the last four-power controls.

"We are in their marrow," shrugs Kornblum to me. "It has been said we are part of the unwritten constitution of this place."

He sits in an ambassadorial office overlooking the Rhine, a perch from which U.S. envoys have monitored one of the great democratic experiments of the twentieth century. Put most simply, he says, the question was whether one could one take a country that had gone wrong, provide it with a proper system and institutions, put it within a supportive Western community, give it some seed financing, and then essentially let it go off on its own—with occasional orientational nudges.

More than anything else, what the American presence did after World War II was neutralize the combustive mix of a continent that kept getting its balance of relationships wrong. By inserting itself as a central player, Kornblum says, it made the rest of Europe less nervous about a Germany which, after all, was now divided. And Germans felt safer with themselves. How could matters go too wrong with such a mighty chaperone? It was largely because of America's continued presence that reluctant German neighbors such as France and England withdrew their objections to unification and let it go forward.

"Our role here is defining," says Kornblum. "And aside from that, Germany has become the most American country in Europe."

I raise an eyebrow. More American than the English, with whom we share a language, literature, pop culture, and movie stars? From Shakespeare to the Beatles, from the American Revolution to World War II, British and American histories have been intertwined. How can Germany be as American as all that? And look at all the problems Germans are having reforming their economy. German overregulation doesn't look very American to me.

Kornblum shrugs. "Germans are pragmatic, like Americans. They do what they need to do. Where they differ is that they are slower to accept and embrace change. That resulted in a far slower development of a venture capital market and in job creation levels that lagged so far behind those of the United States that the unemployment rate, at some 11 percent by 1999, was about double the American levels. Yet, slowly and more methodically, Germany follows the American lead in questions of corporate restructuring, the building of an equity culture and company management based increasingly on shareholder value. Greater cultural differences would have rendered a French takeover of an American company of the Daimler-Chrysler scale nearly impossible."

Over the years, I've spoken with a growing number of American officials who consider Germany their most natural partners in the world, more so even than Great Britain or Canada. They reckon only Germany (with the world's third largest economy) has enough strength to be a truly useful partner, plus a similar enough outlook for the partnership to last. (They argue that the second largest economy, Japan, has a much more inscrutable value system.) America also needs Germany for its central geographic position in the middle of Europe, a perch from which it can influence all the politics of Europe that matter to America.

Germany is also similar to America in that it is a federal country, giving it a division of power similar to the United States. No other major country in Europe is so federalized. The United Kingdom and France are built around London and Paris, while Germany has its Berlin, Munich, Hamburg, and Frankfurt to match America's Washington, Los Angeles, Chicago, and New York. It also has become more ethnically diverse, and thus more similar to America, with its eight million "foreigners," an increasing number of whom are becoming citizens. Germany is far more reluctant than America to embrace such demographic change and call itself a melting pot, but it is Europe's America if one measures such a thing by its attraction to would-be immigrants.

Feeding this partnership is America's own unwitting Germanness. Some sixty million Americans have some sort of German heritage. If one disregards language and simply looks at the number of immigrants over the years and the impact of those immigrants on the country, America is probably more a German-American country than a British-American one. And those immigrants, in turn, create family ties that have always connected the two countries. Demographic change in America these days is driven more by Asian and Latin American newcomers, but the American structures and practices they'll inherit have been heavily shaped by Germans. The Protestant work ethic has its roots in Germany, as do the American school and medical care systems. As Kornblum says, "We have lots of underlying similarities we seldom point out. Our entire national science system was built up by German immigrants. The German immigration to America was one of the great involuntary economic development programs the world has ever known. We were nothing better than average in the sciences before this immense inflow put us in the first category."

All of this would seem to make Germany and America natural partners. Already they have emerged as the most important players in spreading NATO membership eastward and in trying to save Russia from economic and political ruin. While America still provides Europe's most important security guarantees, Germany is increasingly emerging as the irreplaceable, stable anchor at the middle. It championed the creation of a single currency and greater integration of the West and now leads expansion of the European Union to the East.

For some time, conventional wisdom had it that Germany's toughest decision would be whether it defines France or America as its more important partner. France sees the European Union as a rival to America, the more powerfully so because of the new single currency. America sees Germany as a potentially global partner in the great coming tasks, ranging from absorbing an ascendant China to wrestling with radical Islam.

In the U.S.-French rivalry, some American officials feel the dice are loaded in their favor. Even as Germany continues to look officially for any means of cooperation with France, its private sector gravitates toward the United States. Germany's relations with France are still based more on fear and guilt than on common hopes and values. Their bond thrives where governments dictate the rules: biannual meetings of national leaders, joint military operations, and subsidized student exchange programs. Yet when Daimler was looking for a partner that would give it global presence, it bought Chrysler and not Peugeot or Renault. Bertelsmann turned to Random House to give it global reach. French, once the chosen language of the German monarch Frederick the Great, is increasingly passé. The current global game is an American one, and the Germans, more than the French, have the culture and size to play it.

France's special strengths are its culture and its heritage, and these are being worn away, replaced by a "universal culture" that looks strangely American. This culture has proved far easier for the Germans than the French to embrace. Psychology plays a role. The French consider the Americans as competitors. Though the Germans might well move in this direction as well, Germans have often regarded the Americans as partners. America has demonstrated at critical points of history that it trusts the Germans far more than do its closest European neighbors. For example, while British leader Margaret Thatcher and French President François Mitterand were opposing German unification, U.S. President George Bush was unreservedly supporting it. Europeans, even as they join the Germans in a common currency, worry about Germany's size and influence; Americans don't share this concern.

Americans often believe more in Germany than Germans do themselves. One German banker privately whispered to me at a dinner to celebrate an anniversary of German unification that he thinks German democracy will always be unstable "because, of course, the system is not our own." (Even Joschka Fischer has written of the problem of Germany's "borrowed democracy.") The banker's point was that Germany is unable to establish a stable democracy on its own, that its democracy had not evolved gradually and matured in Germany as it had in other Western countries. He used the metaphor of a tree with heavy democratic branches but with roots that aren't sunk deep. If the winds blow too hard, the tree can topple. I argued with him that German democracy has had fifty years to sink its roots and seems to have done quite well in doing so. The banker countered that unification and Germany's acquired influence in Europe have put tremendous new pressure on the branches.

Ambassador John Kornblum bristles at the thesis that Germany lacks democratic roots. "It just isn't true," he says. "There were lots of democratic traditions in Germany. The Hanseatic League, the city-states. They were some of the earliest forms of democracy. The institutions of the Holy Roman Empire were democratic to some degree." And as Thomas Mann wrote, Martin Luther's "each man his own priest" was an early form of democratic thinking. "All you have to do is bounce around this country for a while and you see democratic behavior way down at the grass roots," says Kornblum, who has been traveling the country for more than thirty years. He is adamant on this point.

"Now that doesn't mean that there aren't aspects of authoritarian behavior, or that there are no institutions which aren't quite right yet," says Kornblum. "But you can say the same thing of France, Britain, or the United States . . . But is there a democratic core in this society? Yes. Is the society still unsure of its structure and role in the bigger environment? Also 'yes,' and that is why we Americans are so important. But to say that without us the place would be the Third Reich is just plain wrong. It is a modern society with all kinds of contradictions. Go to Jackson, Mississippi, and see how democratic—or not—some of their structures are. . . . Every modern society is essentially a sort of chaos. The questions are the roots and the direction of a given society. And the real question, of course, in the back of everybody's mind, is whether, if certain controls were taken off, this would again become a land of werewolves. I don't believe it."

There are, of course, important ways in which Germans will always be different from Americans. Perhaps the greatest dissimilarity I've noticed between the two countries is Germany's relative lack of a healthy, national self-confidence. That prompts the country to sometimes lurch into ill-guided decisions, such as its premature recognition of Croatia, which most American diplomats believe heightened the chance of the Balkan war rather than heading it off. And Germans are so afraid of rapid change or of altering the system that has brought it such stability—the state regulations and inflexible tax and labor laws—that the country has adjusted only slowly to the globalization of the economy and to the information era, reducing the potential for entrepreneurial job growth.

America's society and business were able to transform themselves more quickly to the information society and the Internet age than were Germany's. That is neither good nor bad—it is simply part of reality. Americans embrace new ideas and product and lifestyle innovations so quickly that they often make changes that aren't always positive for society. Germans consider, mull, and regulate change more. They make fewer mistakes, but they seldom introduce global innovations.

What drives German change these days is the most "American" part of German society—the corporate boardroom. Daimler Benz's Jürgen Schrempp and SAP's Hasso Plattner have done more to change the way the country works economically than any cabinet minister. Fear of political instability after the war resulted in an electoral system that put a great deal of power in the hands of the parties, leaving the political grassroots little capacity to throw out groups of politicians whom they consider out of step with the times. The party puts up national "lists" that ensure that its more senior candidates, those near the top of the lists, face little to no chance of being ousted, even if their local constituencies vote heavily against them. The United Kingdom's more direct parliamentary voting system helped bring on the Thatcher revolution and then the Tony Blair–driven moderate Third Way that shifted the politics of the Labour Party toward one center.

Because Germany's political elites are so rarely cleaned out and replaced, they can drag their feet on reforms and stand by helplessly watching unemployment rise while still keeping their jobs. But while German politics remains stuck in the mud, German business moves forward, restructures, and modernizes because it must do so in order to survive in a global market place. Germany's new generation of corporate elites has more often than not cut its teeth in international operations. Daimler Benz was the first to list on the New York Stock Exchange and thus accept the much more transparent American international standard for accounting practices.

By the time SAP made the same move a few years later, the NYSE threw a party. It knew the German company operated in one of the dullest branches of international software—accounting and business software—and the stock exchange was looking to jazz up the image. So it organized a thoroughly American beach party, dumping sand over Broad Street with a few palm trees and music by Kool and the Gang. SAP couldn't see what this had to do with its business, and at first rejected the hype. But the Stock Exchange was paying, and if this is the way Americans sold stock, so be it.

Just as German industry adopted the American word and practice of "streamlining" in the 1960s, diversification in the 1970s, and downsizing in the 1980s, so did it embrace the American concept of "shareholder value" at the end of the 1990s. It's no accident that this coincided with the emergence of an equity culture of the sort that has created so much wealth in America. And the Euro would only make Germany all the more American, giving it a currency of global weight and attractiveness that would make Frankfurt more of an international financial capital.

But Germany still runs behind America in many future-shaping trends. By 1998, Germans owned twenty-six personal computers per one hundred residents compared to nearly double that percentage in America. While some 18 percent of Americans used digital networks, only 5 percent of Germans did so (by comparison, the numbers in France were 15 percent and in Great Britain 8 percent). Still, the number of on-line users in Germany had doubled in 1997, and this growth would likely continue throughout the decade and beyond. Job creation also lags. While America created 11.8 million jobs from 1991–1997, Germany lost 2.6 million jobs in the same period.

The government's lack of innovative spirit plays a role here, but it is also true that the engineering-minded Germans have less zest for the world of services: only 10 percent of German exports by 1998 were in the highly paid, quickly growing service sector, while the American share was two and a half times greater. Nearing the end of the century, the high-end market for services in Germany was ruled by foreign, usually American, stars. The two leading business consulting companies, the top four accounting companies, and the largest six advertising firms were all foreign, and mostly American. The next wave of Americanization, the drive of the service industry, was already surging into Germany.

What these statistics miss, however, is that Germans often run and staff those businesses. German business is taking the challenge, and it believes that once its politicians shake the cobwebs from their heads, the country has just the landscape for the twenty-first century: a highly educated, well-trained population operating in an economy with considerable weight and a communications infrastructure in some ways superior to America's—a telephone network with 48 million connections, a fiber optic network that is more than 170,000 kilometers long, and blanket ISDN coverage that few countries could match.

German businessmen complain to anyone who will listen that their society still needs a fundamental shift in attitude. They lecture the voters on this more than the politicians. One such effort is a 1998 book called *Die Zweite Wende*—the second turning point, the fall of the Berlin Wall having marked the first one. Authors Lothar Späth (chief executive of Jenoptik AG) and Herbert Henzler (of the American management consulting company McKinsey) tell how Germany missed a once-in-a-lifetime opportunity to use East Germany as a place for free market experimentation à la America. Instead, it forced its own overregulation, overtaxation, and oversubsidization on its eastern German neighbors. And then it blamed them for not prospering. "Basically, we took the faulty industrial policies of the West and applied them to the East," write the authors. "At the first turning point, models were introduced in the East that had already had their day."

The authors urge Germany not to fumble the opportunity of globalization and the information era as well. "The second turning point has to succeed better than the first," says Lothar Späth. *"Reculer pour mieux sauter*—take a step back, in order to jump better, say the French. Let's take the stalled reform as the pause before the leap. But we must leap."

It is that kind of roll-up-your-sleeves pragmatism among the business class and among Germany's young elites—an almost American can-do spirit—that encourages me and people like Kornblum. "I like this new Germany," he says. "It gives me a very positive feeling. I was gone for ten years—and I notice, in comparison to before, a loosening up . . ."

But is America in Germany's marrow as Kornblum argues?

Is America as essential to Germany as is, to the human body, the tissue filling the bones? Perhaps. For without this American ingredient, Germany would walk differently. It would be less flexible, less confident, less democratic, more suspected by its neighbors, and more isolated in its first postwar try at continental leadership.

But marrow is an integral part of the bone—without it, the bone would dry up and crumble. Is America that to Germany as well? To answer this question, one must look at Germany's evolution and America's role at different points in history, for this role has been critical to the German fate ever since Americans entered World War I in 1917. Already in the Weimar Republic, German intellectuals began to complain about the excessive influence of American mass culture on Weimar's ideas of fashion, style, leisure, entertainment, and other things modern.

Germany's response to things American has always been a mixture of disdain for its "more shallow" culture and envy of its energy and optimism. At the end of the eighteenth century, Goethe waxed poetic about the New World to an American friend in a letter. Though written before the Civil War, the poem is telling in its tone:

> *America, thy lot was cast by powers,*
> *Happier than those of our old continent:*
> *Thou hast no ruined towers*
> *No basalt monument.*
> *Thy heart endures no pain,*
> *In the heyday of life,*
> *From memories that are vain,*
> *Unprofitable strife.*
> *Then use the present happily!*
> *And when your children thirst for poetic glories,*
> *May some good genius keep him free*
> *From knights, from robbers, and from ghost stories.*

Some pop-culture historians link the advance of Americanization with the spread of Coca-Cola. By that measure, Germany started early. The first Coke plant went up in 1923. Even after Hitler took power ten years later, the Americanization didn't stop. Jazz, the influence of Hollywood films, and Coke continued to infiltrate the Third Reich. By 1939, when Hitler's troops invaded Poland and began World War II, Germany was Coke's second largest world market. During the first years of Hitler, dancing to America's swing music was a soft way to rebel against the stiffness of Nazi culture.

Meantime, American companies had invested some $500 million in the country, a hefty amount in those days. They saw the merit in Germany's geographic position. And many American officials encouraged them, for they viewed Germany, which was straining at the Versailles bit, as a potential bulwark against the Bolshevik threat. Washington even took financial steps to stabilize the first German republic. It guaranteed the Rentenmark, starting in November 1923, and it provided loans at relatively soft terms. European neighbors criticized the United States for being soft on the postwar Germans, but Washington already saw its national interest in supporting German democracy.

The Nazis tried their damnedest to avoid a clash with America; the First World War gave warning enough that you didn't want America against you. But Hitler's rhetoric and actions flew in the face of U.S. ideals to an extent he failed to calculate. The Americans "regarded the repression of democracy and the persecution of Jews . . . as a declaration of war on humanity," says the historian Michael Stürmer.

He notes that Germans were ill equipped to understand the Americans' curious foreign policy mix of national interest and moral mission, which was giving them an ever-more global definition of their calling. Because of that, the Germans didn't take seriously the threat of America's armed intervention until it was too late. It was only when America entered the war following Pearl Harbor that the Nazis cracked down on the spread of American music and values.

At war's end, Germany's warmth toward American occupiers grew as much out of relief as affection. Germans who fled from the Soviet to the American zone—millions of them—congratulated themselves on having escaped Red Army brutality, the wholesale raping of German women, and pillaging of German businesses. For people who had few choices after the unconditional surrender, landing on the American side was a lucky break.

Newspapers that promised loyalty to American values gained licenses. American funding established chairs of political science at universities to promote democracy. NATO and later the European Community complemented the redrawing of German borders to shift landscape westward, toward America.

Yet it was the unplanned force of American culture that had the greatest impact. The Austrian-born filmmaker Billy Wilder tried to argue exactly this to U.S. government employers who had sent him from Hollywood to his former home of Berlin to help along "re-education" of Germans. In a memorandum, he sneered at America's heavy-handed propaganda and efforts to keep out of Germany any films and plays that might highlight America's own problems.

"So now we are slowly opening up the movie houses in Germany," he wrote. "We are showing them newsreels which carry along with the news a lesson, a reminder, and a warning . . . Attendance ranges from capacity to satisfactory. And yet we all realize that once this novelty has worn off (in Berlin it has worn off already), we shall find it increasingly difficult to deliver our lessons straight. Will the Germans come in week after week to play the guilty pupil? . . . Now if there was an entertainment film with Rita Hayworth or Ingrid Bergman or Gary Cooper, in Technicolor if you wish, and with a love story—only with a very special love story, cleverly devised to help us sell a few ideological items—such a film would provide us with a superior piece of propaganda . . ."

Many years later, in 1979, it would be an American television series about the Holocaust that would take the country by storm, showing a new generation the human tragedy of genocide. And then in the late nineties, another generation would get its Holocaust lessons from Hollywood. An American of Eastern European Jewish origins, Stephen Spielberg, produced *Schindler's List,* and one German teacher after another took entire classes to screenings. Time and again, Wilder would be proved right: it would be the unequaled capability of American filmmakers to reach a wide public that would re-educate Germany, far more than any official dictum. Love and adventure stories in Technicolor washed across the ocean, unintentionally brimming with America ideology, not from the preacher's pulpit but as part of a gripping plot.

In the case of Billy Wilder, the film that grew out of his visit to postwar Berlin was *A Foreign Affair,* a movie whose vivid portrayal of the time has prompted many of my German friends to see it several times (though it was rejected by Wilder's official minders). It shows an oafish congressional delegation that an army corporal dismisses as "a bunch of salesmen that's got their foot in the right door." It paints GIs as materialistic colonizers deploying nylon stockings and cigarettes for sexual gain. The most attractive character is Erika, a German lioness of malleable morals, played by Marlene Dietrich. She had been a night club performer with Nazi connections to the very top. Dietrich's heroine fell well outside the bounds of American official sanction, but she provided Germans a view of themselves that they understood. As she says in the film: "Bombed out a dozen times. Everything caved in and pulled out from under me: my country, my possessions, my beliefs. Yet somehow I kept going. Months and months in air raid shelters, crammed in with five thousand other people. I kept going . . . it was a living hell."

The evolution of German film isn't a bad way to track German change. The best-known German filmmaker of the 1960s and 1970s was Rainer Fassbinder, who on the face of it would seem to be entirely un-American. His films were dark and brooding, angry and intellectually elitist, usually with something despairing to say about the current state of society—hardly Hollywood. Yet Fassbinder in a 1971 interview credited America with his (at that time) very un-German attachment to narrative.

"The American cinema is the only one I can take really seriously," he said, "because it's the only one that has really reached an audience. German cinema used to do so, before 1933, and of course there are individual directors in other countries who are in touch with their audiences. But American cinema has generally had the happiest relationship with its audience . . ."

All his late films on one level or another wrestled with a German society that was conforming more each year to American norms. Wim Wenders (who with Fassbinder and Werner Herzog was the vanguard of the German New Wave of cinema in the 1970s) is similarly fascinated by his American "stepfather." The genre wasn't American, more that of European art films, but the subject matter was: his production company was called "Road Movies"— in English. In *Paris, Texas,* he used the writer Sam Shepard to bring him "forward movement, which is very American in a way," he said in an interview. In *The American Friend,* he cast in his lead role Dennis Hopper, an actor who had won over a generation of Germans in *Easy Rider.* His *Alice in the Cities* used American music, including a concert by Chuck Berry in Wuppertal. German filmmakers grew increasingly fascinated with America.

Perhaps it all had to lead to Wolfgang Petersen, who by the end of the 1990s was not only making mainstream American films but unabashedly patriotic American films, more "commercial" than any German filmmaker before him. He had won some international notice with his submarine war-action film *Das Boot* in 1981. But by 1997, he was making *Air Force One* with Harrison Ford, about an American president who almost single-handedly must save his friend, the Russian leader, and Russia's nascent democracy from a crazy group of fascist Russian nationalists. There is nothing German left in his American filmmaking, unless it is the perfectionism he applies to it.

Germans not only liked American culture, they had made it their own. By the end of the 1990s, German insomniacs' favorite show had become *Late Night with Harald Schmidt,* such a clear rip-off of America's David Letterman show that its host never troubles to deny it. Schmidt, like Letterman, takes cameras out on the street for loony meetings with everyday Germans, he makes fun of people in his audience, he conducts absurd side-conversations with his musicians, he smacks his lips when he sips from his coffee cup.

His guests have included the irreverent basketball player Dennis Rodman (who pulled off his shirt and described the history of his various tattoos), and the sex symbol Pamela Anderson, whom he dressed in red tights and, in one of his sillier skits, liberated while garbed in a Superman outfit. The line between American culture and German culture was not only blurring but disappearing.

The newsmagazine *Der Spiegel* described the phenomenon in weightier German tones: "Harald Schmidt has become an addiction for the info-elites as well as for youth without future prospects" and his style is "travesty with a cathartic healing impact." *Spiegel* commented, "The Copernican turning point for German humor has already begun."

Dozens of radio stations and daily papers carry the best lines from the show; shops offer Harald Schmidt books, best-of-Harald-Schmidt CDs and videos, T-shirts, coffee cups, and calendars. If anyone doubts the American inspiration for his show, Schmidt dispels that in a 1997 interview in *Stern* magazine with talk-show host Jay Leno. Leno is surprised at how much Schmidt, a cabaret artist before starting his TV show, knows about late-night American television, particularly the legendary Johnny Carson, the father of their genre whom Leno has replaced.

"You know [Carson]?" Leno asks with astonishment.

"I've watched his farewell program . . . at least twenty times, kneeling before it by candlelight," says Schmidt of Carson's finale, a thirty-year retrospective. "Every time [I watched], I learned something new." Later he says, "When I see you with stars like Demi Moore, Mel Gibson or Julia Roberts, every day sitting on your couch, I grow green with envy."

Stern doesn't need to explain to its readers who these people are—they have become part of German culture.

The word that pollster Richard Hillmer, of Infratest Burke, uses is *Verinnerlichung*—the internalization of American influences. "Few Germans would call the Internet American, yet mostly that's what it is," he says. And certainly Germans surf it using American English. "Americanization no longer comes with the tensions that suggested themselves to earlier generations. We idolized Kennedy and we were disgusted by Vietnam. Now America, as symbol, both positive and negative, doesn't play the same role. Today our polls show that everyone has friendly feelings toward America—East Germans as much as West Germans."

And again, what is merely a trend elsewhere in the world—the spread of American culture—grows deeper roots in Germany, at first because its own culture had been discredited by the Nazis and with time because of the closeness between the two societies that this starting point established—a base on which one built.

The author Peter Schneider started getting America into his marrow when as a six-year-old child he first saw the Yankee conqueror in the form of soldiers driving jeeps through his Black Forest village. Until that time, for the boy, Americans were only the pilots who dropped bombs from the fearsome planes. He had remembered most vividly a time when in the last weeks of the war he and his mother had been on a train which had to stop because of shelling, leaving child and mother to run in terror for cover in a nearby woods. The contrast between that scene and the boys who now appeared on the jeeps impressed him.

"The soldiers were so loose," Schneider says. "I mean, one foot was on the gas and the other leg hung out of the jeep. They threw sacks of sugar and salt on the street that one could then pick up. An amazing gesture, wonderful, of course."

The victors were generous in spirit, optimistic, easy-going. One wanted to be like them. They set up tents and distributed soup. Schneider particularly recalls huge supplies of Camels that were left out so that one could and did easily pilfer them; their owners seemed to expect it. It was a modest transfer of wealth, but not insignificant in those first, desperate postwar days.

"The feeling was simply overpowering—it all meant freedom, the war is over. The first English sentence, that I learned when I was six, was, 'Have you any chewing gum?' I learned the sentence, and I got chewing gum. Magnificent, this lesson." The message: learning English pays dividends. "How congenial it all was. And then came the air lift, when Berlin was threatened in 1948," and American planes and men broke the Soviet blockade of the city.

The Americans were suddenly knights in white armor.

Schneider as a teen considered himself to be particularly hip, so it was only natural that he should search the city where he lived, Freiburg in the Black Forest, for a James Dean–like T-shirt. What he means by that is one with sleeves into which one could roll a pack of cigarettes up against one's shoulder. He couldn't find one in town, so he bought a sleeveless undershirt instead and wore that. "I created a sensation when I wore it in public," he smiles. "In those days only women exposed their shoulders that way."

Schneider's parents after the war were looking back to a peaceful and happier past through films like *Der Förster von Silberwald* (*The Forester of the Silver Forest*), but Schneider's generation was getting its kicks from Marlon Brando's *The Wild One* and the music of Fats Domino. His father, a musician, tried to show him how mindlessly simple these tunes were, but Schneider loved them anyway.

The generation of Schneider's father found American culture to be vulgar and disorderly, but these elders had lost all authority to offer an alternative. The American stepfather ruled, and his teachings were informal manners, casual appearance, and anti-authoritarian behavior. Hannah Arendt wrote that America, for the Germans, was the dream of the lower classes and a nightmare for the country's traditional elites. The shell-shocked aristocracy and like-minded intellectuals saw American culture as the common man moving in on their traditions. But the young saw it as a liberation from their parents.

America was everywhere after the war. Armed Forces Network became one of the most popular radio stations in the country. American comic books flooded the market; Donald Duck and Mickey Mouse infected the young four decades before Eurodisney would open outside Paris. The loftier aspects of American culture began reaching intellectuals and converting them, at a time when their country was throwing its energies into the *Wirtschaftswunder* and producing little important literature. The German market celebrated Norman Mailer's *The Naked and the Dead*, Salinger's *Catcher in the Rye*, the works of Henry Miller, Ernest Hemingway, John Steinbeck, and the plays of Arthur Miller, particularly *Death of a Salesman*. And at the level of mass-market culture, American film had no rival: stars like Paul Newman and Marilyn Monroe became German matinee idols. The most popular films of the 1950s included *Gone with the Wind*, *From Here to Eternity*, *Moby Dick*, and Humphrey Bogart's *Casablanca*.

But the German elite also feared an excess of Americana. Teenagers poured into cinemas for movies like *Rock Around the Clock*, then afterward paraded through their cities' main streets shouting "Bill Haley" and "Rock 'n Roll" until police disbanded them. More alarming yet was the violent subculture of young German James Deans. They called themselves *Halbstarke*, loosely translated as "rowdies." They wanted to embody Dean's character James Stark, in *Rebel Without a Cause*.

A Bill Haley concert in October 1958 provided a shock: a young generation shaking up tightly ordered German society with their new-found weapon of American youth culture. During the show at the Ernst-Merck Halle in Hamburg, the standing and dancing crowd began to fight with volunteer ushers who tried to move them back into their chairs.

A reporter for the intellectual weekly *Die Zeit* reported the events with horror: "Crowds of people streamed forward like screaming flows of lava. In no time, Bill Haley and his musicians were surrounded by a wall of people closing in on them . . . It looked like a pack of predatory animals looking for a victim . . . The youths were brandishing chair legs, iron rods, boards, and many other weapons . . . then police arrived and a wild chase ensued through the aisles." The author proposed an ancient cure for such mass hysteria: isolating the raging people or perhaps thrashing or showering them with cold water.

As I read this report from more than four decades earlier, I fast-forward to a contemporary event that shows just how far Americanization has progressed (or Germans have sunk, depending on one's point of view). My teenage eastern German cousin from Leipzig, Claudia Müller, drags me along to Berlin's annual "Love Parade," a "techno" music festival. She wears a miniskirt and elevated shoes, while an earring pierces the navel on her bare midriff.

She's one of the more conservatively attired among the million-plus revelers on the wide Boulevard of June 17, a human bath of neon-color hair and dress (when dressed at all), vibrating to the incessant, throbbing rhythms of the electronically pulsating music that was blasting off the backs of the human-infested platforms of flatbed trucks.

Some say one can only speak of Americanization in *western* Germany, because the easterners—17 million of the 80 million—were insulated from all the democratic development, the sixties movement, the fast food, and the hard rock. But Claudia at age seventeen shows how quickly a new eastern German generation is catching the bug.

I ask her why the English-named "Love Parade" also has an English-language slogan, "Let the Sun Shine In." Claudia explains that everything simply sounds better in English. She has never been to America herself, but she is sure that she wants to work there as an au pair. She is picky, however, and insists that she must work in San Francisco and nowhere else. Several years earlier, a teenager from eastern Germany wouldn't have been allowed to go to America at all, but now she can narrow down geographically the places she'd be willing to go. She has even written class papers on San Francisco, and on AIDS. She knows all about America.

She recites to me in her schoolgirl English the speech she gave in school on San Francisco: "I would like to visit San Francisco, the city of hills and natural wonders. San Francisco is one of the most cultural cities in the world. It will be so interesting to see the Golden Gate Bridge, which accommodates over a hundred thousand cars every day. Other interesting things are the islands in the Bay. None is more known than Alcatraz . . ."

I interrupt her. Why does she so badly want to live in America? "I want to get out," she says, speaking of Taucha, the sleepy suburb of Leipzig in which she lives. "People are so uptight and stupid. It starts with the dumbest things. If you walk barefoot through the streets in the summer, people look at you like you've killed someone." They look at her strangely when she wears her "Destroy"-brand elevated shoes—similar to the pair she wears to the parade, jet black and with steel toes—making her impressive height all the loftier. The locals don't understand the safety pin jewelry that she has pierced through her belly button, or the three earrings in her left ear. She's sure Californians would easily accept her search for individual freedom.

The "Love Parade" itself strikes me as a sixties-like event updated for a new youth without political motivation. It is European cool and intellectual anarchy grafted onto American individualism and free spirit. The parade is heavier in atmosphere than such an event would be in America, with fewer smiling faces and less easy laughter, though lighter than it would have been a decade earlier in Germany. This "Americanization," if that is what it is, is based on a form of music that has never been as popular in America; the country's Americanization is being Germanized. This techno-party strikes me as a melding of two cultures into a third to the point that the line between them can no longer be discerned.

Four decades earlier, German authorities had frowned on Bill Haley's fans dancing in the aisles, and the police cleared the streets of them. Now the police merely ensure order; afterwards city-directed teams spend days cleaning up the litter in the parks. City fathers view the massive party as a logistical and sanitation problem—to be humored for the economic boon it brought to their city.

I sit after the concert at an outdoor table of a pizza restaurant with my cousin and a friend who worked at the Berlin senate, Susanne Michel. Claudia has been more of a spectator than a techno freak; she prefers rap and soul, the sort of music that connects her with America. It is the music of the oppressed, she says, and she considers herself to be oppressed as well. Puberty, differences with her parents, and an uncertain future in a world of unemployment have unsettled her.

She talks about her favorite rap singers: Snoop Doggy Dogg and Warren G. She tells us stories about their violent worlds, recounts tales of those who were killed by members of one gang and the revenge killings that followed. Susanne, too, knows these groups and their histories. It is only the American in our trio who can't participate in the conversation.

Claudia doesn't understand all the words of American rap. Because of that, she likes German rap bands, like Cappuccino. She can have American culture in her own language these days.

Jeanett Frössinger is a product of this era of blurring cultural boundaries. She was born in 1965, four years after the Berlin Wall was built. I am meeting her to discuss the future of German foreign policy at Adenauer House, the head-quarters of her Christian Democratic party, where she is head of the foreign and security policy department. Her degrees include a bachelor's in journalism from Temple University and a master's from Johns Hopkins University in Baltimore.

When I phone to arrange the meeting, I am confronted by a home answering machine message laced with Bruce Springsteen music, "Blinded by the Light." When we chat later over lunch, she tells me Springsteen had been that defining figure for her that Bob Dylan had provided Joschka Fischer.

"As a teenager, you think about everything and you are in conflict with everything," she says. "All I heard about the United States made me believe that things were somehow better over there. I came to that conclusion, though I'd never been there. And I blame that on Bruce. Or at least on the stuff he did before he got more commercial. Bruce allowed you to be a soft rebel. There was no earring in my nose. I didn't dye my hair pink. After a while, all you care about and see, all the clothes you wear, the music you listen to, it has to do with America on some level. When I asked myself what I really wanted to do after German high school graduation, it was going to the United States to see for myself this country that so infiltrates your thinking and lifestyle. I was thrilled by the positive attitude of people—to live and let live.

"America produces a lifestyle that's exciting because so much develops and changes. Germans sometimes laugh at that, thinking that true culture has to be at least a hundred years old. This is the country of poets and philosophers, after all. Germans hang on too much to the past, while much of the living art happens somewhere else, namely in America."

Frössinger grew up in a town near Heidelberg, an area that was influenced by a large concentration of American bases and soldiers. Her manner is *un*German to its core: brash and optimistic, full of life and humor. Her long blonde hair falls California-like off her shoulders, and she vivaciously relates a battery of the sort of "dumb blonde" jokes any American can tell, but funnier.

Her English accent is unapologetically American; the preference of a new generation over their parents' more stilted Oxfordian tones. She is senior enough at the CDU to have two secretaries working in her office. How she treats them fits with German tradition—using only the formal *Sie* form of address and no first names. With me she shifts languages and moods and is easy-going and familiar. She knows where her American style fits and where a German style is more appropriate, and she seems to be able to change them in mid-sentence.

She recalls how America's message of hope and optimism infected her as a young teen in a society that seemed rather dull in comparison. But now all that American-bred self-confidence translates into a greater German self-assertiveness. She lectures me that Americans must stop thinking that they always knows what's best for Germany and the world.

Our fiercest argument comes when I suggest that Germany, like America, has become a country of immigration and should find a way to more quickly integrate its foreign residents through naturalization. "Why can't you Americans realize that we have a different tradition and history?" she argues. "You were a country built up by newcomers. Our change has to come in a different way. The laws we have in place are liberal enough for our context." She opposed the red-green government's moves to speed up the process.

She supports the European Union not because she considers the concept sacred, as did her parents' generation, but because it makes sense. She wants her country to have a greater voice on the world stage, and she realizes that it is through a stronger European Union that it will be taken most seriously.

Yet at the same time she yearns for Germans to become more American in some ways. She speaks of an article about a shopping mall that opened near Dortmund—one of the largest such centers in Europe. Even though the region had 20 percent unemployment, few locals applied for jobs because they didn't want the long commute that would be required. "Trying to get a German to move is a big challenge," she says. "That would never happen in America."

Yet when Jeannet first visited her dream country, America, as an au pair, she faced the shock of many young Germans going out into the world. She suddenly had to carry a burden of history that she'd never experienced at home. On her flight to New York, she sat beside a middle-aged Jewish man from Arizona, who had been in Germany researching his family history. "He told me that he could still feel the Nazis all around him as he traveled through Germany," she recalls. "I felt so uncomfortable. I hadn't ever sensed these Nazis he spoke of. But I didn't say anything like that to him. Instead, you immediately want to say you are sorry, but you know how inadequate that is. He made me feel guilty about it all for the first time."

As fate would have it, she landed as an au pair in a Jewish home in Philadelphia. The family father had just hit it rich, and at age sixty-five had married a woman twenty years his junior. "From the very beginning," says Jeannet, "his wife didn't like the idea of a German girl in the family. She was uncomfortable, and she made me feel it." The most awkward moment was Yom Kippur, the Day of Atonement or cleansing of sins that goes back to the time of Moses. She didn't allow Jeannet to sit at the table with her invited guests as they broke the fast—because she was German. "There wasn't a plate for me. No one said anything. Just no plate. I felt so sad. And angry. They treated me as if I had killed all the Jews myself."

She found solace in an elderly Jewish man whom she met in a nearby park where she took the family's six-year-old boy each day to play. He befriended her and provided instruction on Jewish history and holidays to help her deal with the family. Years later, she still recalls how he bought her an ice cream on her birthday, though her "family" ignored the day. He took her to his old-age home and introduced her as his "niece from Hollywood." The two of them grew so close that he invited her to the bat mitzvah of his grand-daughter—only to withdraw the invitation later because his daughter couldn't accept having a German girl at the event, a daughter of the Holocaust. "It was sometimes not easy being a young German in America," she says.

Jeannet looks at her watch: she has a full afternoon ahead. I notice that the watch isn't telling the proper time—in fact it is several hours off. Jeannet laughs. She's just returned from a trip to the States, and she always leaves it on American time for a couple of weeks to remind her of a lovely trip. "I like to think of people or things from America for a while. But I do the same thing when I go to America. I keep the watch on German time. I'm nostalgic for home when I'm there."

However, she has no dual loyalties. She's German and proud of it. She simply loves America and what it has given her and her country.

With all this Americanization, one must ask oneself, why are so many Germans still so dour, so gloomy, so humorless, so pessimistic, so, well, unAmerican? In fact, President Roman Herzog's most attention-getting speech of 1997 essentially told his audience that Germany wasn't yet American enough.

The setting is dramatic: the newly rebuilt Hotel Adlon in the shadow of the Brandenburg Gate, the hotel on which the film *Grand Hotel* had been based sixty-five years earlier. German presidents play largely a ceremonial role. Their only power is their bully pulpit, and Herzog uses his to take on what he calls a lack of civic courage and "a feeling of paralysis" hovering over the country. He recognizes that Germans need to change their attitude, their *Weltanschauung*, if they are to tackle the task of European leadership.

He quotes an American newsmagazine to make his point. "*Newsweek* speaks of 'the German disease.' That is certainly exaggerated. But this much is correct: whoever reads our media has the impression that pessimism is our general attitude of life . . . We again need vision."

Vision? It is a word that was long out of favor in Germany, and is only beginning to return to civilized conversation. Germans had stopped wanting vision after they recognized that Hitler had a little too much of it. Another word that one doesn't use much anymore is the one for leader: *Führer.* A host of other words have been thrown on the trash heap of history along with it: Honor, Courage, Vision. Americans love those words, but in Germany they are loaded with unwanted historic connotations.

Herzog, knowing this sensitivity, explains:

"Vision is nothing more than a strategy for action. Vision can mobilize unrecognized strengths: I only need remind you of the vitality of the 'American Dream.' "

Herzog, it seems, is calling for reassessment along the lines of the American model. "We have to get down off our high horse and stop thinking that the solutions for our problems can only be found in Germany. Focusing on our own navel doesn't teach us much new . . . Most traditional industrial states have similar problems to our own. A number of them have proved that these problems can be solved . . . in the U.S.A. a well-aimed strategy set loose a new growth that created millions of new jobs."

Herzog had been prepared for the criticism that would follow his speech. Many argued America was hardly the model for a country that didn't want inner city ghettoes.

When I visit Herzog some months later, we sit in a gilded reception room at his Belvedere Palace in Berlin.

"The lesson of the market economy and beyond that," he says, "the lesson of free society as a whole is: give people freedom, and they will make the best of it . . . and then comes the question, but what happens when they don't do enough with this freedom and instead they go on vacation? And that is a little bit our situation at the moment . . . For years, we'd been telling people to join political parties when they complain they can't change anything—that they don't make a difference. Yet that is nonsense. One has to say instead: do something yourself. If you don't trust the system, do something outside of it. That was really the point: to pierce this depressive basic attitude, this passive stance."

"What you are telling them is to be more American?" I say.

He concedes that is so, but to put such language in a speech would have been a death sentence for the whole matter. Herzog accepts that Germans are already the most American of European countries. The youth are particularly so, much readier to take the initiative than their parents.

It is mostly for that reason, he says, that he wants politicians to reduce the role of the state. The German electorate is growing older on average, and they thus hold on stubbornly to a status quo that must change. He concludes Germany can only transform itself if more of the task is handed over to younger people and taken from the hands of government.

Herzog suspects Germany's youth in time will find it has more in common in world outlook with the United States than with neighboring France. Above all, Germany needs America for its primary mission of the twenty-first century—the integration of Central and Eastern Europe into the West. He regards the United States as a sort of chaperone on the world stage for the German coming-out party.

"I have a pretty banal metaphor. If I am leaning far out of the window, then I need someone to hold me by my feet so that I don't fall out. And we must lean far out of the window in Eastern Europe for moral reasons, but also out of the motivation of stabilizing the uncertain part of our continent. We can't do that alone, even within closer European Union. I would prefer being held by the Americans."

He sees a coincidence of interests that will hold the two countries together for years to come. Each successive younger German generation grows more American in its world outlook, less burdened by historic uncertainties, and more certain they have what it takes inside of them to do good. He believes, like Fischer, that the world would see a German foreign policy that came more to resemble that of America—one more driven by altruism. For years, Germans have dreamed of the disappearance of the nation-state, because they considered that political unit overtaken by history. They almost hoped it was so, because they couldn't feel proud of their own nation-state.

But Herzog sees the German nation-state re-emerging, but this time as perhaps the least self-centered figure on the world stage. "I already said it back in 1988, and I feel it even more now, that we are creating a concept of nation in Europe that for the first time isn't egotistical. The French and Italians still have a wholly egotistical idea of nation. In Germany, it was that way as well before." But history has made Germans deal multilaterally in a way in which they wouldn't stand out, a practice that could now serve them well. "For the first time, we see the necessity and the chance to have a nation that is there also for others. In this case, for East Europeans. There is an altruistic element to us now that has always been there for the Americans, even if it sometimes has expressed itself in some funny ways."

So, it seems to me, Germany's president wants his country to act more like America on the world stage, but leaving out "the funny ways."

Peter Schneider loves America but hates the way it understands Germany.

He loves Germany but hates the way it understands itself.

Schneider is troubled that, this many years on, the stereotypical German still goose-steps through the American subconscious. If Germany is to play the role of America's healthy partner, he argues, Americans must celebrate the extent to which they had helped turn Germany into the world's great democratic success story; they had themselves changed the paradigm.

In an article in the *New York Times* written during a stay at Washington's Woodrow Wilson Center, Schneider lectured Americans in his usual whimsical style on how badly they misunderstood Germans.

When he returned to Germany, he deployed the same style in *Der Spiegel* magazine in which he told his countrymen to loosen up a bit and recognize their good sides and above all stop this continual self-flagellation, this tedious pessimism.

At his daughter's Berlin school, for example, budget cuts resulted in a lack of books. Yet when parents were asked to provide some emergency contributions to help out, they protested the request. "The problem is the German attitude that one has to cling to fixed principles—the state is responsible for schoolbooks—rather than embrace a bit of American pragmatism: where the state fails, the individual must step up to the plate.

"To a certain degree the Germans are victims of their envied, efficient state, and they are struck dumb when this state doesn't lay schoolbooks before its children on the table," he writes in *Der Spiegel.* "How will one achieve anything with this mix of arrogance and incompetence? Every group hangs on with panic to its falling privileges. Each defends its early retirement, its thirteenth monthly salary [a bonus paid to virtually every German], and to positions from which they can't be fired—as if these were sacred human rights."

Sitting over tea in his Berlin writer's studio, Schneider says the *New York Times* article and the *Spiegel* essay that followed were part of a personal campaign that grows out of an obligation to his two children. At the time of his America trip, they were aged fourteen and nine. He resents the burden of guilt they must both carry internationally for the accident of being German, even though they have Polish relatives who were murdered by the Nazis. He fears German economic paralysis endangers their future at home, and he's sure American stereotypes unfairly brand them abroad.

He repeats what he wrote in his *New York Times* article, responding to a column by Richard Cohen about Daniel Goldhagen's book, *Hitler's Willing Executioners.* "Goldhagen has revived the notion," wrote Cohen, "that there is something indelibly spooky about Germans, a gene in the culture that outsiders cannot detect that gets passed from generation to generation."

Having read this, Schneider says, "I immediately wanted to have myself tested for this gene. Does every German have to fear that, no matter what we say or do, we are secretly disposed, deep down inside, to persecute minorities? And can we conclude that all non-Germans are by contrast comparatively immune to such impulses?" He calls what Americans practice on the Germans "enlightened" prejudice.

As a German in America, he notes that he avoids the vocabulary of the Hollywood German, not daring to shout "Halt" to his son even if he is heading into traffic. "You try not to seem earnest or profound. You show some humor even if you've none to spare." But despite a half century of German civilization after the Third Reich and more than its share of greatness (Beethoven, Bach, Thomas Mann, Kant), what Americans see in their mind's eye when they think of Germans, Schneider argues, is "a blond, handsome fellow with cold blue eyes, wearing a brown or black uniform, clicking his heels and shouting, 'Right away, Herr Kommandant!' "

Most Americans, I argue, connect modern Germany more with BMWs and Boris Becker than with Adolf Hitler. Americans let out hardly a peep when Daimler Benz bought Chrysler and Bertelsmann bought Random House.

Yet American network television rarely touches a German story that doesn't have a Third Reich peg of some sort, he argues quite rightly. He speaks of a victim of this anti-German propaganda, a black American friend, a lawyer, who returned from vacation in the Caribbean and spoke of how shocked he had been to hear a handsome young couple on the beach whispering endearments into each other's ears in German.

"He didn't think you could talk lovingly in the German language," smiles Schneider.

I joke with him that I had never considered him such a patriot before. He is, after all, a veteran of the German left.

"This doesn't insult my patriotism," he says, "but my intelligence."

Schneider has always been a little ahead of his time. The book of his that is best known in America, *The Wall Jumper*, recognized the evil of the Berlin Wall while much of the intellectual left was still looking to Eastern Europe for its role model. His witty observations, written into snappy, well-constructed sentences, are both more terse and more humorous than one usually finds in German literature. German authors often consider it their task to tax rather than entertain their readers.

Schneider is considering a new book, one about the relatively few Germans who hid Jews during World War II. They numbered perhaps ten thousand in Berlin, a small fraction of the population, even considering the numbers directly involved in the Holocaust, which Goldhagen estimates at two hundred thousand. Yet Schneider says he owes it to his children to write about them—the young generation needs to know that positive German role models exist in history.

"Many children in today's Germany have all sorts of mixed backgrounds. My children aren't genetically what you can understand under the heading of German. Their mother is Polish and many of her family have been murdered by the Germans. And still they go out in the world and have to apologize that they are German? It's not just."

Schneider says a friend of his, a famous German writer who prefers his name not be used, says that Germans offer a service for the rest of the world that no one wants to give up. "One always needs someone from whom you can distance yourself. *They* are the bad and *we* are the good. And because we are the good, there must also be bad. The Communists are no longer there, so one reached again for those who were there before."

I note, however, that modern American film-making has turned to extra-terrestrials.

"But when you look closely," he says, "the aliens are all German. Look at *Star Wars*—the uniforms, how they talk, they are all Germans. The bad aliens are just different-looking Germans. And Hollywood lives from these myths." The problem, he says, is that Hollywood captures the imagination of the world, and captures the imagination of German youth as well. They end up hating their own country because movies teach them to.

Schneider sees the impact on his daughter. She had turned so much against the idea of being German that she insisted on speaking English to her father most of the time. She sought and received enrollment in the English-language John F. Kennedy School in Berlin rather than going back to school in the German system.

When she was in the midst of a confrontation with her parents on Christmas Eve, I retreated with her and her brother to the street outside to play basketball against the side of the building. Whoever could hit a designated square—a plaque for a doctor who worked within—scored. I was Karl Malone, and they were Michael Jordan and Scotty Pippen. They themselves chose the names, which they knew far better than those of the stars on their national soccer squad. The evening was saved.

"I'm not appealing to Germans to forget the past, but instead I'm calling for them to also seek its positive elements. There is no creativity in guilt. You have to love yourself to be creative. I sometimes envy the Americans their naive optimism that simply leaves out parts of their own history. It is an ability the Germans don't have," Schneider says.

Schneider remembers a time when he was with his young son in Florida, and the boy heard German at a neighboring table in the hotel cafe. He excitedly ran up to the people there and began to talk to them, happy to hear his own language. Schneider envies that spontaneous joy—he had long since learned to avoid all other Germans when on holiday. "Germans want as little to do with each other as possible."

Then two years later, when he first came home to the familiarity of his German home and neighborhood, his son uttered a sentence, a confusion of English and German, which Schneider says is the healthy easiness he hopes his country can someday adopt. "He said in this indescribable mix of languages: *Ich liebe* Germany. And I said to myself, that's what the future could look like."

A little bit of modest love of country. Only with that, argues Schneider, can Germany tackle all that it must: the construction and launch of a new capital in Berlin which will be Europe's most important, the hosting in Frankfurt of the European Central Bank and the leadership of a single European currency project; the key position in expanding European institutions to Central and Eastern Europe. Germany, in short, needs to embrace itself if it expects others to embrace it as the central power again at the center of the European continent.

His recipe for the future is a surprisingly American one: "He who needs to take on something great, even if only because he is forced by history, needs also to dare something great. And that doesn't require pride or megalomania. Something much more simple is called for: creativity, enthusiasm, a sense for beauty and—in bearable measure—love for self. Who doesn't love oneself can certainly not love anyone else."

I liked the recipe: a modest amount of American-like affection for the new and improved Germany.

HITLER'S OFFSPRING, AMERICA'S STEPCHILD

Memories fade—and the health of nations
as of individuals depends on some measure
of release from the wounds of the past."
    —FRITZ STERN, *DREAMS AND DELUSIONS*

As things stand today, my type of Germanness
is most suitably at home in the hospitable . . . racial
and national universe called America. Everything
else would have been alienation from my character. As an
American, I am a citizen of the world, which is what
the German is by his nature . . ."
    —THOMAS MANN, 1945, LIBRARY OF CONGRESS

When I awake, I find my ex-convict cousin waiting outside my bedroom door. It is only seven in the morning on a Saturday, and he says he's been up all night. He looks it; his face is pale and damp with sweat, and his body shakes from fatigue.

"My God, Franz, what hit you?" I say.

He opens his mouth to talk, his thick tongue coated in white. He chokes back tears and speaks with a parched voice. "You can't publish these chapters the way they stand."

Franz Kramer, my sixty-year-old cousin, had arrived with his partner Uschi just two days earlier to visit me in Brussels, where I had returned to the *Wall Street Journal Europe* as editor after having finished the bulk of the work on this book. We had visited the Grand Place and strolled along the battlefield at Waterloo. Just the night before we'd stayed up late drinking brown Belgian beer and eating cream- and wine-soaked mussels. That afternoon, we planned to drive to the coast.

Yet Franz's visit had another purpose: he was to review the chapters I'd written about him and his father for errors. I'd also made copies of the small mountain of documents I'd found about his father's Nazi past. I'd given him the pages shortly before he'd gone to bed. I'd put off giving them to him, partly because he seemed so little interested. He knew his father's history, he had told me, and he doubted I could tell him much about it that he didn't already know.

Yet now he stands before me with a pained look, as if I'd shoved a knife in his back, twisted it, and then left it there. "I wasn't going to read a thing until the morning," he says. "I looked at a couple of pages before going to bed and couldn't stop. It's awful, simply horrible." It was a version of his father's past that was far more gruesome than anything he'd ever heard or suspected. His emotions had bounced wildly back and forth from disbelief to horror. "What my parents told us about Father being released from prison due to lack of evidence was a lie," he says.

Franz talks and talks, as if there aren't enough words to express his troubled emotions. I walk him to the kitchen and try to calm him down as I prepare a pot of coffee and pour him a tall glass of mineral water. He tosses the liquid down his throat, which seems to have been parched dry by the heat of the ugly truth.

After finishing my chapters, Franz says he turned to the stack of more than three hundred pages of documents that I had copied for him.

Throughout the night, he read them: the protocols from interrogations, witness statements, expert opinions, court documents, and, to his surprise, confessions from his father. "The testimonies were so disturbingly exact in the details that they made me shiver. And then the judgment! Acquittal on a technicality due to a statute of limitations, and that just because they couldn't prove that my father had committed his crimes as a civil servant."

Law, he says, had seldom seemed so distant from justice. Franz had once told me that he forgave his father his past, but that was before he knew the details. How could anyone forgive such atrocities? he says. He'd never think of his father in the same way again. He *so* wanted to sleep and have it all go away.

By the time he had finished with all the documents, it was four in the morning. The pounding of his heart prevented sleep. "I had no idea it was this bad," he says. "My father always avoided talking about his role in the Nazi period, or he answered in a way that made it impossible for me to reach any conclusions. And Mother either fed me half-truths or lies. She must have done so consciously. But why? To protect Father? To protect herself? Or to protect us? This question is *so* important to me, but it will never be answered. I'll never be able to come to peace with what I've read. I can only constantly ask myself: Would I have been any different than my father—any better than my father—if I had lived then?"

Once Franz calms down and has some water and coffee in him, he wants to negotiate. He's got nothing against what I've written about him, and his own life of crime, or about his father. What I've written is the truth, after all, and I'm free to record it, but he asks me to remove his and his father's names. He can't bear the thought of his neighbors turning against him for a whole host of new reasons, twenty years after he'd gone clean and spent his last day in jail for comparatively petty crimes.

I try to persuade him, explaining that history isn't made up of anonymous quotes and pseudonyms, but my heart isn't in it. He's so distraught, like a man standing before the gallows, that I can only consent to change the names and even, at his request, remain vague about where he lives (which I've done throughout this book).

He brightens somewhat. Like most Germans I know, he prefers general responsibility to specific blame of one's family.

"Thank you, Fred," Franz says as if I have just given him back his life. "People can be so cruel about these things. Even now."

"My intention wasn't to ruin you, Franz," I say. "I was only trying to understand Germany."

Or was I?

An obsession with the German past is as understandable as human nature, whether one has German blood or not. No country has proved quite as compelling a stage for the *ur-Kampf* between Good and Evil. The extremes represented by Beethoven's *Ode to Joy* and Himmler's Buchenwald are so mind-twisting as to have become a cliché for mankind's co-habitation of brilliance and brutality.

And Germans, who are themselves as taken as outsiders are with their own perceived exceptionalism, only feed this fascination. Some Germans object angrily that the international spotlight on their ugly history needs to be turned dark. But such protests run up against a new generation of German young that disagrees. Their interest in the past was much of the reason for the box office success of *Schindler's List*, attended by one school class after another. They drove Daniel Goldhagen's *Hitler's Willing Executioners* to the top of bestseller lists. Like me, they can't help but wonder what it is in their heritage that made it all happen. As Mephistopheles said to Faust as he signed away his soul in blood, *Blut ist ein ganz besonderer Saft*—"Blood is a juice of a very special kind." Germans remain absorbed by the effort to analyze this elixir, though with increasing distance.

For the past is also a slowly fading photograph. Germany's historic 1998 elections did more than simply remove Helmut Kohl from office. A set of German voters, many of whom were born after the building of the Berlin Wall, had elected a new set of leaders, none of whom had personal experience of the Third Reich. The Green party that joined the coalition as a minority partner was born out of the 1968 movement and only became a national force in the late nineteen seventies. It provided the coalition its face to the world: foreign minister Joschka Fischer, a man born three years after the war, and a year before the creation of the Federal Republic of Germany.

Few countries have such distinct historic lines drawn between generations:

a typical family can include a great-grandparent who was a Nazi and fought in the war, a grandparent who built Germany's economic miracle out of the rubble on the Western side of a divided Germany, a parent who campaigned against the Vietnam War and knew nothing but democracy and affluence, and a child born into a reunified country who will know the Berlin Wall only from postcards.

Yet for all of those differences, Germany's Third Reich years won't disappear as a factor in determining twenty-first-century German identity. That experience is built permanently into virtually every German and European institution. The single currency grew out of Europeans' desire to keep Germany from going it alone, and Helmut Kohl pushed it forward against German public opposition because he shared this concern himself.

Yet for a country again called upon to lead Europe, the self-doubt of the past is an insufficient compass. The challenges ahead require Germany to transform its historical conscience from a restraint to a motivator. As a psychiatrist might counsel a patient wracked with insecurity (which, on some level, Germany still is), Germany must learn to access and properly understand the roots of the healthy experience of its last fifty years. Though no book can draw the roadmap for Germany's future, my personal search for the new republic turned up a few signposts worth watching.

First, for all its desire for new beginnings, the new Germany must avoid a natural inclination to bury and forget its ugly past. Even German newborns are Hitler's Offspring. This feature of their emotional landscape is as impossible to deny as the Rhine River's place on the physical map. Germany's reduced size, its more Western leanings, the smallest details of its parliamentary system, its devotion to Western institutions, its conscience and its national personality are all products of this dozen-year trauma.

An increasing number of Germans argue in favor of a *Schlussstrich*, an arbitrary line between the bad past and the good future. Yet to etch such a line, even if it were possible, would be to cut out a vital part of the country's anatomy, or its soul, without which postwar Germany would breathe much differently, and not nearly as well.

To again quote Hans Frank, the Nazi Governor General of Poland, before he was hanged at Nuremberg: "A thousand years will pass and the guilt of Germany won't be erased." The wise German voices are trying to transform

the unhealthy aspect of guilt with an instinctive national responsibility. The
world needs a Germany with a conscience that drives it, not with complexes
that tie it in knots. The historian Fritz Stern was right when he wrote,
"Memories fade—and the health of nations as of individuals depends on
some measure of release from the wounds of the past."

The recipe offered in this book by my cousin Marcus Bleinroth, the
young diplomat, is a good one. "There is no German identity without historical guilt. My Germanness is defined by it. But I don't have a complex
about it. Perhaps it has given me a heightened sense of responsibility . . . I
have decided to turn it into something positive. In all the important global
problems, such as saving the environment, we must play more of a positive
role because of who we are."

Second, Germans' quest to be "normal" isn't sufficient for a country
that will need to rise far above the mediocrity of the average. Germany must
seize the opportunities that lie before it to guide a single currency project and
to expand the European Union eastward if the continent is to turn the coming hundred years into a European Century, which is a good possibility.

Yet that won't happen without more visionary leadership than the world
has seen under Germany's Gerhard Schröder, the country's first chancellor,
whose personality wasn't forged by the war and its immediate aftermath.
When given the opportunity to extradite a Kurdish terrorist, who was wanted
for murder in Germany, Schröder explained he wouldn't do so because of the
danger of domestic unrest. The country's large population of Kurds might
well have taken to the streets. Yet if Europe's de facto leader and the world's
third-mightiest economic power can't extradite a single terrorist because of
domestic fears, it is unlikely to rise to the occasion of far more difficult decisions that stand before it in the twenty-first century.

That said, the tone Germany sets is likely to be a more pleasing one due
to a new generation that has more humor, modesty, and flexibility than outsiders view as traditionally German. Movie houses and television screens are
awash with a new breed of comedy and comedians, feeding off a people that
has at long last begun to laugh at itself. In my chapter on "normal Germans,"
the psychiatrist Stephan Ehebald, with tongue firmly implanted in cheek (I
think), traced his country's problems to premature potty training. The mathematician Norbert Heldermann took me to one of his country's most breast-

beating monuments, the über-Prussian Hermann's Denkmal, so that we can have a good chuckle at what Germans used to think was appropriate behavior.

Yet there is little humor in his showdown with his neighbors over whether to turn a green area before their homes into parking spaces, a battle that had found its way to the courts when this book went to press. The modern German love for cars was running up against the ancient attachment to green areas, and for both sides compromise came hard. One could write another book listing the many examples that remain to reinforce tired German stereotypes: headstrong, stubborn, inflexible. And for all the new-age, late-night talk shows, Germany remains a thoroughly serious society. That's often tiresome, but not altogether bad, as long as Germans also take their role in Europe more seriously as well. After all, Germany made all the difference in Europe in the twentieth century, and the twenty-first century will be no different.

I attended the country's coming-out party in Bosnia, the first engagement of its combat troops outside German borders since the war. The historic moment couldn't have been richer: German troops were actively engaged in trying to create peace in a place where they had left behind a legacy of World War II atrocities. More to the point, then-Defense Minister Volker Rühe drove the process of NATO's eastward expansion in concert with the United States. He understood the context: Germany was morally obligated to embrace Poland not only for the harm Germany had done to it in the past, but also for the heroic role Poles played in bringing down Soviet-style Communism and helping pave the way for German unification. As he said, linking Germany's pro-democracy protests before unification to the Poles' historic shipyard strikes, "There would be no Leipzig without Gdansk."

The most positive first instinct of Germany's new government after its 1998 election was to embrace its many "foreigners" with the idea of dramatically liberalized citizenship requirements. Within a few years, Germany could have three to five million new citizens. The growth will be particularly great among its largest "foreign" population, the Turks. By accident, Germany has become an immigration country through taking hundreds of thousands of guest workers, asylum seekers, and ethnic Germans from the former Soviet bloc in the postwar half century. But for all of them except the Germans, naturalization had long been complicated by an abiding philosophy that citizenship still begins with bloodline—that juice of a very special kind.

The new laws go a long way toward changing the legal underpinning of a widespread German aversion toward its largest minority, the Turks. That could allow Germany to better tap the talents of its immigrants rather than focusing on them primarily as a problem. Perhaps then Germany will become a little more American still—a more multi-ethnic state with all the creativity and social tensions that brings.

It might also lead Germany to deal more creatively with what will arguably be its biggest foreign policy challenge in the next century: preventing Turkey from turning anti-Western, a role America has suggested to Germany on many occasions.

That leads to this book's final, and—for Germans, at least—its most controversial finding. Germany isn't only Hitler's Offspring, it is also America's Stepchild. And the country's Americanization in the shadow of this powerful parentage has been one of its most positive forces. Intellectuals of the left and right will rail against this observation, but it is again impossible to deny. As Joschka Fischer himself said, he learned his democracy from America, and his left-oriented politics were more a result of Bob Dylan than they were of Karl Marx.

The writer Peter Schneider, who introduced me to this image of the "Stepfather," explained that World War II cost his generation its authority figure, for the parents were complicit in the crime and in the national failure. America was the closest thing to an ersatz, a well-meaning interloper that helped give its German offspring certain guidelines and nurturing which, when added to Germany's own experience and habits, resulted in the current system.

Like any stepchild, Schneider argued, Germany rejects the authority and the model set by the stepfather while at the same time unconsciously emulating him. But beyond helping to establish institutions and democratic practices, instincts German already had, America also helped imbue the country with its naive but refreshing belief in self-improvement and new beginnings. It believed in Germans when many others didn't.

For the future, President Roman Herzog said Germany and the U.S. have a common mission in expanding democracy and free market economies, based on Western values, eastward. The metaphor he used was a powerful one: Germany leans out of the window toward the east and America holds it by the feet so that it doesn't fall. The message: Who else could Germany depend upon not to let go of its feet as it ventures into its new, more ambitious role?

Intellectuals complain that Americanization has dumbed down their country, giving it a superficial culture and economy that, by its harsh competitiveness, widens the gap between rich and poor. They condemn *amerikanische Verhältnisse*, the widely used catch phrase that conjures up visions of drug-soaked, gun-toting youth in violent ghettoes. Many Americans fear that with Helmut Kohl's ouster, voters have removed a generation that was devoted to this transatlantic relationship and replaced it with one that will prefer to "liberate" itself from America.

Yet as the previous chapter illustrates, the relationship is internal as well as bilateral, and in that respect the two countries have never been closer. In some respects, Germany is emerging as the America of Europe, the country that is its continent's decisive force. Yet nothing is that simple: Germany has less absolute weight on its continent and a history that makes it more suspect to its neighbors. It knows it can only lead through coalition-building, not a bad habit for a century where multilateral institutions will be key in determining everything from monetary to environmental rules. That said, Germany is more like an America in Europe in that it is gradually growing more willing to lead. Tellingly, the new foreign minister calls for a "value-oriented" foreign policy, which he counts as more American than European.

German intellectual elites who reject the notion that "Americanization" can be a positive force should read Thomas Mann's speech of 1945 before the Library of Congress. "My type of Germanness," he said, "is most suitably at home in the hospitable Panopolis, the racial and national universe called America. Before I became an American, I had been permitted to be a Czech. That was highly charming and commendable, but it had neither rhyme nor reason. Similarly, I only need to imagine becoming a Frenchman, an Englishman, or an Italian in order to discern how much more proper it was that I became an American. Everything else would have been too narrow and too certain an alienation from my character. As an American, I am a citizen of the world, which is what the German is by his nature, notwithstanding . . . his timidity in the face of the world, of which it is hard to say whether it is rooted in conceit or innate provincialism, an inferiority complex in the face of the world community. Probably both."

What has changed is that Thomas Mann today could find much of the "hospitable racial and national universe" of which he speaks without leaving German borders. Mann's German nature of 'being a citizen of the world' has found a new opportunity.

I am accustomed to covering other people's affairs—Israel's invasion of Lebanon, the Soviet occupation of Afghanistan, Poland's liberation drama, the end of the Cold War. Even when a bullet or bomb came a little too near, I had the comfort of knowing it was never intended for me. I had kept my stories at arm's length.

But during my search for the new Germany, after years of considering the country just another one of those foreign stories, I lost much of my distant perspective. The country was part of my heritage, part of my makeup. That said, I came away from it more grateful than ever before to be born American. Helmut Kohl once spoke about "the mercy of a late birth," meaning that he had escaped the awful choices of the Nazi years. I had enjoyed "the mercy of an American birth." By the grace of my parent's prewar emigration, I didn't bear that psychological tattoo that every German is born with, not as visible as the horrible Auschwitz branding they imposed on others but just as indelible in its own way.

At some point in every young German's life, he or she learns that Germany committed a crime of unfathomable proportions. Few Germans forget their first meeting with a Jew or the first time that someone asks them what their fathers or grandfathers did during the war. It may seem unfair to them that the world still points a warning finger at Germany, but it is a reality each learns comes to live with, if not entirely accept.

It is my responsibility, as it is for any citizen of this world, to know what happened in the Third Reich and to learn its lessons. It is all the more my responsibility as an American of German heritage. For a German, however, that responsibility is less a matter of choice than obligation. Learning the lessons is a rite of passage.

As I ended my search for the new Germany, however, I drew back once more to the reporter's safe distance. The best final destination for such a story, I decided, is Weimar, the closest thing Germany has to a place of pilgrimage.

The poet Anna Segars referred to it as "the best and worst place in German history." It was where Goethe wrote *Faust*, and where the Nazis held their first party conference. Franz Liszt composed there, and Nietzsche's sister moved there from Latin America with her failing brother to establish a nationalist, intellectual salon. Every great literary figure in Europe dropped in at some point in the nineteenth century. Hitler himself visited thirty times or more to claim German classicism for himself.

And each time, Hitler stayed at Hotel Elephant—as did Goebbels, Goethe, Göring, Schiller and the rest—an elegant hostelry where I would overnight as well. Yet on the facade, one can spot the hooks where a swastika once hung. And the balcony remains where the Führer himself stood over adoring crowds that cheered him on from the market square below.

Weimar today prefers to focus on Goethe, who spent his best years here; he's even said to have etched his initials in a tree in the woods above the town that would later house the Nazi concentration camp called Buchenwald. Infamy was seldom set in such serene surroundings. It is clearly Goethe's Weimar and not Hitler's that Chancellor Helmut Kohl and others were thinking about when they granted the town the status of European Cultural Capital for 1999. The plan: to show, through Weimar, the country's great cultural city, that Germany's identity at its core is European, literary, and musical. Not only was there a single European currency, there would also be a single culture.

Justus Ulbricht is a hip historian in his thirties who is part of the effort to prepare Weimar for its starring role, and he isn't going to let them get away with it. He complains that everyone has used Weimar for propaganda purposes over the years—its monarchs, its Nazis, and its Socialists. He's putting a stop to it by drawing up a program that will highlight both sides of the city: *Kulturstadt* and *Unkulturstadt*.

We sit at a small round table in a café that lies at the middle of the heavily subsidized building and renovation spree that engulfs Weimar. It all started in this town, he tells me, when the young Charles Augustus lured Goethe to his cultural backwater with a rich pay package, including generous housing and ultimately a long list of public positions, among them parks commissioner and architectural consultant. Charles Augustus's mother was ambitious for her son, and she reckoned it could do his image good to have Goethe in his court, and she was right. He was the magnet who attracted all that followed, right down to today's tourists. Yet Weimar has always embodied the strange tension in Germany between the progressive and the reactionary.

When the authors of the Weimar constitution chose the city as their setting, for example, it wasn't only because of Weimar's cultural heritage. It also happened to be so conservative that they knew they were less likely to be disturbed there by the troublesome Bolsheviks. Walter Gropius came to Weimar from 1919 to 1925 to create his Bauhaus school of design—he figured its record suited it for such a calling. But conservative city fathers eventually ran him out of town with his apostles, considering their work a little too radical.

Even East German Communists played the Weimar game. They shut down the Nietzsche archives, for the philosopher's works had been too co-opted by Hitler to be part of the creation of the Socialist Man. They then proceeded to co-opt the rest of Weimar for their own purposes. Goethe, their reasoning went, would have been a Marxist if only Karl Marx had come before him.

The East Germans convinced themselves that the mission of their little bit of the Soviet bloc, misleadingly known as the German Democratic Republic, was the fulfillment of the Utopia that Faust talks about in the second part of his classic work. "The people, the party said, were writing the third part of Faust," smiles Ulbricht. "East Germany was the realization of Goethe. They felt they were carrying the torch of Faust further, but Goethe never would have touched it."

So now unified Germany picks up the Weimar torch and decides to carry it in the name of Europe. Ulbricht's resistance includes the staging of a Goethe exhibit at the site of the Buchenwald concentration camp, on the pretty hill above town, and a Buchenwald exhibit at the Schiller House. The point: to show that the murderous camp can't be as easily separated from Weimar as many would like. The locals don't like the approach, he says, but his plans are going ahead anyway.

"We want to show that Weimar wasn't only the home of culture but also of anti-culture," says Ulbricht, whose humanist father gave him the first name Justus—Latin for Justice—to get him off to a morally proper start. "There are many who criticize us for this. They want to make Weimar a cultural Disneyland. But it is important to show how classicism has been abused over the years. And it is also important to show why, despite a history of classicism in Germany, that a Buchenwald could happen. We want to make clear that barbarism wasn't just up there"—he nods toward the dreaded site in the hills above town—"but also down here in Weimar. They are tied together more closely than most people know."

And it wasn't just that the slave labor from the camps often came to town to do odd jobs, such as cleaning up war rubble or removing dead bodies. Weimar's surrounding region of Thuringia also gave Germany its first SS minister, its first Nazi chief of police, and its first Nazi culture minister, says Ulbricht. After Hitler took power, Weimar didn't require any political bloodletting; no need to purge anyone when the local leadership was either National Socialist or happy enough to become so.

"No protests against the Nazis here, no political resignations, no resistance," says Ulbricht. "The inhabitants of this city—the heart of German culture—took part themselves in the dismantling of the inheritance they created. That's the chilling part that we want to show."

Germany's promise has never been far removed from its doom, something worth remembering as the country prepares for the new century. It would seem as if nothing could go wrong for Germany, but the country has had good preconditions before.

Renate Müller-Krumbach is the keeper of the Goethe flame as the director of Weimar's twenty-five museums and public sites. They include Goethe's own spacious house (the town's number-one tourist attraction), where she meets us in a small, top-floor office that has been made out of one of his children's bedrooms. She presides over what she regards as "the best address in German history." No unsavory ghosts here, she says.

"It is such an honorable house, perhaps there is no other place like it in Germany. They all visited here—Schiller, Wieland, Liszt. Every major European literary figure came here. This house must be handled like a pharaoh's tomb—with reverence. To work here is beautiful for the soul. So few black spots. When it is closed at night and I walk through, I get such a special feeling. There is one room I wouldn't dare open—his special work room. I imagine that he is behind there working by candlelight as he did, completely concentrated. It so intimidates and impresses me that I don't dare touch the door and disturb him. It is so moving."

But it also strikes her that Goethe had many peculiarities that one might now call typically German, characteristics that in another setting have brought less favorable results. "This close co-existence of good and evil is what moves one here," she says. "And the perfection of the German in the role of both good and evil is what is particularly remarkable. Goethe was a man who led his entire life in an exemplary way. Everything he collected, everything he wrote, was accounted for, every sheet of paper, every piece of art, every book was catalogued. And the Nazis up the road were just as orderly and disciplined in how they ran their camp. Yet what comes out here is good and what comes out there is evil. What unifies them is the extreme order and discipline behind both."

She sympathizes with the townspeople, who must bear the burden of being the symbol of all good and evil in the German soul. Weimar had disappeared from most tourist maps for years, locked away in East Germany where it was difficult to reach, due to the challenging visa approval process and the lack of tourist rooms. Yet now Weimar is again the central attraction for studying the tortured German soul.

"It's a big burden for such a small place that wishes the shadow of Buchenwald would just go away," says Dr. Müller-Krumbach. Why, she wonders, couldn't the burden be shared with Nuremberg, where the best Renaissance architecture coexists with a history of the early Nazi rallies and postwar trials? Or with Munich, where baroque meets Dachau? Weimar isn't alone in representing Germany's contradictory content.

"With his character type, Faust," says the professor, "Goethe described the German. Like Faust, every individual has two poles, the good and the bad, but the German handles them with greater thoroughness than most people. The good is beautiful, but the bad is devastating. Goethe arrived here to live in the most Protestant area of the world imaginable—the lofty heights of Lutheranism. This is where the Faustian idea reaches its highest level: Have I done wrong? Have I done right? This agonizing over cause and effect is so typically German. This justification of actions. Why is it that there is so much bad in the world? Why do I have such a bad character? This constant questioning of oneself. This introspection. This is Germany. Catholics confess and it's over with."

I note that a good percentage of Germany is Catholic: Bavaria, the Rhineland.

"Yes," she says, "but we have a more Protestant character as a nation. As a Catholic, you can delegate guilt: accept it, regret it, and then confess it. But the Protestant can only confess to himself. He intensively asks himself questions about what it is all about. Life comes from the light and from the heavy sides. But the German spends much more of his energy on the heavy side of life."

I noticed that she, like so many of my German friends, was also referring to Germans in the third person—as if she doesn't belong to them. I mention this to her and she smiles. "They aren't convinced by themselves, the Germans," she says, keeping her pronounal distance. "If we existed only from Goethe, Luther, and Schiller, we would be able to say 'we.' But Germans have been told for decades now that they are criminals, and it takes root in one way or the other. I, for one, am glad we aren't so enthusiastic about ourselves."

The history of Buchenwald "has cost the Germans a great deal of their self-confidence," she says. "It's a stigma. When something like that happens, a people is ashamed for who knows how long."

I had been at the camp that morning: the neat rows where the barracks stood are still well marked. Within the building that held its crematorium is the room where doctors carried out their scientific experiments on the dying and the barely living. Shortly before I had arrived, roofers found ashes from the burned dead in urns in the attic. So metaphorical; Germans were unearthing new evidence of their sour history, even so many years later.

Not far from the inmates' desperate lodgings, over the concertina wire and fences and into the living area of the guards and the administrators, the commandant had built a sweet zoo where Nazi children could while away an afternoon with well-fed animals. At the same time, inmates starved but an apple's throw away. I had looked at the cement remains in the earth of a bear's pool, and I pictured innocent children around it, laughing and throwing bits of food to the creature, while humans were treated worse than animals. So much has been written about the camps over the years, but visiting one never fails to reinforce the sickness of the human spirit at that time in Germany.

Allied troops had forced the locals in Weimar to come and look at the camp and its survivors in the last days of the war. They wanted to rub Germans' faces in the brutalities committed in their name.

I ask the professor whether she thinks Germans, knowing their worst side, have become a better people. The Holocaust seemed to have built in a censor and a guard-rail for the new Germany: Germans know racism sounds uglier in their mouths. Most Germans realize politics must remain forever more within the safe confines of strong Western institutions.

Dr. Müller-Krumbach frowns. "We haven't become a better people, but we are a more careful people. When you lose some of your self-confidence, perhaps it is not so bad. You think more about your neighbors and your impact on your neighbors. The question is how long this stigma lives on, and then what becomes of it."

We talk some about German nature, about the lack of spontaneity and easy joy that still pervades society. I paraphrase for her the Thomas Mann theory that much of German tendency toward gloom, humorlessness, the lack of ability to let down one's collective hair and have fun, comes from the fact that Germans never experienced a successful revolution like the French or the Americans. They've never had a time when the common man triumphed clearly over oppressive authority.

"Oh, I disagree," she says. "It is good we haven't had a revolution. Revolution is so disorderly. Germans are so terribly pedantic that they would never be able to deal with it. They lack the playfulness" that is needed for revolution.

She then tells the story about the *Revolutzer* and the *Lampenputzer*. The essence of the story is that the lamp cleaner didn't want to stop cleaning the lamps merely for the sake of revolution. Who would clean the lamps if he didn't? And for this sense of duty of the *Lampenputzer*, the revolution is lost.

She considers Goethe's relationship with his apparent lover of many years, Charlotte von Stein, to have been typical of the sort of pain the German enjoys bearing, even in the pursuit of pleasure. He wrote her twelve to fourteen hundred letters, she says. "Unbelievable creativity. He never repeated himself in a single one. Can you imagine that?" But the relationship was never consummated, she insists. Charlotte had been a married woman during their entire friendship. It seems that she sought Goethe's company because her own husband lacked the spirit and intellect she desired. But I couldn't believe that their relationship had remained platonic all those years.

"I think if he had been happy with her," she says, "it never would have been as much fun for him."

I look for a bottom line in our discussion—and for my book. Where is this new Germany going?

The professor is a modest and thoughtful woman. She has lived most of her life in East Germany, as a professor whose nonconformism with the party prevented her rising far. Now she has been elevated to one of the country's loftiest cultural positions. She views history as the basis that every country builds upon, and not just Germany. Germans, she says, have accomplished a great deal over the years, considering the modest reach of their land and their limited natural resources. Germany has what she calls a "thick" culture, with a long list of great accomplishments. But it also has a large share of historical failures. So the challenges ahead—European leadership, globalization, a UN Security Council seat—these sorts of things may go beyond what its base will support.

"Because of this uncertain foundation, this history, I would suggest that the Germans try not to build too high in the future," she says. "The more certain the foundation, the higher you can build the tower. If the history is sound, if I am happy with it, then I can more comfortably construct my goals higher and higher."

Then it follows, I conclude, that the more good history Germany accumulates now, the higher it can build.

She nods her agreement.

And it can construct its dreams to a loftier height now, after five decades of democracy and good citizenship in Western institutions, than it could have after the war. That is why unification could occur without great danger. Germany had enough good years behind it to give it a chance.

"So how high can Germans build their tower at the moment?" I ask. "And out of what materials?"

The professor smiles at my game. She plays along.

"The Germans find their soul in the woods—nature, trees, plants. It softens them. That is what makes them happiest." So the tower should be built of natural materials. "The tower can't be built of cement—in no case. That would be too hard. But it also can't be built of sand. The German needs security. The house must be built of wood, and the foundation should be the strong, sturdy earth of the forest."

And how high ought the structure to be?

"Not so very high just yet," she says. "The tower must be elevated enough so that we have a perspective over the land around us. So that we understand it. But not much higher. Above all, it should not be so high that one has the temptation to feel superior."

Not a bad recipe for Germany: to construct modestly and solidly, but with flexible materials. It shouldn't grow too lofty in its ambitions, but construct high enough to gain the perspective from which it must help lead Europe. As history's wounds heal and its confidence grows as an exporter of stability and democracy, Germany may at long last achieve its historic potential. And that will be critical, because the strains of introducing a single currency and of expanding Western institutions and values eastward will require a steady, confident, modest hand.

A forgiving God has presented Germany a series of lucky breaks: the peaceful breakdown of the Soviet bloc allowed the country to reunite bloodlessly, a war in Bosnia (for all its horrors for others) allowed Germany to send its army on a mission of peace to a place where it once committed atrocities, a new group of Russian-Jewish emigrants demonstrates vividly to the world that even Jews are comfortable in the new Germany, and the expansion of NATO and the European Union allows it to reach out to eastern neighbors whom it has done so much harm to in the past. It is safely embedded in Europe, has a tight relationship with its most powerful partner, America, and is surrounded by neighbors with whom it has warm links and no border conflicts.

A new German drama is about to begin. The last century's most heinous criminal is free again after fifty years of probation and supervision. The once-wicked Third Reich has been re-educated, reformed, and restored to a remarkable degree of economic and political power. Fate has sweetened the plot even further, making our show's star the decisive factor at the center of a Europe that is struggling to come together more closely while at the same time expanding.

All the plot elements are in place for this twenty-first-century thriller.

Some may call it "Germany's Last Chance."

It is certainly Germany's Best Chance.